An
Illustrated
History
of
American
Psychology

An Illustrated History of American Psychology

John A. Popplestone
Archives of the History of American Psychology

Marion White McPherson
Archives of the History of American Psychology

WCB **Brown & Benchmark**
PUBLISHERS

Madison, Wisconsin • Dubuque, Iowa

Book Team

Executive Editor *Michael Lange*
Developmental Editor *Sheralee Connors*
Production Editor *Karen A. Pluemer*
Photo Editor *Shirley Lanners*
Art Processor *Jodi Wagner*
Visuals/Design Developmental Consultant *Marilyn A. Phelps*
Visuals/Design Freelance Specialist *Mary L. Christianson*
Publishing Services Specialist *Sherry Padden*
Marketing Manager *Steven Yetter*
Advertising Manager *Brett Apold*

Brown & Benchmark

A Division of Wm. C. Brown Communications, Inc.

Executive Vice President/General Manager *Thomas E. Doran*
Vice President/Editor in Chief *Edgar J. Laube*
Vice President/Sales and Marketing *Eric Ziegler*
Director of Production *Vickie Putman Caughron*
Director of Custom and Electronic Publishing *Chris Rogers*

Wm. C. Brown Communications, Inc.

President and Chief Executive Officer *G. Franklin Lewis*
Corporate Senior Vice President and Chief Financial Officer *Robert Chesterman*
Corporate Senior Vice President and President of Manufacturing *Roger Meyer*

Cover design by Sailer & Cook Creative Services.

Cover photos from the Archives of the History of American Psychology Collections (left to right): *Photo 1* AHAP Photographic File; *Photo 2* Marion E. Bunch Gift. Photograph by Morton May, Jr.; *Photo 3* from *Scientific Monthly,* April 1930, Copyright © AAAS; *Photo 4* Courtesy Evan Calkins; *Photo 5* Cedric A. Larson/John B. Watson Papers. Identification with the help of Charles Brewer; *Photo 6* National Training Laboratories Archives. Photograph by Mort Kaye Studios.

A Times Mirror Company

Library of Congress Catalog Card Number: 93–70759

ISBN 0–697–21127–4

Printed in the United States of America by Wm. C. Brown Communications, Inc., 2460 Kerper Boulevard, Dubuque, IA 52001

10 9 8 7 6 5 4 3 2 1

Edwin G. Boring at the beginning of his career.

Archives of the History of American Psychology, University of Iowa Libraries Record.

This book is dedicated to Edwin G. Boring (Ph.D., Cornell, 1914), author of the precedential volume, *A History of Experimental Psychology*. The first edition, 1929, is an account of the emergence of psychology as a science between 1860 and 1910, and the second edition, 1950, extends the coverage for an additional 40 years. For a considerable period, this was the best-known and to many people the only textbook devoted to experimental psychology. In this role, it brought the history of modern psychology into relief, helped to credit it, and by integrating details and perspective certified it as scholarly. For each person, theory, and activity, Boring develops purposes, functions, and continuity—consistently documented with thoroughness. Even those who disagree with Boring's interpretations are awed by his literacy and scholarship.

Edwin G. Boring, in his later years, at the 49th meeting of the Society of Experimental Psychologists in 1953, at the University of Texas. Boring was particularly pleased with this photograph.

Archives of the History of American Psychology, Frank Geldard Papers.

Table of Contents

Foundations

Last Quarter of the Nineteenth Century to World War I

Development

World War I Through World War II

Maturity

Third Quarter of the Twentieth Century

Preface

People perceive the field of psychology in many ways. Some believe it suggests techniques for manipulating people; some look to it for guides for child rearing; some conclude that it is the source of information about and assistance in handling private but socially forbidden thoughts and impulses; some think of it as the supernatural or psychic; and some see it the way psychologists themselves do: as a field of science that is responsible for acquiring and applying knowledge about the variable behavior—both overt and covert—of human and subhuman organisms. Psychology's subject matter is too large to describe in its totality here, but its scope includes such diverse matters as how organisms learn, why they fear, how they dominate and submit, what they imagine and dream, how they judge distance, what range of sounds they can hear, and what pulls them toward certain goals but pushes them away from others.

A psychologist is a professional person who was educated in a graduate department of psychology of a university and who typically is a specialist in only one or a few areas of the field. Some psychologists devote their careers to research and teaching in their areas of specialty whereas others devote their careers to the application or practice of the knowledge and skills they have mastered. At present, there are more than 100,000 professional psychologists in North America. Modern psychology began to take shape only a little more than 100 years ago; this volume describes in words and illustrates with pictures many of the highlights of psychology's recent past. This book may serve different purposes for different readers: it may open up a view of the field for those who are not psychologists and sharpen the memories of those who are.

When we started to plan this book, we came face to face with two conflicting realizations: that the wide range of activities of psychologists are much too numerous to review in a single short volume, and that any selection among them would force our own preferences on readers. Since we had to make choices, we are pointing out our selections so as to make it easier for the consumer to understand the text and to track the biases.

The first task in planning this volume was organizing it. Historical accounts usually present the content in chronological order, dividing it into various sections (eras) bounded by specific dates. Simple reliance on the calendar would have been convenient, but it also would have distorted the record since historical epochs should be characterized by similar events or themes, but divisions that are based solely on dates are apt to create a false, rather than an actual, consistency.

The search for different periods started easily because historians tend to agree that psychology as a laboratory discipline began during the last quarter of the nineteenth century when a few scientists tried to adapt the procedures and apparatus used in laboratories of physiology and physics to research in psychology. Unfortunately, scholars have not been equally specific about the end of this borrowing phase, but a scan of historical events indicated that World War I changed the field.

Psychologists tackled some of the practical problems that the war created, particularly those related to the selection and placement of military personnel. Since there were few, if any, precedents for this work, the psychologists, for the first time, had to create special procedures and apparatus for their work. Their success in developing both an autonomous subject matter and new methods for studying it gained so much momentum that we accepted it as evidence that the initial period was giving way to a second. We recognized that this transition occurred at about the same time as the war, but we did not want to specify exact dates for either the beginning or the end of this Founding Era since there is generally some overlap in the beginning and the takeover of all changes in science.

A survey of the important events that had occurred before World War I indicated the topics that we should cover or structure in a book format. These are the European education of the founders, the establishing of American laboratories, the struggles to define the subject matter of psychology and to construct a theoretical framework for it, and the first efforts to build psychological tests.

This definition of the limits of the Founding Era encouraged us to identify the next phase. A review of happenings after World War I revealed an increased interest in trying to discover the best ways of conducting psychological research. One simple example illustrates this shift. Early experiments on memory measured how much subjects remember, a measurement restricted to a *physical* dimension. But, as they accumulated knowledge, psychologists began to measure the effect on memory of such *psychological* variables as familiarity of the material, its pleasantness or unpleasantness, and its manner of organization.

Psychology grew enough at this time to justify naming this second period the Era of Development. The field's self-improvement was broad in scope, but development was so heavily concentrated on methodology that the refining of experimental procedures became the dominant theme. A concern with *how* to do psychology continues up to the present, but after the end of World War II this concern stopped dominating the field indicating that the Era of Development was bounded at its beginning and end by the disruption of an armed conflict. During these approximately 30 years between wars, the strengthening was going on both in experimental laboratories *and* in the measurement of individuals so that a chapter devoted to both topics was planned.

At about the middle of this century, psychologists' traditional care to restrict laboratory research to single, discrete topics—ones that can be rigidly controlled—started to yield to efforts to master more complex issues, even those hard to manage with experimental precision. A laboratory report became less interesting than a conclusion. For example, research might suggest that missing the bull's-eye during target practice by at least one-third of the width of the target in ten of twenty trials reduces predictions of the level of success in subsequent trials by an average of 50 percent. Psychologists after the war would show less interest in

these findings than they would in the conclusion of the research that a sense of failure, even when measured by personal judgments rather than by a standard meter stick, develops only when there are a series of conditions as, for example, having judged a task as manageable, having expended effort on it, having expected benefits when it was completed, and having informed others about the personal investment in the completion of the task. The shift from restrained but artificially limited topics to more complex ones moved the discipline so much closer to the mastery of psychology as it occurs outside the laboratory that we were prompted to label this period the Era of Maturity.

During this interval, the growth rate of psychology exploded, both in the number of psychologists and the number of new specialized topics that they pursued. The expansion was so widespread that diversity appeared to outweigh an emphasis on any single topic or undertaking. One possible exception was the recurring theme of social concern. However, it was not clear if this concern was a sign of a fundamental change in psychology or merely an artifact of the growth of the field. Because now, more than in the past, a larger number of psychologists entered the applied sectors, their concentration may have made social matters appear to be more important. Nevertheless, the increased attention to the problems of society, whether real or not, prompted us to qualify the era as colored by social welfare and the public interest.

An account of the important developments during this time span seemed to merit three chapters: the first deals with the improved ability of laboratory and clinical apparatus to deliver elaborate stimuli and register a number of simultaneous responses; a second describes experiments that resemble the ordinary or commonplace world more closely than those typical of the past and a third outlines the branching out of psychological services in numerous forms including prevention and therapy.

We are too close to the Era of Maturity to be able to have a long-range view of its duration, but we do not detect any significant modifications of the preference for learning how to understand and control complex events. The question of whether this preference is still the keynote or is only the result of our inability to see clearly remains unanswered.

To summarize, this chronicle broadly organizes modern American psychology in three traditional epochs: its founding, development, and maturity. Each is different: the first involved borrowed methods and pursued simple questions; the second was devoted to the discovery of techniques of acquiring psychological information; the third was more bold spirited, concerned with more complex psychological behavior. We have ended this historical account in 1975, 100 years after Wundt's appointment at Leipzig. It is too soon for us to have the objectivity of distance toward the years since then.

Once our basic organization was in place we began to select the actual material to include. Since the number of words and pictures we could use was limited, we decided to describe a general background that would show major trends, relying on examples rather than lengthy explication and enriching it with descriptions and photographs of illustrative events and subjects.

As the work progressed, we were reminded again and again of the discrepancy between the messages that verbal prose and visual images convey. Neither can cover the whole of the past; each is selective. A narrative history is largely a series of generalizations; pictures can provide only specifics—particular persons, places, objects, and occasions. The different message communicated by text and visuals may complement one another, but they do not prevent misinterpretation since a picture may create a stronger impression than a polished statement of a principle. We have tried to counteract these problems by providing a wide variety of illustrations. Some that show material directly related to the text and some that help to evoke a period, suggest context for the text, or even just delight and astonish.

Regrettably, even the large number of visuals cannot eradicate the possibility of false impression since photographs are taken for personal, often idiosyncratic reasons and older ones often survive only by accident. We have selected items from various collections of historic photographs on the basis of their relevance to the past of psychology rather than on artistic merit. A technically poor photograph may be redeemed by the importance of its subject. We have supplemented these older views with pictures of archival items taken especially for this project. Access to these archival deposits allowed us to show informal documents, historic laboratory equipment, older tests, and even frames from early films.

To gather archival materials, we have drawn on the holdings of several universities, numerous archives, and various commercial companies, but the major source of materials is the Archives of the History of American Psychology, the University of Akron. Quickly surveying the legends of the pictures shows that some archival collections have furnished many more visuals than others. This imbalance comes from differences in the size of deposits but also from personal preferences; some people use cameras only rarely whereas others like to collect and preserve pictures.

Our decision to write about general trends in psychology had the effect of breaking up the careers and contributions of individual psychologists in a way that a history organized around individuals would not. We

have used two aids to help readers find the personal history material that is contained in this book. First, we have placed an asterisk (*) by the name of each person whose work is discussed in different sections of the text; the asterisk indicates that the Index will list the pages on which other information appears. Second, for each psychologist mentioned in the text, we have noted in parentheses the highest degree earned (Ph.D.), the university at which it was earned (Maine), and the date (1928). This information will help the reader locate each person in time and place and will emphasize that contributors to psychology's history are highly diverse in some ways but are always well educated. (An honorary degree is noted only in the rare instances in which it is the contributor's only degree.) This parenthetical identification is included either in the section in which the psychologist is introduced or in the one that gives the most information.

This volume is the result of the cooperation of many individuals; colleagues have shared knowledge about substantive matters and extended numerous other courtesies. Our debt to these colleagues is heavy but gratifying. The names of photographers, others whose efforts and consent allowed publication of pictures, and the people who assisted in identifying photographs are specified at the end of the legend for each picture. The authors are pleased to name in the acknowledgments those individuals and organizations who have assisted with the myriad of details that this project has entailed but are sorry that practicality forces a perfunctory acknowledgment, one that does not allow us to register the keenness of our appreciation.

We must single out one contributor, Joseph G. Benes, Photographic Supervisor, the University of Akron Media Productions, for his effort and skill in creating this book. Almost every photograph received his attention in that it is either a copy he made of a precious original or a new picture that he took. Any photograph without specific credit was either taken or prepared by Joseph G. Benes. He and his staff were indispensable throughout this project.

This book is replete with details—dates, places, names, and sequences of events—and although the accuracy of these details has been checked and checked and rechecked we are certain errors remain, but we are also uncertain as to where they are. Some errors are due to carelessness, some to inconsistencies in the historical facts, and some to differences in the meaning of those facts. We ask for your understanding and suggestions for correcting these mistakes.

John A. Popplestone
Marion White McPherson

Acknowledgments

Individuals:

Leslie Alexander, Louise Bates Ames, James E. Anderson, Marc P. Anderson, Rudolf Arnheim, Magda Arnold, Mitchell Ash, John Barry, Jr., Ludy T. Benjamin, Jr., Charles L. Brewer, Wolfgang G. Bringmann, Bridget Brown, Marion E. Bunch, Evan Calkins, Stuart W. Campbell, Helen L. Carlock, John L. Carter, Norma Chein, Herbert H. Clark, Kenneth B. Clark, Earle E. Coleman, Frederick T. Courtright, Marie Skodak Crissey, Orlo Crissey, Bernard R. Crystal, Vern Davidson, Donald A. Dewsbury, John A. Dillon, Christine Doebbler, David C. Edwards, Dorothy Eichorn, Clark A. Elliott, Rand B. Evans, Judith Fernandez-Latham, Frederick L. Finch, Lorie Fontana, Laurel Furumoto, Joseph F. Giovinozzo, Nathan M. Glaser, Raimund E. Goerler, Gilbert Gottlieb, Gerald E. Gruen, Randall Hagadorn, Katherine Hamilton-Smith, Arthur S. Hanneman, Molly Harrower, Eugene L. Hartley, Ruth E. Hartley, Linda Heider, Lois G. Hendrickson, Mary Henle, Leslie H. Hicks, Melissa L. Hiett, Milton H. Hodge, Shirley Kellogg Ingalls, Beverly Kaemmer, Patricia D. Kellogg, Judi Kincaid, J. W. Kling, Bruce S. Koch, Michael Kozlowski, George L. Kreezer, Penelope Krosch, Cedric A. Larson, Edwin D. Lawson, Joanne M. Lenke, Helen LeRoy, Miriam Lewin, Kenneth A. Lohf, Richard J. Lowry, Nancy F. Lyon, Ayesha A. Maier, Bertha Maslow, William R. Massa, Loomis Mayer, Paul McReynolds, Martha Mednick, Timothy A. Meyer, Willam D. Meyer, Valeria Milholland, Kerri Mommer, Laura V. Monti, Joseph L. Moses, Lois Barclay Murphy, Caroline Murray, G. G. Neffinger, Asher R. Pacht, Nicholas Pastore, Maggie Perault, Janet T. Peterson, Clark P. Pritchett, Jr., Lorrin A. Riggs, Thomas P. Robinson, Judith Rodin, Mimi Ross, Kathleen Rutledge, T. A. Ryan, Peter Salovey, Gary Saretzky, Christine Sauer, Elizabeth Scarborough, Constance Scheerer, Judith Ann Schiff, Neil Sheridan, B. F. Skinner, Edward Skipworth, Wilma R. Slaight, M. Brewster Smith, Helga Sprung, Lothar Sprung, Ross Stagner, Harriet P. Stockanes, Jefferson L. Sulzer, Karen Thomas, Thomas Trabasso, Jill Troy, Loh Seng Tsai, William S. Verplanck, James B. Watson, Gary L. Wells, Michael Wertheimer, Dorritt S. White, and Patricia White.

Organizations:

American Psychiatric Association; American Psychological Association; Bachrach; Boston Public Library; Brown University, Walter S. Hunter Laboratory; Cambridge University Press; Charlottesville *Daily Progress;* Clark University Archives; Columbia University Archives; Columbia University Rare Book and Manuscript Library; Consulting Psychologists Press; Curt Teich Postcard Archives; Duke University Press; Educational Testing Service Archives; Encyclopaedia Britannica; Founders Foundation, AA; Gesell Institute of Human Development; Harcourt Brace Jovanovich; Harper and Row; Harvard University Archives; Henry Holt; Holt, Rinehart, and Winston; Houghton Mifflin; Iowa State University, Department of Psychology; LaFayette Instrument Company; Macmillan Publishing Company; McGraw-Hill; Mort Kaye Studios; National Computer Systems; Ohio State University Archives; Open Court Publishing Company; Presses Universitaires de France; Psychological Corporation; Purdue University, Department of Psychological Science; Richmond *Times-Dispatch;* Riverside Publishing Company; Stanford University, Department of Psychology; Stanford University Libraries; Stanford University Press; Stoelting Company; Swezey Lafayette, IN; Taylor-Sargent, NYC; Teachers College Press; Tulane University, Department of Psychology; University of Chicago, Department of Psychology; University of Illinois Press; University of Kentucky, Department of Psychology; University of Minnesota Archives; University of Minnesota Press; University of Wisconsin, Harlow Primate Laboratory; Vassar College; Wellesley College; Yale University, Department of Psychology; and Yale University Library.

An
Illustrated
History
of
American
Psychology

PART

1

Foundations

–

Last Quarter of the Nineteenth Century to World War I

Psychology has a very long history as a part of speculative, armchair philosophy, but at the end of the 19th century, the times were right to create a new psychology modeled after the many fields of modern science that were coming into existence. This new kind of psychology was most conspicuous in the German universities, but we are also aware of other beginnings.

This new psychology stressed its scientific identity by laboratory investigations using apparatus—just like other sciences. We even find that the psychology of the foundations period has been called "brass instrument psychology."

A remarkable American enthusiasm for this new laboratory psychology occurred and pioneer American laboratories quickly outnumbered those in Germany.

The pluralism and diversity of psychology were also quickly apparent as "systems" and "schools" of psychology were articulated. The importance of these different points of view should not be overemphasized but the fact of pluralism, which still characterizes psychology, should be noted here, at the beginning.

It is also important to notice that, from the foundation period on, psychology has been both a laboratory discipline and a technology that can be applied to advance human welfare. The measurement of human intelligence began at the same time as the foundation of the laboratories.

1

CHAPTER

The European Roots of Scientific Psychology

During the nineteenth century, European universities launched and nurtured research laboratories in a number of sciences. One of the first steps in psychology's entrance into this network occurred in 1875 when the Minister of Culture in Saxony asked Wilhelm Wundt★ (M.D., Heidelberg, 1855) to occupy a chair at the University of Leipzig "in philosophy with special emphasis upon the natural sciences" (Sprung & Sprung, 1981, p. 237). During his 45 years of activity at Leipzig, Wundt succeeded "in establishing both the subject and method of scientific psychology, and in founding it institutionally with a special organ of publication" (Sprung & Sprung, 1981, p. 242). The singling out of Wundt as the "Founding Father" of psychology must not disguise the important fact that contemporaries were also establishing laboratories and building programs in psychology. In fact, William James★ opened an American laboratory in 1875 when he was allocated a small amount of space at Harvard University (Harper, 1950). Although the emergence of a naturalistic psychology can be discerned in many places and in the activities of many people, consensus among historians of psychology points to Wundt as the person, to Leipzig as the place, and to the winter of 1879–1880 as the time of the founding of the first research facility devoted to psychology.

This view of Leipzig, ca. 1931, looks across what was then known as the Augustusplatz and shows the main building of the University. For many years, Wundt lived on this square about 150 to 200 yards to the right of the Paulinerkirche and would have walked past this scene to the Psychological Institute located about 150 yards behind the left wing of the main University building. Time and World War II have altered this scene greatly, although the general relation of the University to the square remains the same.

Archives of the History of American Psychology, Walter and Catharine Cox Miles Papers. Identification with the help of Wolfgang G. Bringmann.

The back of this photograph is annotated by an unknown hand, "Wundt and his collaborators in the Reaction Experiment, ca. 1912." Wundt, in the center, is surrounded by (from left to right) Friedrich Sander (Ph.D., Leipzig, 1913), Otto Klemm (Ph.D., Leipzig, 1906), Wilhelm Wirth*(Ph.D., Munich, 1897) and Ottmar Dittrich (Ph.D., Leipzig, 1898). The large clock-timer and the wall chart suggest that this is not a formal experiment but a demonstration designed to supplement a lecture.

Archives of the History of American Psychology, Anna Berliner Memoirs.

During 1906 and 1907, Foster P. Boswell (Ph.D., Harvard, 1904) attended both the University of Berlin and the University of Leipzig. This one page of lecture notes which he took in a course taught by Wundt attests to the minute analyses that the pioneer experimentalists made of seemingly uncomplicated reactions: in this instance, the hearing of tones.

Archives of the History of American Psychology, Foster P. Boswell Collection.

During his long tenure, Wundt attracted at least 186 doctoral candidates from more than ten countries. The psychology that he advocated was labeled "psychological" or "experimental" in order to distinguish it from the speculative "armchair" psychology that was part of philosophy. Wundt's purpose was to discover the basic elements that make up the mind and to become familiar with their attributes. He pursued this quest for its own merits and with no investment in practical applications.

The Register for Experimental Psychology, "Herrn Geheimralt Professor Dr. Wundt," Summer 1891. This class list shows that four of the students are American, and a fifth, who is British, will have a career in psychology in the United States. This heavy concentration of United States nationals in one of Wundt's classes is unusual, but it does emphasize the German roots of American experimental psychology.

The four Americans are #6—J. L. Steffens (B.A., California, 1889), #8—Harlow Gale (A.B., Yale, 1885), #11—Lightner Witmer, and #18—Edward Pace (Ph.D., Leipzig, 1891). #17—Edward B. Titchener,* born in England, was on the Cornell University faculty for 35 years.*

Archives of the History of American Psychology, Anna Berliner Memoirs.

Wundt's "experimental treatment of the mind" (Baldwin, 1894, p. 364) differed from the psychology taught in America where the discipline was frequently associated with theology: "The mental and moral philosophy in the colleges was almost without exception put in the hands of the president of the college, and he was by unanimous requirement a preacher" (Baldwin, 1894, p. 365). During the 1880s and 1890s numerous American students went to Europe to obtain instruction in a more secular and scientific psychology. They enrolled at such German universities as Berlin, Freiburg, Halle, Jena and Würzburg, but most frequently at Leipzig. They learned the details of the subject matter, acquired skill in linking laboratory data with theory, conducted experiments, and became adept in the use and maintenance of research apparatus. The reminiscences of a few students evoke both the formal content and informal quality of this education.

G. Stanley Hall★ (Ph.D., Harvard, 1878) studied in Germany on two occasions, including a visit during his first postdoctoral year. His evaluation (1912) is explicit and at times enthusiastic:

> Indeed, in these delightful years, there was almost no limit to the field over which a curious student, especially if he was not working for a degree, might roam. . . . he was allowed to drop into almost anything to his heart's content. . . . hearing often very elaborate experimental and demonstrational introductory courses. . . . Fresh from the narrow, formal, rather dry curriculum of a denominational American college, the stimulus and exhilaration of this liberty of hearing was great (p. vi).
>
> Perhaps nothing Wundt ever wrote has caused so many of his admirers and would-be followers more grief and pain than his articles disparaging the applications of psychology. . . . Wundt points as his ideal to Röntgen and his [X] rays, which were discovered by purely scientific studies with no thought of the wide range which their practical applications have since been found to have and to which their discoverer has remained in academic aloofness and superiority (pp. 424–425).

At the 1959 annual meeting of the Oregon Psychological Association, Anna Berliner (Ph.D., Leipzig, 1913) gave an autobiographical account of her academic experiences with Wundt, beginning in 1910:

> Students . . . from foreign countries . . . tried to be as close as possible to the professor. There was no loudspeaker, Wundt spoke in a low voice that was well audible from the high seats where I used to sit.
>
> Psychology was not a profession at that time, and so those who majored in psychology intended to go into academic teaching.
>
> One thing I remember very well, because they talked about it over and over again was that we had to keep all the variables but the critical one constant and that it would be without value to observe at just one point of the critical value, that instead the critical variable had to be changed systematically.
>
> There was a good library inside the [Wundt] Institute where we spent much time reading the journals. It was not customary to use textbooks. Besides the journals, students read the newly appearing monographs like [Narziss] Ach's study on determining tendencies. . . . The backbone of our studies were Wundt's three volumes on physiological psychology.
>
> I succeeded in taking my final examination from Wundt. At first he suggested that [Wilhelm] Wirth★ should examine me on account of my math background, but I did not accept this argument, but just said that I would like to take the finals under him and he graciously consented. He was very kind during the examination and put me at ease. . . . After testing me about the history of philosophy, he asked about the field I preferred. Now, I had worked hard on visual psychology, and it was easy even to quote the footnotes from Wundt's big volume.

The obtaining of a Ph.D. degree also demanded completing a dissertation, but this requirement was a prelude to additional formalities. One of these was publication of the dissertation. Max Meyer★ (Ph.D., Berlin, 1896) explains in an unpublished autobiography

(1935) the problem this requirement posed for him and the solution he found:

> The thesis which I had written and which had been approved by the academic authorities, had to be printed. I of course was too poor to pay the printer. But I found a way out. I sent the manuscript to my former teacher [Hermann] Ebbinghaus,* now in Breslau, who happened to be the editor of a professional journal, the German *Zeitschrift für Psychologie,* and asked him if he considered it acceptable for publication in the journal, under his editorship. He accepted it without any hesitation. So its publication was assured without any cost to me (p. 68).

Completing publication plans permitted candidates to request arrangements for a "defense of the thesis." This was a public event announced on posters, and it was designed to display erudition. Meyer clarifies less formal aspects of the scene. He was told he would receive his degree:

> If I fulfilled only one further condition, that of defending, in the Latin language, before the public, my thesis any other opinions of an academic nature which might be challenged by those who might present themselves and would attack me in the Latin language. The public was not very numerous on the occasion, which happened at eleven o'clock in the morning. There was the Dean in his splendid gown. There was the Deans's clerk. There were three friends dressed like me in what English speaking people would call evening clothes. They were the ones that intended to challenge me in formal disputation and who, of course, had in advance told me what they were going to say. . . . There were three or four other acquaintances and there were three or four strangers who had been led by curiosity and accident into the great Aula of the university building (p. 69)

> After we had thrown enough Latin words at one another . . . the Dean signed and handed me my diploma guaranteed by the Emperor himself; and I was a new man (p. 70).

Once they had obtained their degrees, the students began to contribute to higher education on their home grounds. Much of the impetus for this participation was scholastic, but social vectors were also operating. The Germans welcomed the Yankees and catered to them in some contexts but excluded them in others. Students were readily admitted to institutions and were able to

In addition to establishing the first psychological laboratory, Wundt also founded the first journal for the exclusive publication of psychological material. The inaugural number appeared in 1881, but until 1883 the issues appeared irregularly. The journal was first called Philosophische Studien (Philosophical Studies) *because the word* Psychologische *was in the title of a spiritistic journal then published in Russia. By 1905, this publication was no longer in existence and Wundt adopted the title* Psychologische Studien (Psychological Studies).

This is the cover of the December 1913 issue which contains a dissertation—"On the Perception of Geometric Figures"—by Friedrich Sander, shown on page 6.*

Archives of the History of American Psychology, David Shakow Papers. Identification with the help of Wolfgang G. Bringmann.

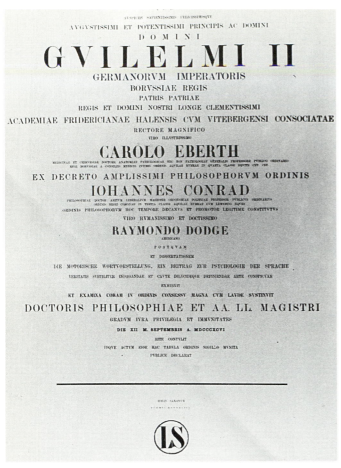

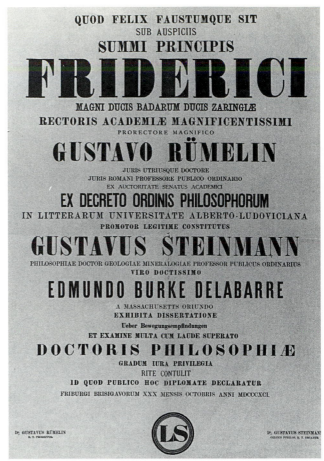

At least two American psychologists who earned German degrees kept copies of the posters displayed to announce their examination. The one on the left (original poster 18″ × 23″) was for Raymondo

Dodge. The one on the right (original poster 19 1/2″ × 25″) was for Edmundo Burke Delabarre.

Archives of the History of American Psychology, Raymond Dodge Papers and Edmund B. Delabarre Papers.

earn a Ph.D. in two or three years but they did not work for the second recognition, the postdoctoral *Habilitation* that is required of aspirants for a German professorship. They did, however, pursue a course that they could control—that of establishing and expanding psychological laboratories in American universities. They worked toward this goal with enthusiasm and diligence but at first were prone to model their efforts after the institution in which they received their

training. As they accumulated experience, they began to innovate and were so successful that the appeal of foreign study was diminished. The exact time required for this autonomy to develop is unclear but a preference for American education was in effect by the turn of the present century (Hilgard, 1987). However, respect for European scholarship endured far beyond that time. One sign of the viability of a European education could be seen in the requirement, until at least the

Three Psychologists Who, between 1896 and 1920, Each Followed a Slightly Different Course of European Education and Employment Across the American Continent

George M. Stratton★ (Ph.D., Leipzig, 1896) died in 1957, in his nineties, the last of the American students who studied with Wundt. The University of California had subsidized his European education. When he returned to the United States in 1896, he founded the laboratory in Berkeley (Brown, 1958).

Archives of the History of American Psychology, University of Iowa Libraries Record.

Max Meyer,★ a German national, came to the United States in 1899 looking for opportunity. He was professor of psychology at the University of Missouri from 1900 to 1932.

Archives of the History of American Psychology, University of Iowa Libraries Record.

William McDougall★ (M.A., Oxford, 1908), a British subject, went to Harvard University in 1920 as a replacement for Hugo Münsterberg.★ He moved to Duke University in 1927 and remained there until his death in 1938.

Archives of the History of American Psychology, University of Iowa Libraries Record.

mid-twentieth century, that American doctoral students demonstrate a reading knowledge of both French and German scientific literature.

The surge in domestic education reduced the number of psychologists who studied in Europe, but it fell far short of ending relationships between psychology scholars from opposite sides of the ocean. In fact, while the number of European professionals who have taken up residence in America is low, many of these emigrés have contributed significantly to the growth of psychology. The pioneers included two stellar individuals: Edward B. Titchener,★ one of psychology's foremost theorists, was at Cornell University from 1892 until 1927; and Hugo Münsterberg★ (Ph.D., Leipzig, 1885; M.D., Heidelberg, 1887), one of the founders of applied psychology, was at Harvard University initially from 1892 to 1895 and from 1897 until his death in 1916 (Hilgard, 1987).

Hugo Münsterberg★ and students at the University of Freiburg in 1891. Münsterberg sits at the table near the center of the picture. Edmund B. Delabarre★ is second from the left. Behind Delabarre's head appears the top section of the apparatus for the Wundt complication experiment and between the two people at the right is a Hipp chronoscope. A small color wheel lies on the table at the bottom-right. On the back wall, like an icon, hangs the photograph of Wundt shown below.

Archives of the History of American Psychology Photographic File, Courtesy J. W. Kling. Permission Walter S. Hunter Laboratory, Brown University.

In the 1930s, refugees from Nazism began to arrive in America. Once again the number was low but the caliber high. By this time, American psychology was so different from the prototype that the contributions of these exiles will be described later in the section devoted to the era in which they were made.

This photograph of Wundt appears in many pictures of classrooms and laboratories of the early period. It was taken ca. 1875–1880 by G. Brokesch of Leipzig, and copies were sold into the 1880s. This is Wundt at the time of the founding of the laboratory (Bringmann, Ungerer, and Ganzer, 1980).

Archives of the History of American Psychology Photographic File.

2

CHAPTER

Pioneer American Laboratories

The first generation of experimental psychologists was sensitized to the necessity of conducting research (there was so much to be learned!). They also recognized that the discipline was new and that their status as scientists could be questioned. The combination of the desires to experiment and to be admitted into scientific circles led to zealous efforts, and the idea of a laboratory was transformed into the reality of laboratories. These physical units varied in the amount and stability of their funding and, thus, in size and equipment as well as in the quality and quantity of productivity.

Historians tend to argue about the time and place of first occurrences, and the founding of psychological laboratories in America has not escaped this sort of controversy. As noted previously, William James★ had a small laboratory at Harvard University as early as 1875. G. Stanley Hall★ also established one at the Johns Hopkins University in 1883. But these dates are misleading because they imply a continuity that did not materialize. Neither the Harvard nor the Hopkins unit remained in continuous operation, and their reopenings were delayed until after at least ten other laboratories that would *not* be interrupted were started. During the 1887–1897 decade, at least 30 psychological laboratories were established at American colleges and universities on both coasts as well as in the south and midwest (Garvey, 1929).

The equipment that was available in any one facility ranged from only one or two to a large number of instruments. An 1893 Harvard University inventory has 240 entries, but the number of instruments appears to be larger since some entries designate more than one item—for example, "five hand stereoscopes" and "a set of twelve tuning forks" (Münsterberg, 1893). The Cornell University register for 1900 totals 375 entries, but some of these are multiples and others are not research tools—for example, a bust of Aristotle and a portrait of Darwin (Titchener, 1900).

The achievements of Granville Stanley Hall★: First doctorate in the United States based on a dissertation in experimental psychology, 1878; first American student to study with Wilhelm Wundt,★ 1879–1880; established at the Johns Hopkins University, 1883, the psychology laboratory frequently cited as the first in the United States; founding president of Clark University, 1888; organized the American Psychological Association, 1892; first president of the American Psychological Association, 1892 (33rd president in 1924); founded American Journal of Psychology, 1887, Pedagogical Seminary, 1891, Journal of Applied Psychology, 1915 (Boring, 1950).

Archives of the History of American Psychology, Burchard DeBusk File.

G. Stanley Hall's bookplate. The original is in colors and gold.

Archives of the History of American Psychology, G. Stanley Hall Documents.

DR. HALL'S STUDY

The study of G. Stanley Hall in the President's House (ca. 1914). The typewriter on the taboret in front of the window and the large speaker horn of the phonograph on top of the revolving bookcase are familiar, but the device just to the left of the record player, on top of the four large books, is not well known. It is a spirometer (see p. 69), a piece of standard laboratory equipment of the period. Why Hall had this device in his house is a mystery.

Archives of the History of American Psychology
Photographic File, Permission Clark University Archives.

THE SEMINARY ROOM

The seminary room in the President's House (ca. 1914). "At Clark, for nearly thirty years, I have met my students at my house every Monday night from seven, often to eleven. . . . From perhaps a dozen to seventy-five or more would be present" (Hall, 1923, p. 327).

Archives of the History of American Psychology
Photographic File, Permission Clark University Archives.

A minimal laboratory. Edmund C. Sanford★ (Ph.D., Johns Hopkins, 1888) published "Some Practical Suggestions on the Equipment of A Psychological Laboratory" in 1893. He estimated that a fully equipped laboratory in an institution would cost (in 1893 currency) four to five thousand dollars. "If a starvation appropriation is all that is to be had, the most satisfactory pieces would probably be: a sonometer [center] and a few tuning-forks for audition [lower left], a color-mixer [upper right] and Wheatstone stereoscope for vision (the later [sic] homemade [upper left], and stop watch [lower center] for time measurements" (Sanford, 1893, p. 436). The minimal laboratory pictured here was assembled (perhaps for the first time) for an exhibit in honor of the 75th anniversary meeting of the American Psychological Association in 1967.

Archives of the History of American Psychology Photographic File.

Ensemble of Optical Apparatus.

This ensemble of apparatus for research on vision was in the psychological laboratory at Clark University in 1892. As the laboratory was started in 1889, all of these pieces must have been accumulated in less than four years.

From an album prepared for the World's Columbian Exposition in 1893, Clark University Archives with permission.

Equipment from the Era of Brass-Instrument Psychology

Helmholtz motor. This motor, powered by an electromagnetic device, generated energy for many instruments. Herman von Helmholtz★ (M.D., Friedrich-Wilhelms Institute, 1842), a German physiologist and an unusually creative and versatile scientist, constructed it.

Archives of the History of American Psychology, University of Michigan, Carl R. Brown Collection.

Helmholtz resonators. The pitch of each of these resonators is different and can be heard by placing the tip of the sphere in the ear canal.

Archives of the History of American Psychology, University of Michigan, Carl R. Brown Collection.

Kymograph. A stylus is placed so that it picks up physiological movements (pulse throbs, muscle contractions) or mechanical movements (from telegraphic keys, metronomes) and scratches a smoked paper mounted on a drum revolving at a constant rate. This particular kymograph is powered by clockwork.

Archives of the History of American Psychology, Marietta College Collection.

Stern tone variators. Blowing air into the resonator produces a tone; changing the height of the piston varies its pitch. The inventor, William Stern,★ devised tone variators for research on the perception of sensory changes (Allport, 1938).

Archives of the History of American Psychology, Ohio State University Collection.

Time-sense apparatus. A sound is produced when the rotating metal arm comes in contact with a terminal. The subject must estimate the duration of the interval between two, or more, of the stimuli. Changing the rate of rotation or the distance between the contacts varies the length of the intervals.

Archives of the History of American Psychology, University of Michigan, Carl R. Brown Collection.

Until about the turn of the century, the hardware that was produced in Europe was considered to be the most desirable. Much of it was visually impressive, a worthy representation of genuine science. Many of the pieces were large, occasionally embellished with marble.

Brass was so prevalent that the label "brass-instrument psychology" was coined. Equipment of this nature could be purchased from more than 50 different companies, most of them in Germany but some in Switzerland, France, England, and the Netherlands.

Instruments—Large and Small

Tuning forks with resonance boxes. Striking a two-tined steel fork generates a sound wave of constant frequency. Many tuning forks have survived because they are durable. Best known are forks 6″ to 8″ tall, but they vary widely in size. The height in one set, for example, ranges from 3 1/2″ to 13″.

Archives of the History of American Psychology, Ohio State University Collection.

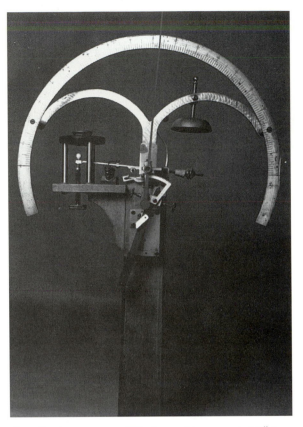

Complication apparatus. This damaged instrument, 54″ in height, is one of the few still in existence. The original was used by Wilhelm Wundt★ in 1861 for an investigation of the effects of attention on perception. A pointer at the top of the instrument sweeps over a scale. A subject must locate the pointer when the bell in the center sounds and attention is directed toward the bell and again when attention is directed toward the pointer. The name of this apparatus reflects this problem of determining how attention "complicates" a reaction (Diamond, 1974).

Archives of the History of American Psychology, University of Michigan, Carl R. Brown Collection.

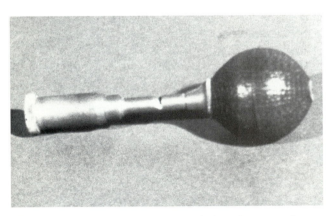

Galton whistle. This small instrument, which produces tones that vary in frequency as the pressure on the bulb is changed, is modeled after one built by Francis Galton★—he placed the piston in the end of a hollow walking stick and the bulb in the handle. Galton blew the whistle on the street and at the zoo to discover the highest pitch to which humans and animals react.

Archives of the History of American Psychology Apparatus Collection.

In America, manufacturing began about 1890 and was carried on by four or five companies, often working from designs produced by such eminent psychologists as Edward W. Scripture (Ph.D., Leipzig, 1891), Joseph Jastrow,★ James McKeen Cattell,★ Lightner Witmer,★ and G. Stanley Hall.★ This cooperation, however, generated only a few orders and production did not increase until the beginning of the twentieth century. About that time, Christian H. Stoelting, a manufacturer, began to take an active personal interest in psychological equipment. He was resourceful in making designs, amenable to continuing collaboration, and a dominant figure in making American manufactured goods the equipment of choice ("Christian H. Stoelting," 1943).

Guy Montrose Whipple★ in a formal pose.
Archives of the History of American Psychology Photographic File.

Guy Montrose Whipple★ relaxing with family.
Archives of the History of American Psychology, Henry H. Goddard Papers.

The first edition of the *Manual of Mental and Physical Tests* by Guy M. Whipple★ (Ph.D., Cornell, 1900) was published in 1910. This book describes the apparatus and the procedures for 54 experiments dealing with physical, sensory, and motor capacity in addition to attention, perception, suggestibility, imagination, and intelligence. Whipple lists 141 items of equipment consisting of both hardware and paper materials such as star patterns that a person would trace while looking in a mirror and charts for measuring astigmatism. He indicates that these items are available from the Stoelting Company. Christian Ruckmick (Ph.D., Cornell, 1913) suggests (1926) that Whipple's *Manual* provoked enough demand for apparatus to allow producers a profit. Carl R. Brown (Ph.D., Michigan, 1928) concurs with Ruckmick that publication strengthened the market but relates the expansion to the research reports that were being published in domestic journals devoted to psychology. Manufacturers had access to this literature, and they gleaned suggestions from it for the construction of a variety of tools that they made available to all investigators (Brown, 1967).

Chronoscopes—Instruments that Measure Brief Intervals of Time

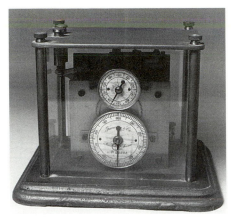

"Amerika" or Münsterberg chronoscope. This instrument which records in units of .01 of a second was designed by Hugo Münsterberg.★

Archives of the History of American Psychology, University of Michigan, Carl R. Brown Collection.

Ewald chronoscope. Ernest J. R. Ewald (degree, place, and year uncertain), a nineteenth century physiologist, devised this piece. It also records in .01 of a second.

Archives of the History of American Psychology, University of Michigan, Carl R. Brown Collection.

Hipp chronoscope. The chronoscope is used in many disciplines. British scientist Charles Wheatstone built the prototype and various individuals modified it. Shown here is the Hipp chronoscope, the modification of Swiss watchmaker Mathias Hipp. This model, in use at the end of the nineteenth century, was one of the most famous (Edgell & Symes, 1906). Although it measured in units of .001 of a second, it looks more like a parlor clock than a laboratory apparatus. It was so expensive and so delicate that its use was restricted to experienced, senior scientists.

Archives of the History of American Psychology, University of Michigan, Carl R. Brown Collection.

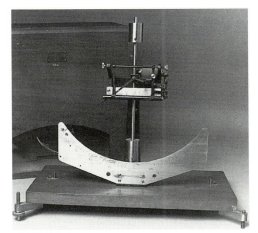

Sanford chronoscope. Edmund C. Sanford★ built this device which was produced in models that vary from a highly valued research instrument to a rough-and-ready tool used at one time in undergraduate drill laboratories. It is sometimes referred to as the Vernier chronoscope.

Archives of the History of American Psychology, University of Michigan, Carl R. Brown Collection.

Bergström chronoscope. John A. Bergström (Ph.D., Clark, 1894) constructed this particular pendulum chronoscope. Several other pendulum chronoscopes, recording in .01 and .05 of a second, still exist.

Archives of the History of American Psychology, Pennsylvania State University Collection.

Dunlap chronoscope. Knight Dunlap★ invented this instrument that is usually referred to by his name. Dunlap, who held an academic appointment at the Johns Hopkins University, preferred to call it the Johns Hopkins chronoscope.

Archives of the History of American Psychology, Ohio State University Collection.

Unusual Equipment

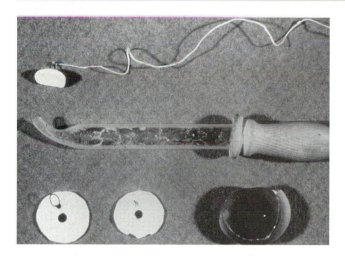

These items are part of the equipment Edmund B. Delabarre★ (Ph.D., Freiburg, 1891) assembled to record eye movements that occur when a subject looks at illusions. Delabarre applied two to three drops of a 2–3 percent solution of cocaine to anesthetize a subject's eye. He positioned a Plaster of Paris cast to cover the cornea of the eye, with an opening directly over the pupil. A thin wire ring embedded in the cast projected to the outside where it was attached to a light thread which led to a lever that moved as the eye moved. This cumbersome technique, reported by Delabarre in 1898, was superseded three years later by photography (Woodworth, 1938). These items were probably not produced commercially.

Archives of the History of American Psychology, Edmund B. Delabarre Papers.

Henry H. Goddard★ assembled this collage of colored paper cutouts on a board 12″ × 18″. Strips of plastic mending tape created the dark stains. On the reverse of the board, Goddard wrote an inscription: "Memory Test—One of the first tests used and made at Vineland, 1906–07." (This collage was used at the research laboratory at the New Jersey Training School for Feeble-Minded Girls and Boys at Vineland. There is no evidence that it was used outside the Vineland laboratory.)

Archives of the History of American Psychology, Henry H. Goddard Papers.

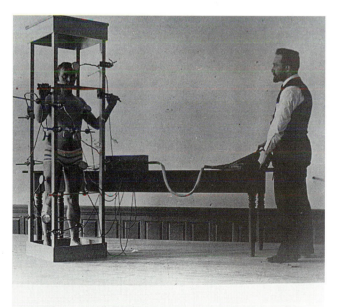

Apparatus for Simultaneous Touches.

This apparatus, designed to stimulate simultaneously various areas of the skin, was used in an experiment on the sense of touch (Krohn, 1893). Edward C. Sanford★ assisted William O. Krohn (Ph.D., Yale, 1889; M.D. Northwestern, 1905) in constructing this equipment. Thaddeus Bolton (Ph.D., Clark, 1894), a student serving as a research participant, appears at the left of the picture. Krohn, at the right, would use the bellows to cause ten tambours (each positioned 1/2″ from various areas of Bolton's body) to thrust corks forward, providing ten points of simultaneous stimulation. During each trial, Bolton was blindfolded in order to prevent him from using visual cues, and he was also required to clench a board with his teeth in order to keep from moving.

From an album prepared for the Chicago World's Columbian Exposition in 1893, Clark University Archives, with permission.

The commercially produced instruments did much to facilitate experimental work, but some experiments demanded unique pieces. Individual researchers designed and constructed these one–of–a–kind tools. Some laboratories provided the assistance of a *mechanician* (in France, *ingénieur*). Some of these custom-built instruments were made from scratch, whereas others consisted of modifications of standard apparatus, and still others were made by cannibalizing parts from various instruments. Unfortunately, many of these fugitive pieces have disappeared and few remain.

A gravity tachistoscope. A tachistoscope allows exposures of visual stimuli that are brief, permitting, for example, only one fixation. The subject would look at the white spot on the panel of the instrument because this fixation point was the center of the stimulus that would be visible when the screen was released.

From Schulze, 1912, p. 205.

A demonstration laboratory, Connecticut Wesleyan University, ca. 1913.

Archives of the History of American Psychology, Walter and Catharine Cox Miles Papers.

A mechanician and a shop were definite assets to the laboratory staff, not only for the construction of apparatus but also for its repair (Sanford, 1893). The equipment, both homemade and commercially produced, was notorious for being, in the terminology of the era, "delicate." In some instances, this adjective referred to *variable, erratic functioning,* and, in other instances, to *a dearth of controls.* The leverage of a dynamometer, for example, would change depending on the size of the user's hand and finger length. Even the best chronoscopes needed to be calibrated frequently. The activation time of a voice key varied with different sounds. The spaced presentation of stimuli was commonly not mechanically regulated but merely monitored by synchronizing each presentation with the ticking of a clock or the beating of a metronome.

A few psychologists complained about these irregularities (Franz, 1900; Wells, 1908), but many more were convinced that instruments could be made infallible, and, with or without the assistance of mechanicians, they worked assiduously to improve them. The early literature is saturated with advice about building and sustaining the integrity of equipment, and mechanical skills became occupational assets for laboratory personnel.

Laboratories served three different purposes: demonstration, drill, and research. For the first of these, instructional equipment was brought into the classroom where basic experiments were demonstrated as shown in the photograph above. Scheduled procedures were carried out in an emphatic, conspicuous manner. The avowed goal was to instruct students in research, but the

Three groups of students work in this "drill" laboratory at Harvard University, not to generate new information but to learn some of the known principles of scientific psychology.

From Nichols, 1893.

On the floor sit two hand-driven color mixers of the size used for individual administration, but next to them (on the far left and far right) as well as on the table in the center are large color mixers for use in a demonstration laboratory.

From Münsterberg, 1893.

polished nature of some of these demonstrations suggested a secondary aim: to display the scientific authenticity of psychology. The drill laboratory was also an educational tool. Members of a class, usually working in pairs, alternately played the roles of experimenter and subject. They were given access to simple, inexpensive apparatus and were required to carry out experiments. The third and most prestigious kind of laboratory was the research facility. Because it offered opportunities to break fresh ground and to generate knowledge, it was essential to the growth of the discipline. These experiments raised new questions and new interpretations which, in turn, led to the development of new equipment and to the design of additional investigations.

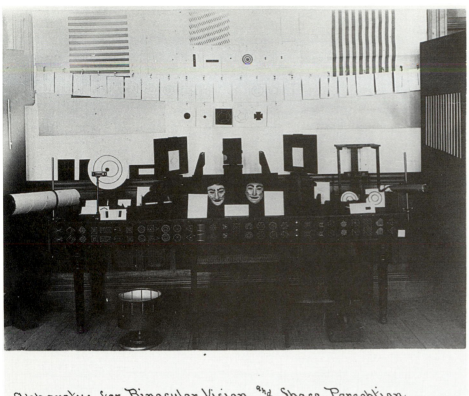

Apparatus for Binocular Vision and Space Perception.

From an album prepared for the World's Columbian Exposition in 1893, Clark University Archives, with permission.

Ensemble of Dermal Apparatus.

From an album prepared for the World's Columbian Exposition in 1893, Clark University Archives, with permission.

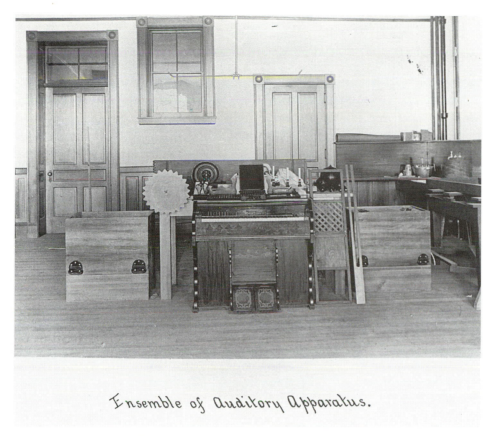

Ensemble of Auditory Apparatus.

From an album prepared for the World's Columbian Exposition in 1893, Clark University Archives, with permission.

Apparatus for Color and Light and Shade.

From an album prepared for the World's Columbian Exposition in 1893, Clark University Archives, with permission.

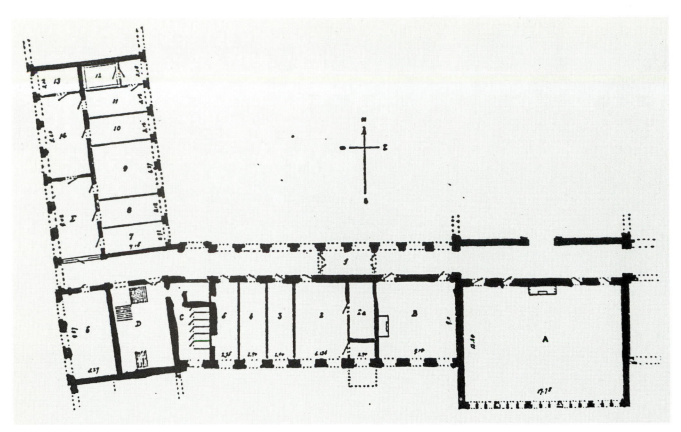

George Stratton* had just returned to the University of California from Germany when he described the new quarters of Wundt's Psychological Institute, first occupied in 1896:

> *Rooms 1 to 5 are . . . for experiments in optics, room 1 having north light, while the others open toward the south. No. 2a is the dark room. . . . No. 3 is the Director's Room. In rooms Nos. 4 and 5 are kept . . . optical apparatus. . . . C and D are occupied by closets and stairs. . . .*

The meetings for the introductory course . . . are held in room 6. Here, too, are the central batteries and the larger pieces of apparatus for demonstration. . . . No. 7 is the First Assistant's room.

> *Rooms 8 to 12 are arranged . . . for work in acoustics. . . . No. 12, the silent room with double partitions and doors . . . .*

> *In room 13 are lockers for tools and for chemicals. No. 14 is the well-lighted library and reading room.*

From Stratton, 1896, pp. 867–868.

Since progress in all sciences depends on the exchange of information, pioneers, as early as 1892, formed the American Psychological Association as a forum for communication. They wrote textbooks, reported the results of research, and printed numerous details about the construction of laboratories and apparatus. Specialized journals were established; some of the first ones are still in existence. The early experimenters, in contrast to those who are working at the present, did not have to compete for publication space. They were able to publish the same article in more than one journal, and they were allowed to write at length free from the restrictions that modern authors must contend with, such as having to follow a standard format; write in an abbreviated, almost telegraphic, style; and generally restrict reports to quantified results anchored to specific hypotheses. Rather, they were free to fill their papers with lengthy explanations of their own beliefs and speculations as well as with drawn-out descriptions of what went on in the laboratory. There

was no prescribed style for research reports, and procedural details might be deferred until the final discussion section. Some citations were omitted, incomplete, or even inaccurate. Practices were so fluid that what is called a *trial* today was frequently referred to as an *experiment,* and, thus, one article might report multiple experiments.

The shortcomings in carrying out and writing up experiments did not come from a lack of effort or standards but from a failure to grasp some complexities of methodology. Scientific precision had to be developed. Researchers had to grasp the importance of reporting all data in as complete, objective, and accurate a manner as possible. They had to learn to recognize that all variables must be identified and treated consistently, to anticipate irregularities, and to make allowances for them *before* starting an experiment (Popplestone & McPherson, 1983). As psychology in America grew, many of these refinements came into being.

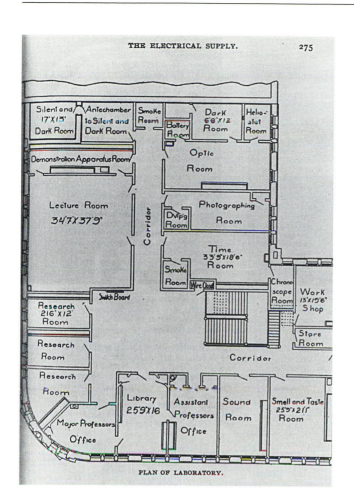

THE ELECTRICAL SUPPLY.   275

PLAN OF LABORATORY.

In 1906, the Leland Stanford, Jr., University opened a new psychological laboratory, an event sufficiently important for Lillien J. Martin (A.B., Vassar, 1880) to publish a description of it. Martin was a Stanford faculty member from 1899 to 1916, but from 1894 through 1914, she made five trips to study in Germany—at Göttingen, Würzburg, Munich, and Bonn. In 1913, the University of Bonn granted her an honorary doctorate (Merrill, 1943).

Martin comments that one of the most important improvements in the new laboratory was the wiring for alternating, direct, and battery currents. The last of these was included because "expense, awkwardness of manipulation, inconstancy and irregularity make the two previous currents unsatisfactory for much experimental work. . . . The laboratory has, therefore, been supplied with various forms of battery currents." The "Smoke Room" is an area set aside for putting the carbon on the recording paper that would be stretched on kymograph drums.

From Martin, 1906, p. 275.

George Malcolm Stratton (Name)   (**Room No.** 1.)

Assoc. Prof. of Psychology, and Director of the Psychol. Laboratory, (Title)

announces regular appointments at the University, for the half-year beginning in the month of *January*, 1900, as follows:

Title of Course.	No. and Sect.	Time.	Room.
General Psychology	2, I	Mond. Wed. Frid. 8:30	1.
Introd. to Psychol. Experiment	6	Wed. 4:30, Sat., 8:30–10:20	7
Psychological Conference	13	Mond. 10:20–12:10	9
Psychol. Laboratory: Advanced	15	Mond. Tues. Wed. Frid. 1:55–3:45	7–14.

Consultation Hours and Room: *Immediately after any of the above Exercises, in the rooms stated.*

The laboratory appears to have been Stratton's main responsibility.

Archives of the History of American Psychology, Knight Dunlap Papers.

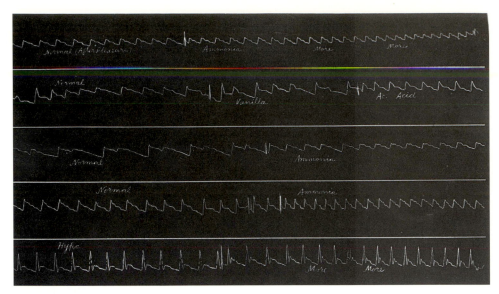

Kymographic tracings on carbonized paper of pulse responses to odors.
Boris Sidis (Ph.D., Harvard, 1897; M.D., Harvard, 1908)
reported data from his doctoral dissertation as well as some collected
less formally in the Psychology of Suggestion *(1898). Shown*
here is a kymographic record of sphygmographic, or pulse, tracings.
Sidis presents these tracings as a record of both stimuli and results.
The stimuli are odors, but there is no information about the
conditions under which they were delivered. Neither is there any
quantification of the amount, although in Record A note "more" and
"more." The bottom tracing, E, was made under hypnosis, and the
differences among this and the others led Sidis to conclude, "The
upper consciousness does not feel the pain, but the subconsciousness
does" (p. 108).

From Sidis, 1903, Plate II.

Systems and Schools of Psychology

At the time that psychological laboratories were being founded, there was widespread disagreement about the subject matter of psychology. The boundaries between psychology and other new fields such as anthropology, neurology, child development, and psychopathology were vague. Some people believed that the subject matter of psychology should be restricted to adult humans. Others thought that children and animals should be included. Still others affirmed that psychology should deal only with the reactions of individuals and exclude social phenomena. While some people would restrict research to the analysis of conscious *experiences,* others would examine mental *acts,* and still others would feature the purposes of *reactions.* Whereas some people accepted psychic phenomena as a legitimate part of psychology, others did not.

A few psychologists tried to manage this uncertainty by formulating a system of psychology, a *point of view* about the most appropriate definition of the field, the most suitable research methods, and the proper interpretation of the experimental results. Various systems were developed, and, although they offered different—and sometimes conflicting—positions, each was promoted by at least a few psychologists as *the* valid conception of psychology, and each group of supporters was called a school.

The devising of systems and the forming of schools helped to define the young discipline but also encouraged controversy and this, of course, generated some linguistic confusion. The words *school* and *system,* for example, are often used synonymously. Obviously, the terms do have much in common, but in precise usage, *system* designates a framework for organizing ideas and *school* is reserved for those who advocate a system. The words *system* and *theory* are also sometimes used as equivalents, but there is a difference in scope. *System* stresses the systemization of the entire discipline, or at least major portions of it, and *theory* stresses the systemization of a particular segment of the discipline.

The pervasiveness of this contention, which was at times intense and even bitter, is difficult to assess. Some psychologists appear to have been preoccupied with defending one position, but there were many more who were not deeply committed to any single point of view and were guided by features they selected from various sources. This choice of eclectic synthesis has, however, not received as much attention as the controversies about systems in histories of the period (Woodworth, 1948). Whatever the actual force of the arguments may have been, there was a period in which schools of psychology were a conspicuous feature of the field.

Structural Psychology

One of the first systems, structural psychology or structuralism, was a modification of the viewpoint that Wilhelm Wundt★ taught. Its best known proponent was Edward B. Titchener★ (Ph.D., Leipzig, 1892), who came to Cornell University in 1892, shortly after a laboratory had been started. He patterned it after the one in Leipzig. Titchener was a domineering figure—the system as refined at Cornell was his and he put it forth with an authoritative stance buttressed by a high level of productivity. During Titchener's 35-year tenure, more than 50 doctoral degrees were awarded and 176 studies were published by students working in the laboratory. Titchener authored 27 books and 216 articles, and he both coedited and edited the *American Journal of Psychology* (Dallenbach, 1928; Pillsbury, 1928).

The goal of structuralism was to ascertain the basic or elementary constituents of the normal adult human mind which was thought of as a compound of momentary mental processes. These processes could be analyzed by the method of introspection, an esoteric technique in which highly trained individuals attend in a very concentrated manner to their own consciousness. These individuals were called *observers* (*Os*) because their direct access to their own consciousness enables them to observe what is in the mind. As the introspective data accumulated, Titchener decided that there are three basic mental elements—sensation, image, and affection (feeling)—and that all varieties of conscious experience are made up of these elements arranged in different compounds. Broader issues of both how and why the mind functions were acknowledged as interesting, but, since they did not fall within the domain of structural psychology, they were dismissed as of no interest to psychologists. To many modern psychologists, this system appears artificial, pointless, and irrelevant. This negative evaluation is understandable today, but it was not warranted in Titchener's era inasmuch as structural psychology was one of the first organized efforts to conduct laboratory experiments on elusive, poorly understood, mental phenomena.

Meticulosity was one of the most outstanding characteristics of introspection. *Os* were told to ignore both the meaning of what they experience as well as the stimuli that provoke the experiences and were ordered to concentrate on the nuances of their awareness. The introspective reports that they produced disclosed shadings and gradations of consciousness that are rarely discriminated outside the laboratory. To illustrate, hearing was found to consist of both noises and tones, with the latter varying in pitch, loudness, timbre (quality), and volume. The sound of a tuning fork is a tone, but the sound of a soap bubble breaking is a noise. If the bubble is small it is a sharp pop, and if it is large, it is a thud. The contrast between different colors is increased when they are equally bright. There are only four distinct tastes: sweet, bitter, sour, and salt.

Cornell University Professor Karl Dallenbach★ (Ph.D., Cornell, 1913) made this plaque of Edward B. Titchener in the style of a relief of Titchener's mentor, Wilhelm Wundt,★ made in 1905 to commemorate the 50th anniversary of Wundt's medical degree (Bringmann, Ungerer, & Ganzer, 1980).

Archives of the History of American Psychology, Cora Friedline Papers.

Titchener was renowned for a rigid formality and an addiction to decorum and to cigars. Students revered, respected, and held him in awe—a mixture that nourished anecdotes. Cora Friedline (Ph.D., Cornell, 1918) reports that during one of the conferences concerning her thesis a cigar ignited Titchener's beard, which at the time was unusually long, and he did not notice it: "And, of course, I couldn't interrupt such a very important man in the middle of a sentence. So I waited patiently until he reached the end of a sentence and I said 'Dr. Titchener, I beg your pardon, but your whiskers are on fire' " (Friedline, 1962).

Archives of the History of American Psychology, Cora Friedline Papers.

Titchener customarily advised students in his home. This picture of the study where the conferences took place discloses why it added to the Titchener legend.

Archives of the History of American Psychology Photographic File.

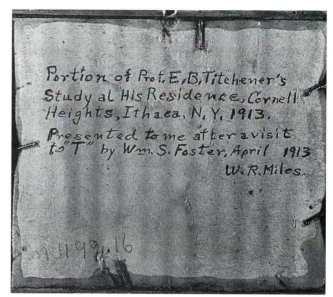

The note, written by Walter Miles,★ transforms a picture into a souvenir. The former owner of the photograph, William S. Foster (Ph.D., Cornell, 1913), served on the faculty at Cornell.

Archives of the History of American Psychology, Walter and Catharine Cox Miles Papers.

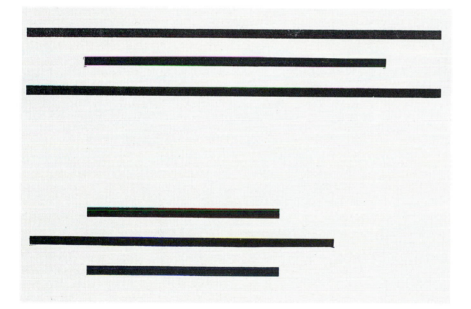

The middle lines in these two clusters of three are equal in length, but they appear unequal because of the length of the lines above and below them.

Archives of the History of American Psychology, University of Michigan, Carl R. Brown Collection.

Stimulation of only one eye produces aftereffects in the unstimulated eye. When moving from a darkened room into daylight, an individual's color sensations have a tinge of blue (Titchener, 1901a).

The structuralists were aware that the mind does not always mirror the external world accurately. They were familiar, for example, with distortions of size, direction, and depth that people experience when looking at some objects and scenes. Structuralists believed these illusions were misperceptions, and they studied them intensively because they saw that understanding them was one means of understanding normal perception. Although illusions were known to occur in various senses, most of the experiments were concentrated in vision, and geometric designs were the devices most commonly used to investigate visual distortions. They were selected because they are not only readily available but they eliminate extraneous and uncontrolled cues found in realistic drawings. Titchener demonstrated the popularity of these readily available items by assembling more than 100 designs used to investigate optical illusions.

The research made it clear that it is easier to measure an illusory experience than to account for it. The perplexity of this problem is indicated in the description (1942) by Edwin G. Boring★ of 12 different theories of the Müller-Lyer illusion shown on page 32 that were formulated in the brief period of 1889–1902.

A ruler shows that the man and the boy are the same height.

Archives of the History of American Psychology, University of Michigan, Carl R. Brown Collection.

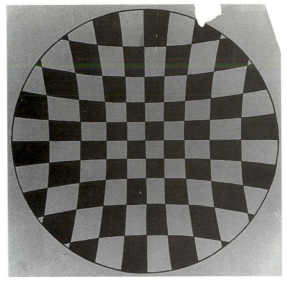

Chessboard illusion. Hermann von Helmholtz★ designed this illusion to demonstrate how perception compensates for distortions caused by the shape of the lens of the eye. The curved lines create an impression of depth, but the lines on an enlarged design, when viewed at close range by only one eye, appear straight. The poster shown here is 16 1/2″ × 16 1/2″.

Archives of the History of American Psychology, Ohio State University Collection.

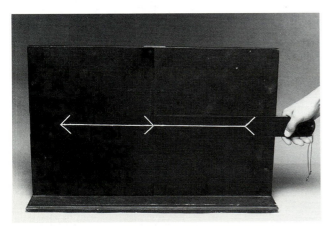

The Müller-Lyer illusion. One of the most frequently used geometric illusions, this was first published in 1889 by Franz Carl Müller-Lyer (M.D., Strassburg, 1880). When the line has arrow-feathers, it appears longer than when it has arrowheads. This model is made of wood and the right side is adjustable, and the task is to move the right side so that the two horizontal segments appear to be of equal length.

Archives of the History of American Psychology, Hobart and William Smith Colleges Collection.

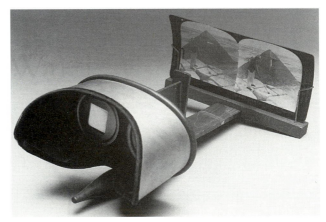

The interest in illusions spreads beyond the laboratory. A stereoscope makes a single, solid object or scene look distinct, enlarged, and in relief. Stereoscopes were commonly used for both pleasure and education. Oliver Wendell Holmes (M.D., Harvard, 1836) invented a model for the hood stereoscope that is pictured here. Holmes (1861) was extravagantly enthusiastic:

> *To this charm of fidelity in the minutest details the stereoscope adds its astonishing illusion of solidity, and thus completes the effect which so entrances the imagination (p. 14).*

> *Of all the artificial contrivances for the gratification of human taste, we seriously question whether any offers so much, on the whole, to the enjoyment of the civilized races as the self-picturing of Art and Nature,—with three exceptions . . . dress . . . architecture . . . music (p. 16).*

Archives of the History of American Psychology, Hobart and William Smith Colleges Collection.

PSEUDOPTICS
THE SCIENCE OF OPTICAL ILLUSIONS.

This is a series of psychological experiments for the classroom and the home, prepared under the direction of Prof. Hugo Munsterberg of Harvard University.

The first box, Part No 1, contains four sections A, B, C, D, made up in this way: Section A, Illusions of Length; B, Illusions of Direction; C, Illusions of Form and Size of Figures; D, Illusions of Movement.

The second box, Part No. 2, contains sections E, F, G, H, made up as follows: Section E. Illusions of Speical After Effects; F, Illusions of Color Mixtures; G, Illusions of Light and Color Through the Influence of the Surroundings; H, Illusions of Indirect Vision.

Part No. 3, comprises three sections I, J, K, arranged as follows: Section I, Illusions of Multiple Vision; J, Illusions of Perspective; K, Illusions of Stereoscopic Vision.

On each portfolio is a full description of the experiments which it contains, so that any boy or girl who possesses a set of this material can perform all the experiments without further instruction. One important peculiarity of Pseudoptics, and its chief difference from books with their illustrations is found in the fact that here everything is transformed into a real experiment. Nothing is shown as a diagram only, but the experimenter has always to act in connection with it. There is no better way to learn than by acting and there is no better result of our acting than learning.

These experiments and the material for their exhibition are planned on a scale liberal in size and durable in construction, equally useful in the classroom and the home and are cordially recommended by such men as Profs. J. Mark Baldwin of Princeton, E. W. Scripture of Yale and William James of Harvard.

The methods of performing the experiments, which easily number one hundred or more in their various modifications, are clearly described and the principles involved in them and illustrated by them are explained in language not too scientific to be understood and yet not so popular as to lose its educational value.

		Price
The whole set, comprising three parts,	.	*$5.00
Part No. 1,	.	*2.00
Part No. 2,	.	*1.75
Part No. 3,	.	*1.25

One of these theories asserts that the wings attracted attention so that judgment was based on the wings rather than on the distance between the ends of the lines. A second, Wilhelm Wundt's★ explanation, asserts that the eyes move beyond the ends of the line when the angles are obtuse but stop before the ends when the angles are acute. Some of this perplexity was due to the assumption, made by the structuralists, that the perceiver is passive and that the perception is essentially a replica of stimulation. Later views of perception would replace this passivity with an assumption of active reaction to the stimulation.

Titchener was adamant that introspections be made under controlled experimental conditions, and it was this insistence that underwrote his success in laboratory

This entry is from the Catalogue of the Milton Bradley Company *of Springfield, Massachusetts, probably 1896. The* Catalogue *is addressed to teachers and parents, purchasers of materials for children's use and education. Although Münsterberg's Pseudoptics is endorsed by E. B. Titchener★ (1901b) and by J. E. W. Wallin★ (1905), the word Pseudoptics is omitted from dictionaries and glossaries of the psychological literature, and we have found it used only in reference to this set of materials.*

Archives of the History of American Psychology Literature Collection, Milton H. Hodge File.

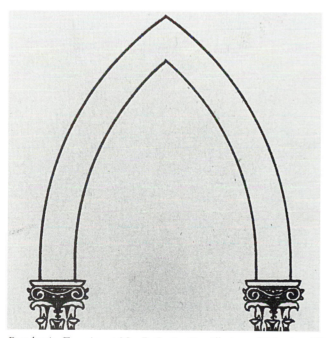 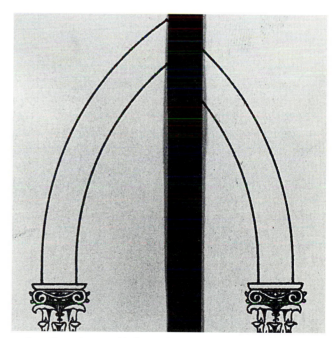

Pseudoptics Experiment No. 7, Section B—Illusions of Direction. The instructions direct placing a black strip lengthwise above and below the arch (on the left). Observing that this placement (on the right) destroys the identity of the segments. The illusion is most apparent when two inner borders are compared.

Archives of the History of American Psychology, University of Michigan, Carl R. Brown Collection.

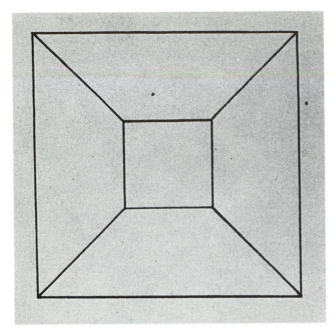

Reversible figure. Looking steadily at this square results in a shift of the relative position of the outer and inner figures—an example of the influence of the perceiver on what is perceived.

Archives of the History of American Psychology, University of Michigan, Carl R. Brown Collection.

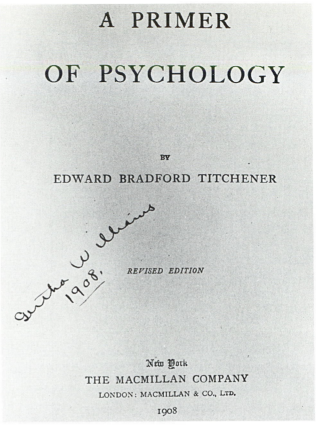

A PRIMER

OF PSYCHOLOGY

BY

EDWARD BRADFORD TITCHENER

REVISED EDITION

New York
THE MACMILLAN COMPANY
LONDON: MACMILLAN & CO., LTD.
1908

As a Mount Holyoke undergraduate, Gertha Williams (Ph.D., Pennsylvania, 1917) was assigned Titchener's Primer. Her mentor, Samuel P. Hayes (Ph.D., Cornell, 1906), advised Williams to obtain graduate education at Cornell University, but she chose to go to the University of Pennsylvania where the dominant figure was Lightner Witmer.★ Although Witmer endorsed introspection, he functioned as a clinician and allowed students to earn academic credit for work in the "Psychoeducational Clinic." Williams described her doctorate as "in psychology with a minor in clinical." Structural psychology may have dominated her laboratory training but her dissertation, "The Problem of Restoration, A Clinical Study" is in the applied domain. During Williams's career at Wayne State University, 1916–1954, she became head of the department of clinical psychology.

Archives of the History of American Psychology, Gertha Williams Papers.

work. He recognized that relevant variables should be isolated, that apparatus should be in excellent working order, and that experimental procedures should be regulated and also recorded with such completeness that experiments could be repeated. These ideals led him to fill the textbooks that he wrote with directives for conducting research. His treatment was restrained by the limited knowledge of the era, but this did not restrict the thoroughness that is found throughout the four-volume *Experimental Psychology* (1901a, 1901b, 1905a, 1905b). This set consists of two volumes each on qualitative experiments and two on quantitative experiments, and in each pair there is one version for students and a second version for instructors.

Titchener's books were used in numerous colleges and universities and were read by psychologists, of various systematic and/or eclectic persuasions, who found in them detailed instructions. They were admonished to repeat observations and advised to explain, and not merely dismiss, irregularities in experimental results. As the field of psychology matured, much of Titchener's laboratory know-how came into widespread use and was categorized as standard operating procedures with the debt to the advocate forgotten.

Those psychologists who relied on Titchener's textbooks for procedural know-how were, of course, exposed to introspective data, and many used the technique, sometimes for its original purpose and in the approved manner and sometimes as a supplement to

behavioral observations they made. In the latter instances, the formalities and restrictions were eroded. In the 1950s, some psychologists became critical of the neglect of subjective information and began to procure personal accounts. They brought back the then outmoded term *introspection,* but, in contrast to Titchener, they included descriptions of both the provocation and evaluation of experiences.

The word *introspection* thus revised is used on the modern scene by two groups who share an interest in studying mentation but are otherwise distinctly different. One consists of psychologists with a humanistic orientation who include "introspective" accounts in investigations of emotionally colored and motivationally intense experiences (Bakan, 1954). The second are the cognitive psychologists who use "introspection" to help them understand how organisms process information when perceiving, thinking, and remembering (Nisbett & Wilson, 1977).

The return of the word *introspection* provides an identifiable, although a narrow and attenuated, bond between Titchener and modern psychology (Radford, 1974). The system of structuralism is obsolete, the fade-out having begun shortly after Titchener's death in 1927 (Boring, 1953). Today, structuralism is, with few exceptions, of interest only to historians of psychology, but laboratory personnel, albeit unknowingly, abide by the rules Titchener promoted for conducting research.

Margaret Floy Washburn (Ph.D., Cornell, 1894). Washburn's doctorate was the first awarded under Titchener. She was the 30th president of the American Psychological Association in 1921—the second woman elected to this office. She was also the second woman in any science to be elected to the National Academy of Sciences. Her contributions disclose a mastery of the psychological literature and theoretical erudition (Hilgard, 1978).

Left: Archives of the History of American Psychology Photographic File.

Right: Archives of the History of American Psychology Photographic File. Permission University of Illinois Press.

Princeton Univ. 1916

This torn photograph was taken at the 1916 meeting of "The Experimental Psychologists" or "The Experimentalists." Titchener organized this group in 1904 and dominated it, setting policies and monitoring invitations to the annual meetings, which were held until one year after his death in 1928. Then the group reorganized as "The Society of Experimental Psychologists" and continued as a self-selected league of no more than 50 members (Boring, 1938).

The air at this 1916 meeting must have been thick with cigar smoke (there are at least five cigars visible in the front row). Women were excluded from such meetings—cigar smoke was ostensibly the reason.

Archives of the History of American Psychology Photographic File.

Functional Psychology

Functionalism defines psychology as the study of mental processes (instead of mental *structure*) and directs research toward the discovery of how the processes work and in what ways they are useful to organisms. It asks such questions as how efficient is memory? is there a safeguard in night blindness? how do animals learn? does fear protect? what cues does an animal receive when its whiskers are stimulated? what kinds of dreams are beneficial and what kinds are harmful? The inquiries about utility that psychologists first entertained were based on questions that had been posed in a variety of contexts, and only gradually were the themes organized into a system of psychology. In fact, the word *functional* is reputed to have been first paired with the word *psychology* by a critic, specifically Edward B. Titchener,★ the advocate of structuralism, when he categorized some concepts—which he denounced—as "functional psychology" (Harrison, 1963). Paradoxically, this labeling directed attention to these concepts and thus encouraged their consolidation.

Once underway, the system of functional psychology gained momentum. The information that was acquired about psychological processes and their advantages and disadvantages was so consonant with the thinking of the majority of psychologists that this point of view became a part of mainstream psychology. In fact, the endorsement and integration were so thorough that, with the passage of time, the system lost its separate identity.

Questions about function were asked long before the emergence of psychology as a scientific discipline, and, as a result, there are both numerous and widely dispersed antecedents of functional psychology. One of these antecedents is phrenology, a pseudoscience. The rise and decline of phrenology is a strange—and instructive—episode in the growth of American psychology. The formal beginning of this doctrine is generally identified as occurring in 1796 when Franz Josef Gall (M.D., Vienna, 1785), a German physician and anatomist, began to lecture in Europe on what he called organology or craniology. This theory was based on a presumed relationship between psychological characteristics and the brain. Gall assumed that the human mind is composed of different faculties and that each of these is localized in a specific area of the brain. He also assumed that the outer surface of the skull and the contour of the brain are the same, and that the shape of the head discloses the nature of various psychological functions. These proposals had a great deal of popular appeal, which was not lessened when

The approach of Franz Brentano (Ph.D., Tübingen, 1864) to psychology is compatible with functional psychology since he asserted that the discipline should be concerned with the activity of the mind rather than with its content. He conceptualized three kinds of mental acts: ideating (for example, sensing, imagining), judging (for example, rejecting, acknowledging), and loving and hating (for example, wishing, resolving). Sigmund Freud★ had "a number of courses with Brentano. The relationship to Brentano is particularly interesting, but difficult to pin down" (Shakow & Rapaport, 1964, p. 42).

Archives of the History of American Psychology Photographic File.

Gall was ordered to discontinue his lectures in Vienna because the Church saw the doctrine as an affront to religion. His ideas came to be considered so dangerous (and important?) that at death in 1828 he was refused a Christian burial (*Dictionary of Scientific Biography*).

Gall's pupil and coauthor, Johann Christoph Spurzheim (M.D., Vienna, 1813), replaced the label *craniology* with the label *phrenology,* and he also elaborated the theory by enumerating additional functions or "powers" of the mind and assigning each a specific location in the brain. In his scheme, there were propensities (for example, combativeness, secretiveness), sentiments (for example, reverence, mirthfulness), perceptive faculties (for example, time, size) and

This PHRENOLOGI bust is molded of plaster. Most of the paper labels on the various areas of the brain have been lost, but "Cautiousness," "Amativeness," "Individuality," and "Semi-Intellectual Sentiments" are still quite legible. The rear of the bust bears the label "APPROVED BY O. S. FOWLER," which refers to Orson Squire Fowler who, with his brother Lorenzo Niles Fowler, founded a firm (just after Spurzheim's death) which would try to bring phrenology to everyone in North America. Historians make a distinction between the objective craniology of Gall and the "moral and inspirational" phrenology of Spurzheim and contrast both with the "commercial," "vulgar," or "popular" phrenology of the Fowler brothers.

Archives of the History of American Psychology, Edwin D. Lawson Collection.

reflective faculties (for example, comparison, casualty). Spurzheim and his successors used information inferred from individuals' skulls to provide advice for the management of a wide variety of personal problems.

Spurzheim came to America in 1832 and spread the doctrine to large, enthusiastic lecture audiences. This journey coincided with a "fever" epidemic of which he was a victim; he died in the third month of his American visit. This dramatic conclusion to a triumphal tour helped to promote phrenology, and the movement grew, even acquiring endorsements by such intellectual leaders as William Ellery Channing, Horace Mann, and Daniel Webster (Walsh, 1972). Phrenology probably reached its height in the 1850s and its longevity was impressive. The *American Phrenological Journal* continued to be published until 1911 and the American Institute of Phrenology existed until 1925 (Dallenbach, 1955).

The acclaim included some transitory approval in scientific circles, but this was dissolved as new knowledge developed. Anatomists learned that the thickness of the skull varies from region to region and that it does not follow the contour of the brain. Research in neurology did not support the notion that psychological functions are localized in specific parts of the brain. Psychology would reject the concept of a mind as divided and limited to the faculties of phrenology. Thus, the legacy of phrenology lies not in its content but in its service to people, or, more accurately, in its promise to unravel the complexities of the human personality and promote human welfare (Bakan, 1966).

A second precursor of functionalism and one that is scientific in origin is Darwinian evolution. Since evolution stresses survival and adaptation, it became almost inevitably, a cornerstone of functional psychology. There are two direct links between this biological doctrine and psychological research: one stimulated experiments on humans and the second stimulated experiments on animals. Both of these sequences were primarily British in origin and the first of them began when Francis Galton★ (B.A., Cambridge, 1844), a cousin of Charles Darwin (B.A., Cambridge, 1831), explored the feasibility of accelerating the evolutionary process by improving the inheritance of humans.

Galton believed that if this were to be accomplished it would be necessary to identify superior people, and he undertook the assessment of individual differences. Galton made a number of measurements, many of which were anthropomorphic—that is, of the size and proportion of the human body, such as standing height, sitting height, extent of the arm span, and weight. He also administered a series of simple tasks, such as visual and auditory acuity, color discrimination, and reaction time. These tests were given to a large number of individuals (almost 10,000!), and procedures were devised for quantifying the "co-relation," or, in modern terms, correlation, among these scores (DuBois, 1970).

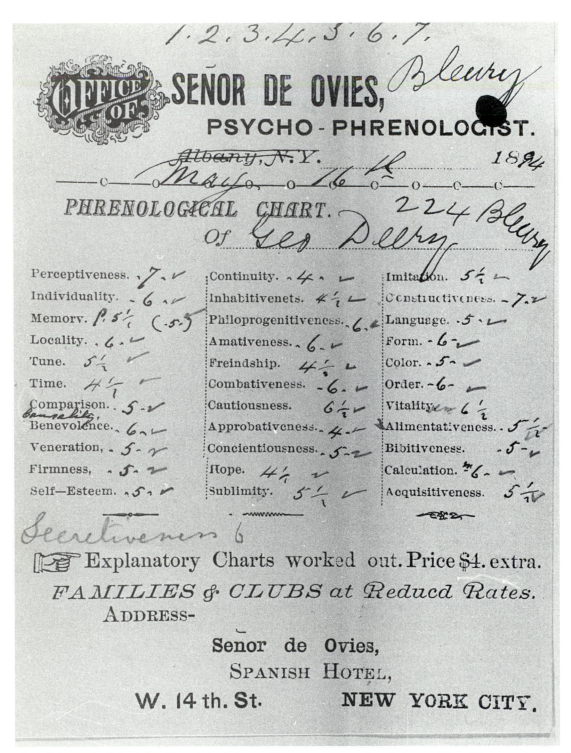

An 1894 report by Señor Julian Segundo de Ovies, psycho-phrenologist. This "Phrenological Chart" quantitatively summarizes a phrenological examination. Each faculty of the mind has been measured and given a score that indicates the amount of each faculty on a scale from 1 to 7.

A qualitative report about each faculty also appears. Following are some of the remarks about two average and two high scores:

Continuity (4):   "You can carry out to completion anything you have commenced—but you can do much better when you have the handling of several things. The wholesale business, buying and selling in large quantities would suit you best."

Approbativeness (4):   "You are not governed by public opinion—you are not insensible to praise or blame; you become suspicious when one flatters you."

Perceptiveness (7):   "You would make a first class detective—and also architect, railroad contractor, carpenter and builder."

Constructiveness (7):   "You ought to possess a remarkable mechanical ability or I should say ingenuity—good at making excuses, getting out of difficulties and be able to manage at a theatre or circus to get a front seat."

Archives of the History of American Psychology, Helen Livingston Memoirs.

Francis Galton,★ a gentleman scholar, earned recognition for his contributions to the fields of anthropology, criminology, eugenics, meteorology, and statistics and for providing information about color blindness, fingerprints, instincts, and mental imagery. He was also an apparatus designer as well as an explorer and has been credited with initiating intelligence testing. Colorful as well as versatile, he tried to measure the efficacy of prayer, attempted self-induction of paranoia, and began a program—but did not finish it—of taking a dose of each medicine in an alphabetic list of pharmaceuticals.

Archives of the History of American Psychology Photographic File.

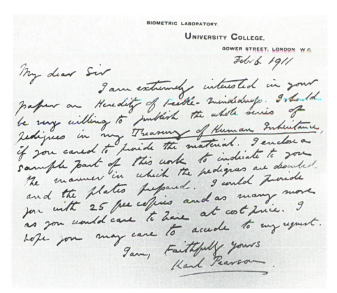

This letter from Karl Pearson★ to the American psychologist Henry H. Goddard★ mirrors the era's conviction that inheritance is dominant. The Francis Galton Laboratory for National Eugenics published "The Treasury of Human Inheritance" as a series of pedigrees of numerous conditions, such as "tuberculosis," "deaf-mutism," "commercial ability," "insanity," "cleft palate," and "legal ability." The letter requests 18 pedigrees that Goddard published in the 1911 Annual Report of the American Breeders Association.

Archives of the History of American Psychology, Henry H. Goddard Papers.

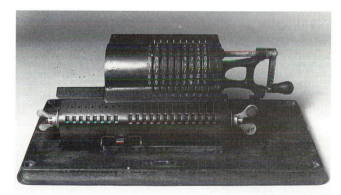

David Wechsler★ owned and used this Brunzwigia Calculating Machine (ca. 1910) for computations published in The Range of Human Capacities *(Wechsler, 1935). As an army student, Wechsler was assigned in 1919 to the University of London where he studied with Charles Spearman★ (Matarazzo, 1981), and he identified his calculator as "a duplicate of the hand [italics added] machine which Karl Pearson used in most of his statistical work published in* Biometrika*" (Wechsler, 1970).*

Archives of the History of American Psychology, David Wechsler Collection.

Galton participated personally in the development of these statistical methods and also made a substantial contribution by virtue of his support of a major figure in the field of statistics, Karl Pearson★ (LL. B., Cambridge, 1881). Galton's tests were too simple to measure effectively a phenomenon as complex as intelligence, but the inaugurating and processing of anthropomorphic data helped to alert psychologists to the feasibility of testing individuals, thereby opening the door to formal examinations of intelligence.

Darwin's belief in continuity between subhumans and humans prompted searches for information demonstrating that people have animal characteristics or that subhumans have humanlike attributes. Both of these possibilities were offensive to theologians, but the naturalists, in defiance, took on the task of showing that there is a behavioral—that is, a psychological—as well as a structural continuity (Warden, Jenkins, & Warner, 1935). They constructed logical arguments and garnered from any available source anecdotes as proof

that animals reason, display high social order behavior, and possess humanlike emotions. Some even made statements as extreme as, "I believe that elephants have immortal souls as much as men, and are, as a species, far more deserving of immortality" (Hornaday, 1883, pp. 508–509). There were what amounted to eulogies

A FRIEND IN NEED.

An example of what the naturalists rejected—from the popular, inspirational Anecdotes in Natural History: The Kind Cow and the Sheep. *"Some gentlemen . . . observed several sheep standing round the head of a cow. . . . The fixed attitude of the sheep attracted the attention of the gentlemen; and as they drew nearer, the cow suddenly raised her head, and the sheep opened a passage for her . . . she reached a large ewe which had fallen on her back, and was unable to rise. The cow gently placed her head under the side of the poor sheep, and gave it a slight toss so dextrously that the ewe was immediately enabled to get upon her feet. After a 'Ba ba' of thanks, and a 'Moo moo' of 'You're welcome,' the two animals walked quietly away. . . .*

"Whenever you see a fellow-creature, or a poor animal, in distress, call to mind the kind cow and the poor sheep. Remember that the Bible says, 'Blessed are the merciful'" (Morris ca. 1873, pp. 44–47).

Archives of the History of American Psychology Literature Collection.

for animal mothers because of the love they display when protecting their young. The ability of some species to see, hear, and smell more acutely than humans was underlined. The intelligence of beavers was said to be shown by their selection of strategic locations for building dams. The spider's "mental power" was demonstrated by the complexity of the web. On each trip out of a nest, bees were observed to stop at only one kind of flower, thereby displaying an aesthetic preference.

Clever Hans of Berlin. Mr. von Osten believed that he had taught his horse, Clever Hans, to think, calculate, recognize colors, and perform other remarkable feats. The horse moved its head to indicate "yes" or "no" and gave more lengthy responses by tapping its forelegs. (Von Osten assigned each letter of the alphabet a number, and Clever Hans ostensibly learned these numbers and tapped so as to spell words.) The demonstrations attracted so much attention that a commission was formed to investigate the matter. One of its members was Carl Stumpf (Ph.D., Göttingen, 1869), of the University of Berlin. The commission did not find deception on the part of von Osten, but neither did it discern what was transpiring. Oskar Pfungst (Hon. M.D., Frankfurt, 1924), a student of Stumpf,★ continued the inquiry (1911/1965) and found that the horse replied correctly only when someone present knew the answer. Pfungst then discovered that people inadvertently provided cues—such as a minuscule nod of the head. If a correct reply was ten, for example, the handler would count the taps and react to the tenth one in a manner different from the previous nine. People today still discuss the lessons learned from Clever Hans (Fernald, 1984; Sebeok & Rosenthal, 1981).

Archives of the History of American Psychology Photographic File.

Some of this anecdotal evidence became so fanciful that naturalists began to argue for direct observations of animals and for more parsimonious explanations—that is, for as few and as simple assumptions about causes as possible. Several of the early psychology laboratories were already in operation when this reform was called for, and experimenters, beginning to observe animals in the laboratory, devised various experimental controls and also endeavored to restrict their interpretations. This replacement of the anecdotal by the experimental method produced more restrained conclusions suggesting, for example, that bees do not have an aesthetic preference but, more simply, go to flowers that have the scent of members of the colony. As the research on animals continued, the focus shifted from the naturalists' concern with evolution to a study of animals *per se*. This change in overall perspective moved the emphasis from the adaptability of the species to the adaptability, particularly the learning, of organisms.

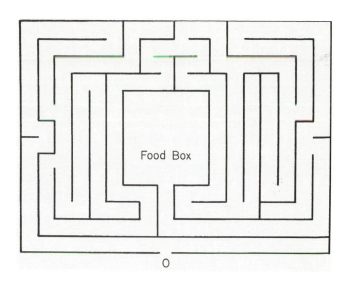

Food Box

0

Ground plan of the maze at Hampton Court—one of the first mazes used in animal research. Willard Small (Ph.D., Clark, 1900) wanted to impose laboratory controls "without interfering with the natural instincts and proclivities of the animal" (Small, 1899a, p. 133). He compiled a diary of the spontaneous behavior of a litter of five newborn rats and used these observations to design experiments (Small, 1899b). He chose a maze because it caters to "the rat's propensity for winding passages" (Small, 1900, p. 208). The floor plan of the labyrinth that Small used (on the right) was an adaptation, rat scale, of a famous maze (above)—still extant in the gardens of Hampton Court Palace—first planted during the reign of William III, Prince of Orange and King of England (1689–1702).
Archives of the History of American Psychology Photographic File.

William James ★ *(M.D., Harvard, 1869) was a versatile scholar. His contributions to psychology were concentrated between 1875 (when he first taught a course with the word psychology in the name and had a laboratory) and 1897 (when his title was changed from Professor of Psychology to Professor of Philosophy).*
Archives of the History of American Psychology Photographic File.

During James's "psychological period," he wrote the monumental Principles of Psychology, *Volumes 1 & 2, (1890). It took him 12 years to write the 1,393 pages. He also produced a textbook abridgement,* Psychology: Briefer Course *(1892), in one volume of 478 pages.*

The "great book" or "James" may well be the most important single work in the history of American psychology. The popular text, "Jimmy," served as the introduction to psychology for large numbers of college students.
Archives of the History of American Psychology, "James," David Shakow Papers; "Jimmy," Psychology Archives Literature Collection.

The seeds of functional psychology were also nurtured by a few pioneer theorists who developed ideas that would later turn out to be useful both to the system and to a more mature psychology. One of the most influential of these individuals was William James, ★ honored in his own time and in the present. James (1890) thought of psychology as a division of biology, and he argued that it should study adaptation. He believed that utility is one of the most valid indices of value, and he talked about the relevance of investigating the role of consciousness, the nature and effects of emotions, and the usefulness of habits and instincts.

A second scholar of influence was John Dewey★ (Ph.D., Johns Hopkins, 1884) who, in 1896, published a theoretical paper, "The Reflex Arc Concept in Psychology." In this, he deplored the custom of analyzing events as links in a chain of elements, such as a stimulus eliciting a response, because, in his opinion, this focus is on artificial abstractions. Dewey suggested that the basic phenomena are acts or functions, and that these sequences are coordinated inasmuch as a response does not mark an end point but rather stimulates a succeeding act.

Many people consider Dewey's article to mark the founding of the system of functionalism, but the principles were not presented in an organized manner until 1903 when James Rowland Angell (M.A., Michigan, 1891; A.M., Harvard, 1892), a student of both James and Dewey, refuted Titchener's previously noted criticism of functional psychology. In his first article on this topic, he proposed some of the basic propositions of the system, and he reviewed this position (1907) in his presidential address to the American Psychological Association, entitled "The Province of Functional Psychology." He did not formulate a formal system and made no pretensions of completeness but these papers introduced a viewpoint that stresses adaptive mechanisms and extends the subject matter of psychology beyond the structure of a generalized adult human mind to include animals and children. That viewpoint also supplements research on the similarities among individuals with research on their differences. This approach to psychology is inclusive, and, in that respect, it contrasts with the exclusive character of structuralism. This openness did not foster a closely knit, self-conscious school, but, again in contrast to structuralism, it encouraged a number of people to integrate functional concepts into a diversity of research topics.

There were, however, a few groups of psychologists who were explicit advocates of functionalism. One of these was based at the University of Chicago where Dewey and Angell were both faculty members. In 1908, these two were joined by another proponent of functionalism, Harvey Carr★ (Ph.D., Chicago, 1905). He became head of the department in 1926 and held that position until retirement in 1938. During his tenure, other systems were also taught, but investigations of adaptive processes and the acquisition of practical information occupied the foreground (Heidbreder, 1933).

Columbia University was also a center of functional psychology, and a favorable atmosphere for the movement began there with James McKeen Cattell.★ He did not formulate a systematic position but enthusiastically pursued research that fused naturally

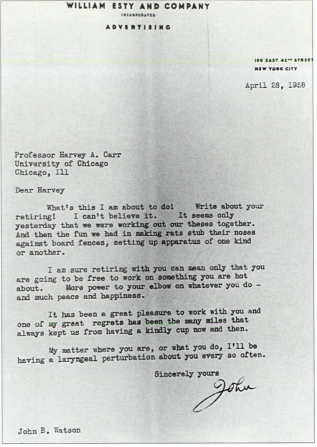

This is one of more than 130 letters sent to Harvey Carr★ in honor of his retirement from the University of Chicago. John B. Watson,★ the well-known founder of the system of behaviorism, wrote this letter. Watson and Carr collaborated on research, and Watson described Carr as one of his closest friends at Chicago, an example of mutual respect between members of different schools—in this instance, the systems of functionalism and behaviorism.

The "laryngeal perturbation" in the last line is a joke among psychologists. In order to avoid the subjectivity of the concept of "mind" Watson defined thought as "sub-vocal speech." Thus, a "laryngeal" reaction would be a thought.

Archives of the History of American Psychology, Harvey Carr Memoirs.

with functional principles, specifically the measurement of individual differences. Cattell's students explored a variety of topics that were consistent with functionalism. Among the most notable of these were two who had also studied with William James.★

One was Edward L. Thorndike★ (Ph.D., Columbia, 1898), who began as early as his graduate student days to investigate learning—specifically how adaptive responses are "stamped in" and nonadaptive responses "stamped out." Thorndike observed that cats learn gradually to manipulate a latch in a way that allows them to escape from a cage and procure food. He related the repetition of the correct response to the

Edward L. Thorndike taught for one year at Western Reserve University and then settled into Teachers College, Columbia University, for the remainder of his career, 1899–1940. He called himself a "connectionist psychologist" but others often called him a "Columbia functionalist." While Thorndike devoted much of his professional activity to the study of learning and the improvement of education, he was a lifelong believer, as were many of his contemporaries, in the power of heredity to limit accomplishment.

Archives of the History of American Psychology Photographic File.

Robert S. Woodworth, shown here as a young man, joined the faculty of Columbia University in 1903 as an instructor and continued lecturing through 1958. His viewpoint is usually described as "functional" although he found that description somewhat narrow and described himself as "dynamic" and "eclectic."

His Experimental Psychology (889 pages), first published in 1938, stood for many years as a best friend for psychology graduate students. Based on an extraordinary grasp of research problems and methods, it covered the range of experimental psychology (Estes, 1981). Woodworth and Harold Schlosberg (Ph.D., Princeton, 1928) revised the book in 1954, and then in 1971, J. W. Kling (Ph.D., Illinois, 1951) and L. A. Riggs★ (Ph.D., Clark, 1936) edited Woodworth and Schlosberg's Experimental Psychology.

Archives of the History of American Psychology, University of Iowa Libraries Record.

Woodworth in his 80's. This photograph was taken in 1958, the year of Woodworth's publication of Dynamics of Behavior. Contemporary Psychology used this portrait to illustrate a review of the book (Mowrer, 1959). A note on the reverse of the original photograph indicates that it was taken by Edwin G. Boring,★ then editor of Contemporary Psychology.

Archives of the History of American Psychology, S. Stanfeld Sargent Papers.

consequence—that is, to rewards of food. He first called this process *trial and success,* but others call it *trial and error,* a label used in the eighteenth century by at least one author (Taine, 1876/1877). Thorndike carried out numerous experiments on learning in various species, and, as this research progressed, he came to be known as an expert in learning rather than as a functional psychologist—a clear illustration of a loss of identity because of a general acceptance (Jonçich, 1968).

Cattell's second outstanding student was Robert S. Woodworth★ (Ph.D., Columbia, 1899) who, in accord with Dewey's criticisms of elements as unsatisfactory explanatory units, replaced the atomistic formula S→R (a stimulus elicits a response) with S→O→R (a stimulus acts through the organism to elicit a response) (Woodworth, 1929). Woodworth was involved in many different areas of psychology, but he emphasized research on how the organism carries out responses (mechanisms) and why particular ones are activated (drives).

From 1891 to 1927, Columbia awarded 106 doctorates in psychology. Although Columbia students and faculty were not restrained by membership in a rigid, controlling school, many devoted their careers, both in teaching and in research, to problems of major importance to functional psychology. In step with their Chicago contemporaries, they succeeded in injecting the system into psychology as a whole (Woodworth, 1942).

John B. Watson★ at 30 years of age, as the Hopkins years begin.

Archives of the History of American Psychology, Cedric A. Larson/John B. Watson Papers. Identification with the help of Cedric A. Larson.

Watson in later adulthood.

Archives of the History of American Psychology Photographic File.

Watsonian and Methodological Behaviorism

Behaviorism was formulated in four widely recognized versions. The first was a system proposed by John B. Watson★ (Ph.D., Chicago, 1903) during the first two decades of the twentieth century. Watson's recommendations were unorthodox in that he stressed two significant departures from tradition. He asserted that the only appropriate subject matter for psychology is behavior and that the mind is an inappropriate—even an impossible—topic for scientific psychology because it is immaterial.

Watson began to think about an objective psychology during his graduate student days at the University of Chicago. He accepted the functional proposals then in circulation at Chicago that psychology should break away from the restraints imposed by structuralism's definition of the field. Apparently, he found experimental work gratifying but was annoyed at the custom that prevailed at that time of inferring the consciousness of animals. He stated, "With animals I was at home. . . . More and more the thought presented itself: Can't I find out by watching their behavior everything that the other students are finding out by using O's [Observers]" (Watson, 1936, p. 276). He believed that procedures that are feasible with animals would also be useful in the study of other organisms that are unable to introspect: infants, children, and adults who do not communicate because of hearing impairment or psychiatric disorder. In this sense, Watson perceived the *restriction* to behavior as an *extension* of the discipline.

Watson's early research reflected this preference in that it included experiments that were designed to disclose the sensory reactions of animals by observing

Robert M. Yerkes with some friends. Yerkes★ was one of America's most eminent and productive psychologists. He contributed to several different areas within psychology and his name appears again and again in this volume.

Archives of the History of American Psychology Photographic File.

changes in responses when sensory cues are varied. In the first of these, rats were deprived—in succession—of sight, sound, smell, as well as feedback from stimulation of their whiskers, and assessments were made of the effects of each interference on their ability to learn a maze (Carr & Watson, 1908; Watson, 1907). In a second program, Robert M. Yerkes★ and Watson (1911) built equipment that displayed different visual stimuli (for example, green vs. red or brilliant vs. dim light) and also measured their physical properties. By rewarding an animal for choosing one of these stimuli, these psychologists were able to discover what differences between stimuli the animal discriminates.

Cambridge, May 24.

Dear Mr. Dunlap:—

I am very glad to report to you that you have passed the Preliminary Examinations...

Yours very truly,

H. Münsterberg.

Professor Münsterberg* writes (ca. 1903) to his graduate student with the anxiety-reducing information that he passed the "Preliminary Examinations"—a critical step in doctoral education.

Watson gave Karl Lashley* (Ph.D., Johns Hopkins, 1914) the major credit for the conditioning research they conducted at Johns Hopkins. In the course of this work, Lashley became interested in tracing conditioned-reflex neural pathways through the cortex, and when he found this task impossible he turned to the relationship between brain function and behavior. He became America's most eminent neuropsychologist, highly respected for his ingenuity in devising ways of disclosing the effects of brain operations (Hilgard, 1987). He delivered his presidential address (1930), "Basic Neural Mechanisms in Behavior," to the American Psychological Association in 1929, the year that he published Brain Mechanisms and Intelligence.

Captain Knight Dunlap* on leave from the Johns Hopkins University during the First World War.

In 1908, Watson went to the Johns Hopkins University in Baltimore as director of the Psychological Laboratory, and there he encountered colleagues who shared many of his opinions about psychology. One associate was Knight Dunlap* (Ph.D., Harvard, 1902), a faculty member who had lost faith in "the old gods of introspection, consciousness, and sensation" (Dunlap, 1932, p. 44). Another ally, who was a student at the time of Watson's arrival, was Karl Lashley.* He agreed with Watson's approach and assisted him in the laboratory. In Baltimore, Watson began to sharpen his thinking about psychology-as-behaviorism, and he delivered a series of lectures at both Johns Hopkins and Columbia University. One of these, "Psychology as the Behaviorist Views It," was published in 1913. This is generally considered to be the first formal presentation of what came to be known as classical, or Watsonian, behaviorism.

In the course of Watson's pursuit of objective methods, he looked into some specialized learning procedures that were being carried out in Russia to induce what were then called conditional reflexes. Because of the language barrier, there was little detailed information about how to do this and Watson and Lashley in collaboration began to explore procedures. Watson was so favorably impressed with what he discovered that he would come to rank the technique as one of the most important methods in behaviorism. This adoption and endorsement make it necessary to describe, at least briefly, the phenomenon.

Ivan Petrovitch Pavlov★ (M.D., Military Medical Academy, St. Petersburg, 1883), a physiologist investigating dogs' digestion, observed that the animals salivated not only when they encountered food but also when they encountered stimuli that were associated with the food: visual, tactile, and auditory stimuli and even Pavlov himself. He thought of the salivary reactions as "psychic" but at the same time insisted that, because they are the result of neurological events, they constitute an objective method of investigation. Pavlov took on the task of finding how to induce these reactions. One of the ways that he discovered consisted of sounding a tone for a few seconds before food is presented as well as during a brief interval while the dog first has access to the food. He found that repeating these paired presentations results in the dog's salivating when hearing the sound alone.

Vladimir Mikhailovich Bekhterev (M.D., Military Medical Academy, St. Petersburg, 1881), a contemporary of Pavlov, also succeeded in eliciting motor reflexes in both humans and animals by repetitively coupling stimuli, for example, eliciting a dog's withdrawal of its forepaw by pairing the sound of a tone with a mild electric shock. Bekhterev referred to this variety of learning as "association-reflexes," but that label connoted mentalism and Watson preferred to refer to conditioned secretion reflexes and conditioned motor reflexes. His successors would adopt the label *conditioned responses,* and refer to the learning of them as classical conditioning.

Researchers soon began to refine and to standardize procedures, and they also developed a specialized vocabulary. The originally effective stimulus—food, shock—is called the U(nconditioned) S(timulus), and the originally ineffective stimulus—light, tone—is called the C(onditioned) S(timulus). A response that is provoked by an US, such as salivating at the appearance of food or withdrawing from a mild shock, is referred to as an U(nconditioned) R(esponse). A response that is provoked by a CS, such as salivating or withdrawing at the sound of a tone, is referred to as a C(onditioned) R(esponse). Once a CR is established, there must be a program for re-presenting the paired stimuli or the organism will learn that the CS does not signal the US, and the CR will fade (Hilgard & Marquis, 1940).

Watson devoted his presidential address to the American Psychological Association to "The Place of the Conditioned-Reflex in Psychology." He flaunted the objectivity of conditioning but also acknowledged the rudimentary status of the technique (1916). He

Pavlov★ greeting visitor(s) to an elaborate research facility that the Soviet government created for him near Leningrad in the 1930s. The institute offered a parklike setting with ample space for dogs, homes for the staff, laboratory facilities, and a house for Pavlov and his family (Cannon, 1936).

Archives of the History of American Psychology, Marion E. Bunch Gift. Photograph by Morton May.

In the foreground, walks one of the numerous contributors to Pavlov's research enterprise. The background shows the laboratory under construction.

Archives of the History of American Psychology, Marion E. Bunch Gift. Photograph by Morton May.

recounted some problems he had encountered and reported difficulty, but not defeat, in conditioning the human pupillary contraction by using a bell and a strong light. Watson stressed this success because the pupillary reflex is not under voluntary control and conditioning it demonstrated that a CR is not merely a

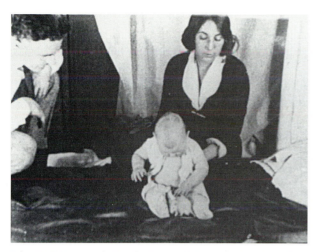

John B. Watson with Rosalie Rayner holding Little Albert who seems to be reaching, with no apparent fear, for the white rat between his feet. Fear of the animal was conditioned by making a noise that did frighten him—a loud clanging one, whenever he touched the rat.
Archives of the History of American Psychology, University of Michigan, Media Resources Collection.

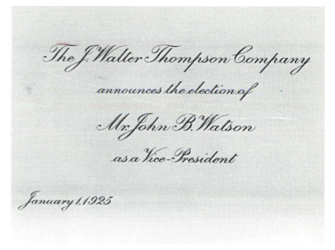

Archives of the History of American Psychology, Cedric A. Larson/John B. Watson Papers.

voluntary reaction. Watson saw the method as scientifically authentic, a dramatic improvement over introspection, and applicable to different species and different sensory modalities.

Watson's research was interrupted by World War I. During military service, he dealt with a variety of psychological problems but none were closely related to the promotion of behaviorism. In 1918, he was able to return to the Johns Hopkins University and resume work on the system.

Watson's first specifications were primarily methodological in that he substituted *behavioral* for *mentalistic* concepts. Thinking, for example, was defined as implicit muscular movements, particularly laryngeal ones. Introspective accounts were replaced with verbal reports, descriptions of the subject's reactions to experimental manipulations. They were deemed to be legitimate because they constituted a person talking, and this is tangible, overt behavior.

This focusing of the spotlight on behavior fostered the formulation of a series of premises that, in combination, formed a system and gave precedence to certain research problems. One of these propositions assigned priority to what the organism as-a-whole is doing—talking, calculating, dreaming, dancing. This was significant in that it distinguished the subject matter of psychology from that of physiology. A second premise affirmed that behavior is induced by stimuli; Watson wanted to be able to predict a response once the stimulus is known and to predict a stimulus once the response is known. This concern with immediate, direct provocation made it easy to minimize the importance of internal variables and to focus on the stimuli that impinge on a behaving organism. It was an easy step from this perspective to the opinion that

experience, or learning, is the most influential determiner of behavior. This modifiability thus directed attention to the learning that takes place in infancy and childhood.

In light of the apparent importance of early experience, Watson began to explore conditioning in human infants. In 1920, with Rosalie Rayner (A.B., Vassar, 1919), he published an account of the conditioning of "Little Albert," 11 months of age, to fear a white rat. The procedures that Watson and Rayner used were much less exact than those used in modern classical conditioning research, but the experiment was nonetheless a landmark in that it indicated that an emotion is learned. Because emotions involve both glandular and muscular reactions, they were considered to be complex; thus, conditioning them became a demonstration of the feasibility of conditioning complicated reactions.

Watson's research ended abruptly in 1920 when the university, reacting negatively to his divorce, requested his resignation. Beginning in the fall of 1920, he began work in advertising and on January 1, 1921, he became a full-time employee of the J. Walter Thompson Company. In 1924, he was made vice president, and, in 1936, he resigned from Thompson to become vice president of a second advertising firm, William Esty and Company (Watson, 1936).

Watson's contributions to systematic psychology were sparse after he pursued a business career, but they did include a chapter written in 1926 about the concept of instincts in psychology. In it, Watson declares that much of what is termed *instinct* actually consists of conditioned responses. In this discussion, he affirms his belief that a behavioral technology was at hand and that it could induce desired behavioral effects. In his own words,

Give me a dozen healthy infants, well-formed, and my own specified world to bring them up in and I'll guarantee to take any one at random and train him to become any type of specialist I might select—a doctor, lawyer, artist, merchant-chief, and, yes, even a beggar-man and thief, regardless of his talent, penchants, tendencies, abilities, vocations, and race of his ancestors.

Watson, 1926, p. 10.

In spite of the brevity of his academic career, Watson had an indelible impact on the discipline. He spoke with authority and conviction, sometimes in overstatements, and, in some instances, by oversimplifying and being offensive. His stance was iconoclastic and self-doubts apparently were alien to him: "With the simplicity and finality of the Last Judgment, behaviorism divides the sheep from the goats. On the right hand side are behaviorism and science and all its works; on the left are souls and superstition and a mistaken tradition; and the line of demarcation is clear and unmistakable" (Heidbreder, 1933, p. 236).

Mary Cover Jones (Ph.D., Columbia, 1926) in her early twenties. When she learned about Little Albert, she began to speculate as to whether or not fear could be "unconditioned." After discussing the matter with Watson, she included conditioning among a number of different strategies in a study designed to remove fear (Jones, 1924a, 1924b).

Courtesy 1919 Vassarian Yearbook.

Jones clarifies her role in the history of behavior modification in this letter to Lois Murphy and Gardner Murphy.* Wolpe refers to Joseph Wolpe (M.D., Witwatersrand, 1948). The participants in the program are eminent developmental psychologists: Robert Sears,* Jean MacFarlane (Ph.D., California, 1922), Marjorie Honzig (Ph.D., California, 1936), and Lois Stolz (Ph.D., Columbia, 1925). (Jones's lecture on behavior therapy was published in 1975).*

Archives of the History of American Psychology, Gardner and Lois Barclay Murphy Papers.

James B. Watson, the son of John B. Watson, at the annual meeting of the American Psychological Association, Los Angeles, 1981. He participated in the symposium "John B. Watson's Life, Times, and Work" and spoke from a son's perspective about his father.

Archives of the History of American Psychology, Cedric A. Larson/John B. Watson Papers.

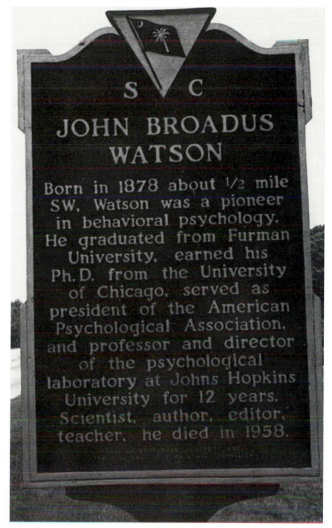

JOHN BROADUS WATSON

Born in 1878 about 1/2 mile SW. Watson was a pioneer in behavioral psychology. He graduated from Furman University, earned his Ph.D. from the University of Chicago, served as president of the American Psychological Association, and professor and director of the psychological laboratory at Johns Hopkins University for 12 years. Scientist, author, editor, teacher, he died in 1958.

This historical marker stands beside U.S. Highway 276, about 1 mile northwest of the small village of Travelers Rest, South Carolina—the birthplace of John B. Watson. Travelers Rest is located approximately 8 miles northwest of the city of Greenville, the site of Furman University.

Archives of the History of American Psychology, Donald A. Dewsbury Gift, Photograph by Donald A. Dewsbury. Identification with the help of Charles L. Brewer.

There were two main criticisms of Watsonian behaviorism. One was the restriction of psychology to behavior. This was a severe blow to the structuralists who saw consciousness as the most important subject matter. The second criticism was directed toward the emphasis on the stimulus and the response with a neglect of the organism. This mechanistic interpretation denied the functionalists' assertion that the organism as well as the stimulus influences a response. The critics thought of these limitations as serious, and their censure was so adverse that Watsonian or classical behaviorism was dubbed *radical* or *naive* behaviorism.

There were various recommendations as to how to achieve procedural objectivity while still incorporating components of traditional psychology. One of the earliest resolutions became a second version of behaviorism, called methodological behaviorism. This is basically a thoroughgoing application of the practice that Watson initiated of converting mentalistic concepts into behavioral ones and eliminating those that cannot be converted: "A conscious state which is not expressed in some form of behavior is, as far as science is concerned, non-existent. The inference of

consciousness is, therefore, unnecessary, since in the last analysis behavior is the only thing that can be classified" (Weiss, 1917, p. 316).

Methodological behaviorism provoked numerous experimental designs intended to yield measures of behavior that cue mentation. An early resourceful example was an attempt to discover whether ring doves react to the Müller-Lyer illusion (p. 32). Using the Yerkes-Watson apparatus for measuring vision in animals, Carl J. Warden,★ assisted by Jacob Baar (1929), trained two doves to peck from an area marked by the shorter of two horizontal lines. When this was accomplished, the experimenters added the Müller-Lyer arrowheads and measured the difference in length that would provoke the birds to go to the segment that appeared shorter to humans. A second illustration involved apparatus designed to measure the ability of different species to learn. The equipment consisted of a cluster of three platforms, and the animal was rewarded for stepping on each of them in a specified sequence. Some species learned to depress only platform 1, whereas others mastered the sequence 1–2–3–2 (Warden, Jenkins, & Warner, 1935).

This kind of approach gained momentum, and finally it became commonplace:

> Methodological behaviorism, like Functionalism, has conquered itself to death. . . . Virtually every American psychologist, whether he knows it or not, is nowadays a methodological behaviorist. That goes for those who glorify John B. Watson as well as for those who belittle him.

Bergmann, 1956, p. 270.

Watsonian and methodological behaviorism were followed in the late 1930s by two additional variations: neobehaviorism and operant behaviorism, the version devised by B. F. Skinner.★ These views emerged in an era when systems of psychology were losing importance and the tenor of the discipline differed from the tenor of the one in which Watson functioned. These differences make it advisable to postpone accounts of them until the milieux in which they flourished are described.

Gestalt Psychology

Gestalt psychology is an enlightened, sophisticated system that organizes the subject matter of psychology in an innovative and singular manner. It originated in Germany, and the identifying word Gestalt has no equivalent in English but has been translated variously as *configuration, pattern, segregated whole,* and *totality.* Currently, the term is commonly written as Gestalt (plural Gestalten), with the capital *G* reflecting the Germanic origin and the lack of italics reflecting the integration into modern English. The unusual nature of the system combines with the translation problems to make an account of how the system developed more informative than a formal definition.

The first publication of the Gestalt point of view was a report in 1912 by Max Wertheimer★ (Ph.D., Würzburg, 1904) of a series of experiments on apparent movement—that is, the perception of motion when separate, stationary stimuli become successively salient. This is a familiar experience and one that occurs in a

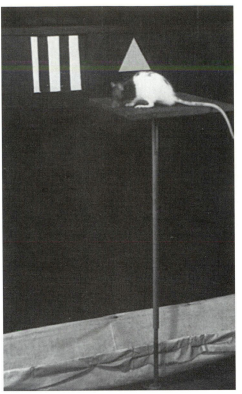

This equipment was built by Karl Lashley,★ Watson's collaborator at Johns Hopkins. An animal faces two designs: one is mounted on a card that falls when the rat jumps against it, and the second is rigid so that a jump against it results in a bumped nose and a fall into a sling that prevents serious injury. The positions of the designs alternate randomly so that the animal does not learn merely to jump to the left or to the right (Lashley, 1938). As the trials continue, the rat more frequently selects the card that falls and leads to food. This change from a nearly chance choice to a consistent selection of a rewarded stimulus allows the behaviorist to infer that the animal has learned to discriminate between the two designs without resorting to subjective concepts such as "consciousness," "mind," or "thought."
Archives of the History of American Psychology, David P. Boder Museum Collection.

variety of contexts. The most common is probably the viewing of a film. This is perceived as motion even though the actual stimuli are a series of still pictures that are projected rapidly and sequentially. A second well-known example of apparent movement is the advertising practice of illuminating a set of motionless arrows at a rate and brightness that causes them to appear to move toward, and thereby calls attention to, a particular commercial enterprise.

The structuralists classified these stroboscopic effects as illusions because they thought they were the result of mistakes in the interpretation of visual sensations.

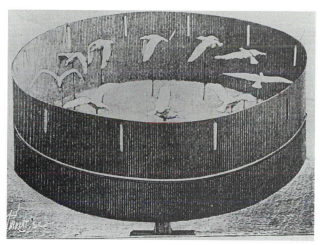

This woodcut shows an atypical stroboscope—in fact, it may be entirely conceptual. This picture was taken from a slide belonging to Raymond Dodge,★ a psychologist famous for constructing ingenious apparatus. In this particular instrument there is no strip of drawings around the inside of the drum, but there is a series of models of successive positions of the wings of a bird (gull?) in flight.

Archives of the History of American Psychology, Raymond Dodge Papers.

Between 1825 and 1850, there was a flurry of interest in illusions, and scientists made various instruments that could trick the eye, including kaleidoscopes, stereoscopes, and stroboscopes. The latter were designed to create impressions of either continuous, decreased, or accelerated speed as well as both forward or backward motion (Boring, 1942). This cylindrical stroboscope is a common piece of laboratory equipment. The viewer looks through the slits at the top as the drum rotates. Under these conditions, the figure drawn in successively different positions on the paper around the inside of the drum appears to dance. A label on the bottom of the drum reads "Patented April 23rd, 1867."

Archives of the History of American Psychology, University of Nebraska Collection.

Wertheimer, rejecting the idea that *errors in judgment* overwhelm *perception,* accepted apparent movement at face value. He thought of this experience as authentic perception dependent upon the Gestalt or configuration, and upon the interrelationships among the stimuli in a particular perceptual field. Wertheimer decided to call this kind of motion perception the "phi phenomenon" in order to distinguish his interpretation from that of the structuralists.

He believed that the best way to investigate these experiences experimentally was to use the method of phenomenology—that is, to observe perception just as it occurs, naturally and unanalyzed. This method is similar to introspection in that both techniques examine consciousness. But it is different because the focus of the phenomenological approach is an ongoing, meaningful experience, whereas introspection searches for the basic elements of the mind—bare and devoid of

meaning. Wertheimer's choice contrasted with the conventional scientific tradition of analyzing subject matter into components, but he selected it because he believed that these rational dissections result in artificial abstractions and destroy what the scientist is really trying to study. For Wertheimer, the traditional approach to the phi phenomenon was an outstanding example of this destruction.

The phenomenological reports that he obtained strengthened his impression that the phi phenomenon is a function of the Gestalt, of the pattern of the entire visual field. They also disclosed that the perception of motion is modified by changes in the timing, brightness, and direction of the stimuli. This research was carried out at the Academie für Socialwissenschaften, later the University of Frankfurt. Wertheimer's interpretation caught the attention of two participants in the experiments: Kurt Koffka★ (Ph.D., Berlin, 1908) and Wolfgang Köhler★ (Ph.D., Berlin, 1909). These colleagues began to apply this orientation both to other perceptual phenomena and to other kinds of psychological responses. Because of this early collaboration, Wertheimer, Koffka, and Köhler are considered to be the founders of Gestalt psychology, and, because of their sustained productivity, they remained the major figures in the Gestalt school.

The Founders of Gestalt Psychology—The Three Gs

Max Wertheimer
Archives of the History of American Psychology, Mary Henle Papers.

Kurt Koffka
Archives of the History of American Psychology, Molly Harrower Papers.

Wolfgang Köhler
Archives of the History of American Psychology, Mary Henle Papers.

The early experiments were, of course, published in German, and it was as late as the 1920s before accounts of the system were available in English. During that decade, Koffka and Köhler also began to lecture in the United States, at different institutions and at various times. Koffka was a visiting professor at Cornell University in 1924, and, in 1927, he accepted an appointment at Smith College where he remained until death in 1941 (Harrower, 1983). Köhler's visits included Clark University in 1925, Harvard University in 1934, and the University of Chicago in 1935 (Henle, 1971). Apprehensive about Nazism, Wertheimer joined the University in Exile (later the Graduate Faculty) of the New School for Social Research in New York in 1933 where he remained until death in 1943 (Wertheimer, 1987). Köhler, also reacting to the German political adversity, became a professor at Swarthmore College in 1935 and stayed on there until retirement in 1958. After moving to America, Koffka, Köhler, and Wertheimer continued to function as leading figures, each serving as a professor, researcher, and contributor to the American psychological literature.

To return to the pioneer work in Germany: the research on perceptual experiences rapidly disclosed a variety of phenomena, so numerous that they can merely be illustrated in this discussion. One of the most important was the discovery of certain perceptual regularities. Dominant among these is the tendency to combine adjacent and similar stimuli into wholes. These units are commonly seen in the foreground and they have attributes that are distinct from those of the parts

Koffka (left) and Köhler (right) attending the Ninth International Congress of Psychology at Yale University in 1929.
Archives of the History of American Psychology, Molly Harrower Papers.

The 1925 meeting of "The Experimentalists" (see page 35) was held at Princeton University in part to dedicate Eno Hall, the home of the new psychology laboratory. Titchener (white beard), the power holder in this group, stands in the middle. Howard C. Warren,★ the Princeton host, stands at his right. On his left is Koffka (in a light-colored suit) and to his left is Köhler. These two Gestaltists, then visiting in the United States, were invited to familiarize The Experimentalists "with their innovative system."

Archives of the History of American Psychology Photographic File.

Two psychologists. Max Wertheimer★ and his son Michael Wertheimer (Ph.D., Harvard, 1952). This photograph was probably taken in 1929 or 1930, in either Karlshorst (a section of Berlin) or in Frankfurt.

Archives of the History of American Psychology, Gardner and Lois Barclay Murphy Papers. Identification with the help of Michael Wertheimer.

that form them. To illustrate, four equally spaced dots : : are seen as a square, but increasing the distance between two of them :   : transforms the square into a rectangle. Köhler commented that the singularity of the organized whole indicated that "the whole is *different* from the sum of the parts" (Pratt, 1969, p. 10). Unfortunately, this description was changed to "the whole is *more than the sum of its parts*" (Pratt, 1969, p. 9). This distortion was widely circulated, severely criticized, and rarely corrected.

Formal principles of perceptual organization were formulated, and these are generally considered to be the most significant contributions of Gestalt psychology. In fact, these principles have been so thoroughly integrated into the discipline that many modern psychologists are unaware of their origin. This sophistication was developed early and was due in part to the Gestaltists' attention to the nuances of stimuli. This orientation contrasted with the structuralists' attention to the nuances of reactions, and, because of this sensitivity, the differences that Wertheimer recognized between the two systems were expanded (Kantor, 1925).

The Rubin ambiguous figure: a vase-profile. People see this image as either a white vase on a black background or as two black profiles facing one another on a white background. Edgar Rubin (Ph.D., Göttingen, 1915), a Danish psychologist, first used this figure in research on figure-ground phenomena. Rubin started work on this problem in 1912, the year that witnessed the publication of the inaugural paper in Gestalt psychology. Many researchers have used the vase-profile and it is illustrated in numerous textbooks in psychology, in some instances identified as "Rubin's goblet" and in others as "after Rubin." Many of the reproductions are more symmetrical than this particular picture, published in Rubin's German translation of his original work.

From Rubin, 1915/1921, Abb. 3.

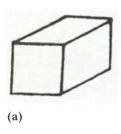 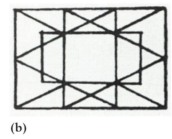 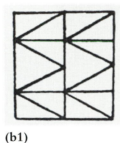 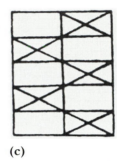 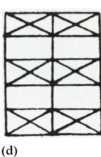

(a)   (b)   (b1)   (c)   (d)

The Gottschaldt figures and some variations. Gestalt psychology holds that the influence of past experiences on visual perception may be less than that of some organizational properties of the visual field. Kurt Gottschaldt (Ph.D., Friedrich-Wilhelms Institute, 1926) conducted some early research on this matter. In one part of the experiment, some participants saw Figure a for three brief exposures, whereas others saw it 520 times. In order to avoid letting the participants know what he actually was looking for, Gottschaldt told them they should memorize the figure so as to be able to reproduce it later from recall. They then saw Figures b and b1 and were asked to describe them. Gottschaldt searched transcriptions of their replies for evidence of the influence of Figure a and found the effects to be very limited in both groups. Gottschaldt (1926/1938), assured that familiarity had a negligible effect on the perception of these designs, examined their phenomenal characteristics and concluded that "internal unity" or cohesion is one condition that past experience does not modify.

Archives of the History of American Psychology, Martin Scheerer Papers.

Gestaltist Greetings! One of the principles of perception is the law of Prägnanz. We are assured that, like the word Gestalt, Prägnanz has no English equivalent, but the law is usually interpreted as designating a tendency in perceptual organization toward as much regularity, symmetry, simplicity, clarity, and stability as the stimulus complex permits.

Köhler, vacationing with his wife, refers to the Law of Prägnanz in a postcard greeting to colleague and friend Mary Henle.★

Archives of the History of American Psychology, Mary Henle Papers. Permission Curt Teich Postcard Archives/Lake County (IL) Museum.

"Köhler's Classic"—an illustrated account of chickens reacting to a relationship rather than to an absolute.

Archives of the History of American Psychology, Martin Scheerer Papers. Artist unknown.

Humankind is not the only tool user.

Archives of the History of American Psychology, Norman L. Garrett Gift. From the film "Learned Tool Use in Monkeys," by C. J. Warden and A. M. Koch, with permission.

The experiments on vision were extended to other senses and analogous results were obtained. For example, a melody is a temporal whole, recognizable even when played in different keys and on different instruments. Closure is illustrated by the tendency when hearing the sequence of taps $-- \acute{} --\acute{} --$ to add one more tap in order to complete a whole. Rapid and successive stimulation of the skin of the forearm at two points produces an experience of synthetic movement similar to the phi phenomenon (Koffka, 1935; Köhler, 1929).

The Gestaltists did not restrict research to humans, and some of the earliest experiments dealt with the reactions of animals to various Gestalten. An important publication by Köhler (1918/1938) reported a series of experiments in which the perception of shade by chickens, an ape, and a 3-year-old child was investigated. In one part of this experiment, grain was scattered on paper of two different shades of gray, but chickens were allowed to peck and swallow food on only one of the two shades. Once they had learned, for example, to peck from the lighter paper, it was replaced with one lighter than either of the training sheets. The fowl responded, generally, by pecking food on the new background—that is, by avoiding the actual paper on which they previously obtained food, thus demonstrating a reaction to relations rather than to an absolute shade. Similar behavior was displayed by both the child and the ape.

These comparisons among species were made at the Anthropoid Station established by the Prussian Academy of Sciences on Tenerife, one of the Canary Islands off the coast of Africa. Köhler assumed the directorship of this facility in 1913, and, because of World War I, he was forced to remain there until 1920. During this residence, Köhler conducted a number of experiments with animals. He was dissatisfied with Edward L. Thorndike's* conclusion that animal learning is not due to the animal's activity but rather to the consequences of its actions, and he started probing this issue by looking for similarities between the intelligence of humans and chimpanzees. Köhler reasoned that animals might display intelligent behavior if they were placed in a situation in which the direct approach to a goal was blocked but an indirect way to reach it was visible. These circumstances would demand that the animal make a detour—that is, turn away from a goal in order to achieve it. Köhler replicated this structure in the design of two similar problems. In one, food is placed outside the cage at a distance that a chimpanzee cannot reach, but there are sticks at different locations in the cage that can be joined to make a tool that is long enough to reach the food. In the second, the food is suspended from the ceiling at a height that cannot be reached, but there are boxes at different locations in the cage that can be placed singly or in piles underneath the food, allowing the animal to reach the food.

The Mentality of Apes (Köhler, 1917/1927) describes in detail the performance of chimpanzees when confronted with these and other puzzles. Typically, the animal tries repeatedly to reach for the food. It also walks around in an aimless and apparently frustrated state. After a period of time, it gives up this task-irrelevant behavior and then proceeds quite rapidly to make the required tool and use it to procure the food. The fact that the chimpanzee, once started on the solution, carries it out in a direct manner suggests that the animal grasps the relationships of the parts to the whole. Köhler interpreted this as evidence of animal insight, as evidence that an organism understands the configuration, that it appreciates the relationships among the parts.

This was a landmark demonstration of the importance of activity on the part of the problem solver. Psychologists—both those who did and those who did not subscribe to the Gestalt system—were intrigued with this contribution of the organism, and they began to generate laboratory information about insight, both in humans and subhumans. The results of these experiments were frequently used to support either Edward L. Thorndike's★ opinion that learning is dependent merely on consequences, or Köhler's opinion that it is dependent on the learner's perception. As a result, much of the research on insight was classified as research on learning rather than on problem solving or thinking. Whatever the choice of topic may be, insight, with its connotation of grasping a configuration—"Ah ha, now I get it"—became, and remains, a basic ingredient in modern psychology.

The Gestalt point of view was applied to many psychological responses (Arnheim, 1966; Asch, 1952; Heider, 1944; MacLeod, 1947), and it induced fundamental changes in such basic concepts as perception, learning, and thinking. Further, there is evidence that Gestalt psychology is again molding research on learning and thinking (Henle, 1987). This reactivation is a product of the modern pursuit by cognitive psychologists of similarities between electronic and organismic functioning (Denning, 1986). Gestalt orientation is more relevant to this effort than other systems, but the process is handicapped because some contemporary theorists do not understand the original formulations (Henle, 1989).

During the 1960s and 1970s, Gestalt psychology began to be (mis)identified as the theoretical basis of what is called gestalt therapy. This started when some of the Gestalt ideas were used incorrectly by the advocates of the human potential movement, groups of psychologists who emphasize affect and prefer self-expression to self-control. The literature of what is called gestalt therapy refers, for example, to the emotionally compelling as the foreground and advises that changing habits demands extracting them from the background and reorganizing them. Unfinished tasks,

unresolved conflicts, and ungratified wishes are labeled "lack of closure." War is called an incomplete gestalt, and peace is designated as closure. This terminology is the product of unmonitored linguistic associations and is not related in any meaningful way to Gestalt psychology (Henle, 1978). Regrettably, this nomenclature has spread and it is now encountered, without correction, in publications of the American Psychological Association (Arnheim, 1974). Readers are reminded of the introductory remarks in this discussion to the effect that Gestalt psychology is an unfamiliar and somewhat unusual system. This leaves it vulnerable to misrepresentation, and readers should ascertain the validity of accounts or remarks about the system.

Psychoanalysis

Psychoanalysis originated in *psychiatry,* but it has also been converted into a psychoanalytic system of *psychology.* This change did not come about until quite some time after the era to which this chapter is devoted. The presentation at this point takes up some of the psychiatric antecedents that are so direct and integral to the psychoanalytic system of psychology that they warrant examination in their own right.

There are various versions of psychoanalysis, but the first, and still the most prominent, formulation is that of the Austrian physician Sigmund Freud★ (M.D., Vienna, 1881). The system began when Freud, reacting to the repeated failures of researchers to demonstrate a neurological basis of psychiatric disorders, undertook a search for psychological precursors. Other physicians were also dissatisfied with the physical explanations then in circulation, but Freud stands apart by virtue of his unrelenting pursuit of the problem. He listened to patient after patient and tried to discover rational explanations for their irrationality. At first, he was forced to rely on hunches and intuition, but gradually he was able to interrelate various bits and pieces and to formulate ordered explanations. Freud thought in an open, flexible manner and his opinions were more like hypotheses than conclusions in that he was willing to reject ideas after they were exposed as weak and refine those that appeared to be satisfactory. Some colleagues accepted his conclusions, others ridiculed him, and still others criticized his position on a few specific issues and constructed what they presented as distinctly different theories of psychoanalysis. Generally, their agreement with Freud was more extensive than their disagreement (Jones, 1953–1957).

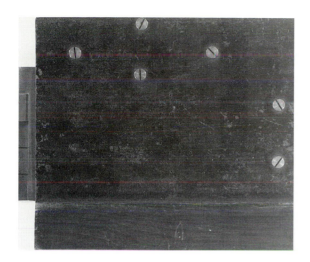

This equipment allows a demonstration of how productive thinking progresses. It was constructed in the shop of the Berlin Psychological Institute for Max Wertheimer in the early 1920s, and it consists of a front plate with attached metal leaves, each approximately 4 1/2″ × 6 1/2″. The leaves can be moved horizontally by pulling the tags at the side. Each leaf is perforated so that light can pass through and different patterns of dots can be formed by the varying position of the leaves. (These photographs were taken on a light-table in order to enhance the effect.)

Wertheimer used these configurations of dots to demonstrate some of the implicit transitions in organization that occur in productive thinking as the thinker progresses from an inadequate, poorly organized grasp of a problem to a mastery of it. These include regrouping the parts, appreciating the requirements of the problem as a whole, distinguishing between arbitrary and necessary components, and spotting inadequacies in the structure (Wertheimer, 1945/1959).

Archives of the History of American Psychology, Rudolf Arnheim Papers. Identification with the help of Rudolf Arnheim.

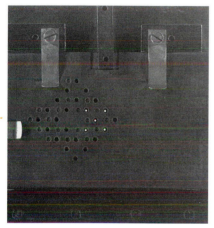

This unit is simple, symmetrical, clear. The five dots are a group, with four on the periphery and one in the center.

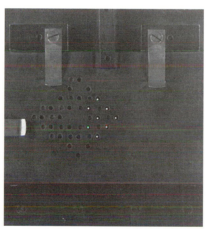

When three dots are added, the middle one retains its physical identity, but the new ones alter the original figure. The configuration is larger and more complex but it is not symmetrical, not right.

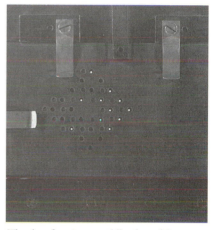

The dots forming an oddly slanted line not only fail to solve the previous perplexity but are disturbing because they seem to relate to one another but not to the remainder of the figure.

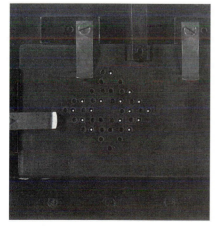

The dots on the left side of the figure change it. They are symmetrical and orderly, but their diamond shape lacks a relationship to the remainder of the pattern on the right.

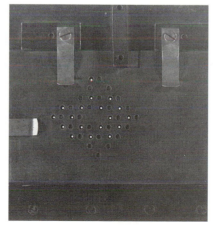

An additional three dots induce a reorganization that is more complete and suggests symmetry. For the first time, all components are starting to hang together.

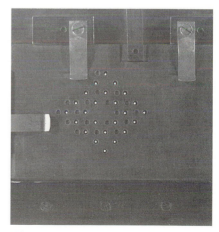

The parts now form a balanced, organized whole. Smaller segments have lost their individual, isolated identity and are integrated into the configuration.

Sigmund Freud, 1906, at 50. In 1956, the Journal of Abnormal and Social Psychology *observed both the 50th anniversary of its first publication and the 100th anniversary of the birth of Sigmund Freud (May 6, 1856). M. Brewster Smith* (Ph.D., Harvard, 1947) was Editor of the Journal on the anniversary. Ernst L. Freud gave Smith this previously unpublished photograph of his father. It was taken on the same day as the portrait frontispiece of* The Life and Work of Sigmund Freud, *Volume 2, by Ernest Jones, 1955.*

Archives of the History of American Psychology, M. Brewster Smith Papers.

The Salpêtrière Hospital (for women) in Paris housed the teaching clinic of Jean-Martin Charcot (M.D., Paris, 1853), probably the most eminent neuropathologist of his time. Freud, age 29 and with an M.D. that was only four years old, received a travel grant, from October 1885 to February 1886, allowing him to study with Charcot. The latter demonstrated that symptoms of hysteria could be both induced and changed by psychological means, specifically by hypnosis. Both this message and the personality of Charcot attracted Freud. The Salpêtrière at this time was of great importance in the creation of modern psychology.

The statue is of Philippe Pinel (M.D., Toulouse, 1773), who was appointed physician-in-chief at the Bicêtre Hospital (for men) near Paris in 1792 and at the Salpêtrière in Paris in 1794. He removed the chains from the patients in both institutions, initiating a new humanistic attitude (Zilboorg, 1941).

Archives of the History of American Psychology, Walter and Catharine Cox Miles Papers.

There were only a few guides when Freud began to look for psychological causes of symptoms, and among them were attempts in France to treat neurotic patients, particularly hysterics, by means of hypnosis. There was heated controversy as to whether their symptoms were due to neuropathology or to psychopathology, and Freud journeyed to Paris in order to become familiar with both sides of the dispute and to observe the effects of a psychological procedure, hypnosis. He appears to have been less impressed by the arguments than by witnessing hypnotized patients recall traumatic episodes and by observing some beneficial effects of hypnosis. When he returned to Vienna in 1886, he opened a private practice, and in this work found that hypnosis

relieved patients of their symptoms, at least for a period of time. The limited success that he achieved displeased him, and so he started looking for other procedures, ones that would produce longer-lasting results and could also be used on patients who resisted hypnosis.

Joseph Breuer (M.D., Vienna, 1867) was one of the first colleagues to help Freud in his search for order. Breuer, a physician, had found that a hysterical patient who experienced intervals in which she was "clouded" became less restless when she recalled fantasies that she had experienced during the abnormal states. Breuer referred to this relief as mental catharsis, and in order to take advantage of it he hypnotized her repeatedly. He then observed that remembering an emotional shock

THE AMERICAN
JOURNAL OF PSYCHOLOGY

Founded by G. STANLEY HALL in 1887

| VOL. XXI | APRIL, 1910 | No. 2 |

THE ORIGIN AND DEVELOPMENT OF PSYCHOANALYSIS[1]

By PROF. SIGMUND FREUD (Vienna)

FIRST LECTURE

Ladies and Gentlemen: It is a new and somewhat embarrassing experience for me to appear as lecturer before students of the New World. I assume that I owe this honor to the association of my name with the theme of psychoanalysis, and consequently it is of psychoanalysis that I shall aim to speak. I shall attempt to give you in very brief form an historical survey of the origin and further development of this new method of research and cure.

Granted that it is a merit to have created psychoanalysis, it is not my merit. I was a student, busy with the passing of my last examinations, when another physician of Vienna, Dr. Joseph Breuer,[2] made the first application of this method to the case of an hysterical girl (1880-82). We must now examine the history of this case and its treatment, which can be found in detail in "Studien über Hysterie," later published by Dr. Breuer and myself.[3]

But first one word. I have noticed, with considerable satis-

[1] Lectures delivered at the Celebration of the Twentieth Anniversary of the opening of Clark University, Sept., 1909; translated from the German by Harry W. Chase, Fellow in Psychology, Clark University, and revised by Prof. Freud.

[2] Dr. Joseph Breuer, born 1842, corresponding member of the "Kaiserliche Akademie der Wissenschaften," is known by works on respiration and the physiology of the sense of equilibrium.

[3] "Studien über Hysterie," 1895, Deuticke, Vienna. Second edition, 1909. Parts of my contributions to this book have been translated into English by Dr. A. A. Brill, of New York. ("Selected Papers on Hysteria and other Psychoneuroses, by S. Freud.")

Freud comments on the origins of psychoanalysis in this lecture which was delivered in German. G. Stanley Hall, ★ *then editor of the* American Journal of Psychology, *arranged for its translation into English and its publication in the journal. Although interpretations and summaries of Freud's writings had appeared in English slightly earlier, this was the first complete paper that could be read by those who were not fluent in German.*

Permission University of Illinois Press.

when under hypnosis helped her when she was awake to recall events associated with the disturbance. She became able to remember the actual transformation of a physical injury into a neurotic symptom, and—more importantly—this awareness brought relief from the symptom. In response to Breuer's urging, Freud began to use mental catharsis. The course of events that is elicited by this procedure convinced Freud that a neurotic symptom is the result of an emotional disturbance of which the patient is unaware (unconscious), and it can be alleviated when the origin is remembered (made conscious). This sequence was reassuring in that it disclosed continuity among events, but it also raised a question that Freud would pursue for an extended period: How does the unconscious sustain its influence?

The collaboration between Freud and Breuer ended when Breuer, learning that his patient had fallen in love with him, withdrew self-protectively from the practice of psychiatry. Freud also noticed that some patients became enamored of him and, reacting with his customary curiosity, he tried to find out why this occurred. Clinical observations convinced him that it was not his personality that attracted patients, but that the analytical sessions triggered the release of emotions initiated in early childhood. This "transference" strengthened his impression that emotional charges are persistent and suggested the possibility of using transference to explain them, but Freud suspected that hypnosis interfered with the transference. This induced him to try out a new method, specifically to refrain from hypnosis and have patients search their memory.

When patients encountered difficulty in remembering, Freud, trying to make the most of what was available, asked them to relax, to suspend effort, and to report their thoughts—whatever came to mind—no matter how embarrassing, unimportant, or illogical. This procedure, called free association, was first used as an expedient, but it turned out to be one of the most effective of the psychoanalytic techniques because, in the course of free associating, patients recall previously forgotten memories. Freud's belief that such recollections could alleviate symptoms induced him to pressure patients to continue to associate to thoughts that he suspected might be emotionally laden.

The pursuit of ways to enhance free association disclosed that dreams are particularly fruitful starting points, and Freud began to examine them in detail. He scrutinized both the manifest content, the dream as it is experienced by the dreamer, and the latent content, the emotional basis of the dream. He conceptualized the latter as disguised and believed that it could be exposed by analyzing both the manifest content and free associations to the dream. Taking on the task of trying to make sense out of dreams forced Freud to deal with the bizarre imagery, the extraordinary symbols, and the idiosyncratic thinking that characterizes them. As every dreamer knows, dream mentation is grossly different from that of wakefulness, and it is classified as primary process to distinguish it from rational thinking or secondary process. In primary process, the laws of physics are violated, and people as well as events are represented symbolically, displaced from their natural settings, and telescoped.

Freud's efforts to understand what these distortions convey about emotions marks a point in the development of psychoanalysis at which various impressions began to form a pattern, one that culminated in a series of guidelines for psychoanalysts to use in interpreting dreams. Applying these guidelines requires technical expertise of a high order, and is much more complex than the oversimplifications that are reported in the popular literature.

Freud's investigations of dreams brought several other gains, and among them was a recognition of the significance of the existence of primary process in the dreams of both normal and abnormal individuals. This overlap promoted the realization that psychiatric disorders are not qualitatively distinct, that there are similarities between healthy and unhealthy people, and that the differences between them are in amount, not in substance. This coherence made it easier for psychologists to develop a psychoanalytic system of psychology (Munroe, 1955).

The evidence that Freud gathered as he moved from hypnosis to mental catharsis to free association to dream analysis comprises the facts or the data of psychoanalysis. At that time, these "facts" consisted of verbal accounts of sometimes faint or fleeting ideas as well as strong and repetitive thoughts—personal, idiosyncratic, and primarily from psychiatrically disturbed individuals. These subjective data are far removed from the objective data that is the traditional scientific base (Heidbreder, 1940).

Freud saw the information he was developing as more of a challenge than a handicap, and he continued his efforts which led to yet another instance in which inquisitiveness developed into a comprehensive explanation. Freud was surprised when several patients reported that as children they had been sexually seduced. He doubted that the children had experienced this exploitation, and he concluded that the patients were recalling fantasies and wishes. This assumption strengthened his opinion that the unconscious strenuously and unrelentingly seeks gratification. He also realized that the unconscious is generally not successful since most people are conventional and conform most of the time. Such compliance led him to postulate the existence of an internal, unconscious restraining force, and, through the years, he formulated this agent in various ways—at one time it was called the censor. Freud observed that success in controlling an energetic and devious unconscious was far from assured, and, as a result, he conceptualized a continuous struggle within each person between compelling and inhibiting agents or forces. Such conflicts would provide a logical

Primary process dominates the wakeful thinking of many psychiatrically disturbed individuals. This drawing by a seriously ill patient provides a concrete representation of ideation that is condensed, incongruous, and unrealistic.
Private Collection.

explanation for illogical acts, such as an alcoholic who sobs because he/she is indulging in another drink and a patient who cries whenever anyone laughs.

Freud's explanations were well received because they helped to make self-defeating, enigmatic behavior intelligible. They were countered, however, because of the postulation of inner forces or homunculi. Since these are impalpable and not part of the space-time world, they violate the mandate of science to deal only with tangibles.

Because of these alien elements, psychoanalytic views were at first condemned and they managed to become a part of psychology largely in a fragmented and less than straightforward manner. Reports of Freud's clinical methods and doctrines began to appear in the American psychological literature in the late 1890s, and, in 1909, Freud participated in a widely publicized conference held at Clark University in honor of its twentieth anniversary. But these initial contacts appear

Psychology conference group, Clark University, September, 1909. This conference of psychologists coincided with programs in physics, mathematics, chemistry, biology, and history. The speakers were eminent and two were Nobel prizewinners. G. Stanley Hall,★ then President of Clark University, invited to the conference a number of psychologists as well as several psychiatrists—a distinguished audience

for Freud's five lectures. Freud received an honorary degree from Clark, and he was deeply gratified by this academic recognition. It was his first and it contrasted with the neglect, criticism, and sometimes even ridicule that he received in Europe (Ross, 1972).

Archives of the History of American Psychology, Permission Clark University Archives.

President Hall (center) and the "Psychoanalytic Delegation" at the Clark Conference. The psychiatrists Sigmund Freud★ from Vienna, Carl Jung★ (M.D., Basel, 1900) from Switzerland, and Sandor Ferenczi (M.D., Vienna, 1894) from Budapest traveled together and, we are told, analyzed each other's dreams to while away the voyage (Jones, 1955). In the United States, they met two friends of Freud: Abraham Brill (M.D., Columbia, 1903), an American psychiatrist, and Ernest Jones (M.D., Cambridge, 1904), a psychiatrist then living in Canada but soon to migrate to England. The cordiality between Freud and Brill and Jones endured, but his relationships with Jung and Ferenczi soured. At one time Freud had seemed to see Jung as his successor, but Jung rejected Freud's theory of sexuality and created his own; and from 1927 until his death in 1933, Ferenczi experienced some personality deterioration and this distressed Freud who was having his own difficulties contending with cancer of the jaw (Jones, 1957).

Archives of the History of American Psychology, Seymour Wapner Gift. Permission Clark University Archives.

to have promoted acquaintance more than influence, and substantive accommodations between the two disciplines were deferred until the late 1940s.

There were, however, some early signs of rapprochement, and one of the first of these involved defense mechanisms. These consist of a series of unwitting psychological maneuvers that fend off disturbing ideas and impulses, for example, substituting

an acceptable for an unacceptable reason for behaving in a certain way. Some of these strategies were first described in an American psychology textbook in the early 1920s, but their source was not identified. Soon the defense mechanisms were included in other texts and ultimately in so many that they became, and remain, a standard part of psychology. These textbooks typically followed the original pattern of reporting particulars about the different mechanisms while failing to deal with their conceptualization in psychoanalysis (Hilgard, 1957).

The unconscious, manifest and latent dream content, and the censor were also introduced early and, again, in a surreptitious manner. A detailed analysis of references to psychoanalysis in a sample of textbooks published between 1901 through 1940 disclosed that the unconscious was mentioned as early as 1901, and by 1911 there were references to manifest and latent content and to the censor (Herma, Kris, & Shor, 1943). The authors of this analysis examined books devoted to normal and to abnormal psychology for evidence of either acceptance or rejection of a psychoanalytic perspective. They concluded that the concepts that were approved were, as in the case of the defense mechanisms, not ascribed to Freud, but those that were disapproved *were* ascribed to Freud.

By the 1940s, more open and direct methods of promoting psychoanalysis came into vogue, but these efforts did not culminate in the sanctioning of a psychoanalytic viewpoint of psychology until after the era covered in this chapter. Further discussion of the changes in psychoanalysis will occur when the corresponding periods are examined.

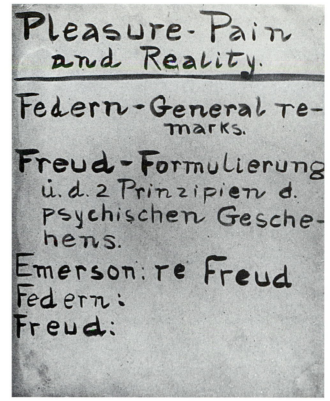

This is the cover of Folder 61 (from a total of 107 folders) of reading notes written by G. Stanley Hall*—a single illustration of the attention American psychologists were giving Freud. "Pleasure—Pain and Reality" deals with psychoanalytic ideas. The two papers by Freud that are included in the folder are dated 1912 and 1915. Emerson *is probably the psychologist Louville E. Emerson (Ph.D., Harvard, 1907), not "the Sage of Concord."*

Hall at one time was intrigued with psychoanalysis. Although he later became disenchanted, at age 76 he wrote the "Preface to American Edition" of A General Introduction to Psychoanalysis by Freud (1920).

Archives of the History of American Psychology, G. Stanley Hall Documents.

CHAPTER 4

The Inception of Intelligence Tests

One of the most influential precursors of the psychological assessment of intelligence was the work of Francis Galton* in trying to identify people who are physically superior. In pursuit of this goal, he administered anthropometric tests—measurements of the size and proportion of the body—initially to visitors at the International Health Exhibition in London, 1884–1885, and then later to subjects in a laboratory setting.

This project demonstrated the feasibility of examining individuals, and two American psychologists became so intrigued with the procedures that they used them as models. One of these was James McKeen Cattell* who had numerous personal contacts with Galton while he was attending courses and carrying out research at Cambridge University in England. The influence is obvious in papers that Cattell wrote and in experiments that he conducted after he returned home to become, in succession, a professor of psychology at the University of Pennsylvania in 1889, and, then, in 1891, a professor of experimental psychology at Columbia University.

Galton's★ first anthropometric laboratory. Visitors paused at stations on the long table on the right of the picture where their measurements were taken and recorded on personal score sheets. Cumulative scores were entered on the large charts hanging on the wall, so that individuals could compare their performance with that of others.

"After the Health Exhibition was closed in 1885," wrote Galton, "it seemed a pity that the Laboratory should also come to an end, so I asked for and was given a room in the Science Galleries of the South Kensington Museum. I maintained a Laboratory there during about six years" (Galton, 1909, p. 249).

From Pearson, 1924, Plate L, Permission Cambridge University Press.

Contemporaries with Similar Careers

On the left, James McKeen Cattell★ (Ph.D., Leipzig, 1886) and, on the right, Joseph Jastrow★ (Ph.D., Johns Hopkins, 1886). Both of these psychologists were born to the Establishment. Their fathers presented formidable intellectual models: William Cattell, President of Lafayette College, and Marcus Jastrow, "The Great Rabbi." Both psychologists were awarded the doctorate in the same year, and in 1888 each established a laboratory at an American university: Cattell at Pennsylvania and Jastrow at Wisconsin. Both became involved in conflicts with university administrators and they worked together to publicize "The Administrative Peril in Education"

(Blumenthal, 1991). Both men were founding members and served as presidents of the American Psychological Association—Cattell was the fourth president in 1895 and Jastrow was the ninth president in 1900. Each had a post-academic career: Cattell as editor of a number of journals and Jastrow as a popularizer of psychology. They both died in 1944, the last charter members of the American Psychological Association.

Left: Archives of the History of American Psychology Photographic File.

Right: Archives of the History of American Psychology, University of Iowa Libraries Record.

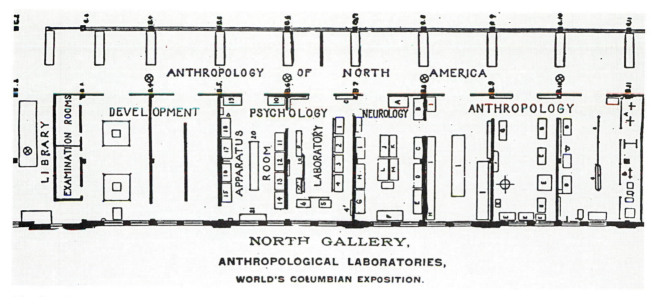

NORTH GALLERY,
ANTHROPOLOGICAL LABORATORIES,
WORLD'S COLUMBIAN EXPOSITION.

This floor plan details part of the mezzanine of the "Anthropological Building" at the Chicago World's Fair of 1893. The bottom of the plan is the outside wall of the building and the top edge is the railing over which a visitor could see the main exhibits on the floor below. Franz Boas (Ph.D., Kiel, 1881) presided over the three anthropology rooms and Henry H. Donaldson (Ph.D., Johns Hopkins, 1895) directed the neurology exhibit. Joseph Jastrow,★ assisted by Mrs. Jastrow and a group of graduate students, assembled and presented the two rooms for psychology.

After Jastrow, 1893, p. 50.

In 1890, Cattell described several tests, including some of Galton's and others that were adaptations of measurements then being made in psychology laboratories. Such tasks demanded only easy, straightforward responses such as reacting rapidly to a light or sound and judging differences in weights, lengths of lines, or intervals of time. Cattell coined the label *"mental tests"* to refer to these measurements, and he suggested, cautiously, that they might be correlated with more complex reactions—that a measure of reaction time, for example, might be a measure of attention. He administered the tests to a few students at Pennsylvania and then developed a more extensive program when he moved to Columbia University (Sokal, 1982).

Joseph Jastrow★ was the second psychologist who pursued Galton's method. Shortly after completing the doctorate, Jastrow corresponded with Galton, and, in 1892, published an account of "Some Anthropometric and Psychologic Tests on College Students—A Preliminary Survey." In 1893, Jastrow replicated Galton's project by administering tests to visitors at the World's Columbian Exposition (The Chicago World's Fair).

Jastrow referred to these measurements as tests of "elementary powers," and, like Cattell, entertained the idea that they might be correlated with more complex responses. He indicated, for example, that speed of responding could be a measure of mental alertness and that muscular strength could be an index of mental effort.

This is the personal score sheet that was filled out by the attendants and given to each visitor who took the tests.

Harvard University Archives with permission.

Other psychologists were also beginning to work with tests. In 1895, the American Psychological Association appointed a committee, with Cattell as chair, and charged it to identify the tests that were the most suitable for assessing what was called "mental capacity." The faith in anthropometric and mental tests was apparently strong inasmuch as the five-member committee recommended, with only one dissenting vote, a list of tests. The dissenter, James M. Baldwin (Ph.D., Princeton, 1887), expressed a preference for tests that elicit complex psychological reactions (Jastrow, Baldwin, & Cattell, 1898).

Baldwin's reservations were supported by the results of a doctoral dissertation, completed by Clark Wissler (Ph.D., Columbia, 1901), in which correlations were calculated for the data obtained in Cattell's testing program. Wissler (1901) found little or no relationship among scores the students obtained on the mental tests and the grades they earned in coursework. Neither were scores on the mental tests correlated. There was, however, substantial agreement among the marks earned in different courses—that is, among grades based on complex psychological responses.

Charles Spearman★ (Ph.D., Leipzig, 1904), an English psychologist, administered various examinations to groups of children and then turned attention to the correlations among their test scores. When he compared his results with those reported in the literature, he noted that Wissler had found smaller coefficients. Spearman began to explore the reasons for these discrepancies. This search led him to the conclusion that the amount of agreement among tests is distorted—either increased or decreased—for a variety of reasons, including errors in the tests and lack of comparability among the groups of subjects who take them. Spearman devised a statistical method of reducing these irregularities, but, since some errors remained, he began to attach little credence to single coefficients and began to examine trends among them. He discovered some systematic relationships on which he based a theory of intelligence.

Spearman assumed that correlation indicates what he called a general factor, or g, common among tests that are correlated. He also assumed that the absence of a correlation indicates a specific factor, s. He thought of

Charles Spearman.★ "Rumors had reached my ears that the attempt was being made to study psychology in quite novel manner, namely, by means of experiment, the method which had proved so extraordinarily successful with the physical sciences. Perplexed though I was as to how such a method could be rendered applicable to the mind, I determined to give it at least a trial" (Spearman, 1930, p. 301).

Archives of the History of American Psychology, University of Nebraska Collection.

intelligence as consisting of g and s, and believed s to be characteristic of simple tasks and g to be characteristic of complex tasks (Spearman, 1930).

Spearman's postulation of two factors contrasted with the commonly held opinion that intelligence is unitary, and attempts to confirm or to modify

Although Lightner Witmer★ (Ph.D., Leipzig, 1893) was educated as an experimental psychologist, he is generally considered to be the psychologist most responsible for inaugurating the specialty of clinical psychology and for establishing the first psychological clinic. Witmer recommended that psychologists determine a child's condition before and at the end of treatment and record the methods of intervention used. In developing these procedures, Witmer was reflecting the increased attention that was being paid to mental retardation. He commented that mentally retarded patients "are better subjects of investigation than normal children. . . . Their mental and physical condition . . . is susceptible of ready description and exact definition. . . . the difference in condition at the beginning and end of treatment is more marked than in normal children" (Witmer, 1896, p. 463).

Archives of the History of American Psychology, Paul McReynolds Gift.

Spearman's views were soon underway. The defenders formed an enthusiastic and prolific but small cadre whose probes of the relationships among coefficients of correlation came to be called factor analysis. They constructed numerous tests that cover a variety of tasks and administered them to groups.

Mental tests withstood the criticisms of factor analysts and others during the first decade of the present century. Not all the reasons for this invulnerability are clear, but some of the strongest support came from psychologists who were involved in mental retardation, a field that experienced a surge of interest around the turn of the century. It is difficult for us today to comprehend how little information was available at that time. There was no generally accepted method of assessing the intelligence of patients and no agreement as to whether intervention would be successful, what kind would be appropriate, or when it should be started. The dearth of knowledge motivated personnel working with patients to give mental tests a trial and to think of them as a source of the kind of information they needed, to conceptualize a measure of muscle power, for example, as a measure of willpower. These expectations, however, were soon defeated because many patients did not understand the test instructions and were unable to cope with the apparatus.

In 1906, Henry H. Goddard★ (Ph.D., Clark, 1899) was appointed director of the laboratory at what was then called the New Jersey Training School for Feeble-Minded Girls and Boys at Vineland. Goddard, like most of his peers, had no prior experience with mental retardation, and, in accord with his graduate education, he tried to use laboratory equipment to observe patients. When this turned out to be unsuccessful, he consulted with several eminent American psychologists, but their assistance was limited. There were so few precedents that research could have taken various courses, and Goddard's perseverance put him in a position to determine one of them: "After two years my work was so poor, I had accomplished so little that I went abroad to see if I could not get some ideas. I came back with the Binet tests" (Goddard, 1952, p. 4).

J. E. Wallace Wallin* (Ph.D., Yale, 1901) worked in many different clinical facilities, including Vineland where he substituted for Goddard in the summer of 1910. He was deeply involved in research on mental retardation and, in the fashion of the day, he tried first to use various laboratory instruments to assess children. When he learned about the Binet tests he began both to revise and administer them. Wallin's papers include a series of 12 photographs that show the use of laboratory-type tests. The three on this page and the next are typical.

Mosso Ergograph. Wallin is using an ergograph to measure "endurance of grip," which at one time he thought was also a measure of "determination" and "grit." The ergograph, originally devised to study fatigue, was invented by Angelo Mosso (M.D., Turin, 1870), an Italian physiologist who, incidentally, has been referred to as the "father of sports psychology." The boy's right arm is secured to an arm rest and he is using his middle finger to raise and lower a weight that is hanging almost to the floor. The pulley arm is fitted with a stylus that scrapes carbon black from the slowly and regularly rotating kymograph, providing a permanent record of the length and frequency of the pulls.

Archives of the History of American Psychology, J. E. Wallace Wallin Papers.

Wet spirometer. This instrument measures vital capacity, the maximum volume of air that is exhaled after deep inhalation. Vital capacity is related to age, sex, and physical condition, and, at the time Wallin was conducting research, it was also believed to be related to intellectual status. The inner drum of the spirometer rises as the child blows into the mouthpiece. The level of displacement can be read on a scale on the side of the instrument. (Neither the child nor the woman examiner are identified.)

Archives of the History of American Psychology, J. E. Wallace Wallin Papers.

The child standing on the base of a volometer is instructed to raise his heels 1/4 inches off the platform. The indicator at the top of the upright shows the elevation of the heels and registers their tremors. When the heels touch the platform, as would seem to be the case in this picture, a buzzer sounds. The test was required to measure "will," "persistency," "determination," and "pluck" or "spunk."

Archives of the History of American Psychology, J. E. Wallace Wallin Papers.

Alfred Binet and an unidentified child. The kymograph in front suggests that this picture is from the period of Binet's research with "brass instruments" and before he developed the age-scale method of measuring intellectual level.

Archives of the History of American Psychology Photographic File, Permission Presses Universitaires de France.

Goddard was referring to the French psychologist, Alfred Binet* (D.Sc., Sorbonne, 1894), the individual who devised what came to be called the age scale method of testing intelligence. Binet was active in a society devoted to the study of children when, in 1904, the Ministry of Public Instruction appointed a commission to advise the French school system about the most effective ways of handling retarded children. Binet saw the need for an examination that would disclose the intellectual level of each pupil. He had been investigating individual differences for 15 years prior to his appointment to the commission, and this research had convinced him that individual differences are more apparent in children's responses to complex than to easy problems. Because there were many unanswered questions about the nature of intelligence, Binet wanted to evaluate a number of different intellectual functions, such as attention, judgment, reasoning, memory, and perception.

The only test then available that measured different psychological functions was one that Henri Damaye (M.D., Paris, 1903) designed as a means of increasing the consistency of diagnoses of mental retardation. Binet was impressed with Damaye's questions because they elicited various functions, particularly reasoning and judgment (Why do you prefer to be French?) and also avoided the effects of unequal education by tapping information that is generally known but not learned from formal instruction (Where are your lips?). Binet was also critical of Damaye because he did not obtain replies from normal subjects and thus had no standard or normative data (Binet & Simon, 1905/1916).

With the assistance of Théodore Simon (M.D., Paris, 1900), Binet devised a series of scales, the first published in 1905 and a revision in 1908. In the year of his death, 1911, Binet published a second revision. Each of these contains questions about a variety of situations that are encountered in everyday life, but there are no complicated instructions or equipment that is heavy and awkward to handle. Each reply was scored either as *passed* or *failed*. Binet and Simon administered the scales to patients one at a time and also arranged examinations of normal children. The number of successes of the latter were used to assign each task to an appropriate year level. Binet chose age for this framework because he thought of it as a *rough* measure of ability (Wolf, 1973). This reliance promoted the label *age scaling* even though this title identifies only one of several procedures that characterize an age scale.

Although Binet and Goddard corresponded, they apparently did not meet personally; Goddard first learned about the 1905 scale when he visited Ovide Decroly (M.D., Ghent, 1896), the director of an institution for the retarded in Brussels. Decroly had just finished administering the tests on a trial basis and recommended them to Goddard. Goddard also visited Sante de Sanctis (M.D., Rome, 1886), an Italian who had prepared a shorter series of similar tests. Goddard was so impressed with both the de Sanctis and the Binet scales that he published descriptions of them (1908a, 1908b) shortly after returning from Europe. In 1910, the year he coined the term *moron*, Goddard also described the 1908 Binet and Simon revision (Goddard, 1910b).

Laure Balbiani Binet, Alfred Binet, and their daughters, Madeleine and Alice. A biographer says, "The fact that Binet was married and had two daughters seems really to be a matter of some moment for psychology. . . . The observation of his own children . . . stands at the head of a series of kindred researches. It is the source of the problem which, in turn, led to Binet's greatest contributions to psychology" (Varon, 1935, p. 25).

Wolf (1973) points out that in the published accounts of this research Madeleine is called "Marguerite" and Alice is called "Armande."

Archives of the History of American Psychology, Theta Wolf Papers.

Théodore Simon examines an unidentified child.

Archives of the History of American Psychology, Henry H. Goddard Papers.

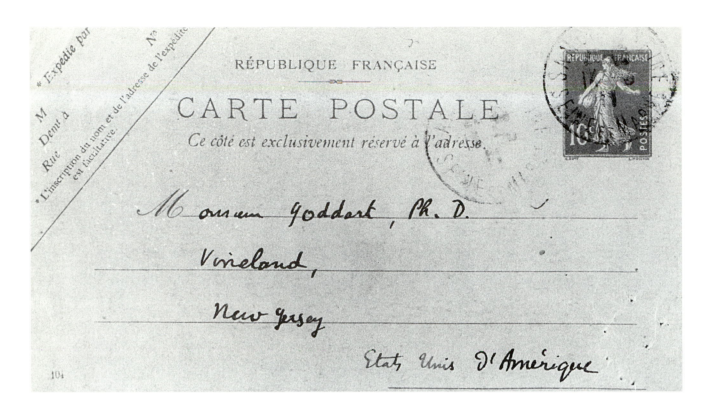

Binet, editor of the French journal L'Année Psychologique, *sent this postcard to Goddart (sic) asking for a manuscript describing his work on measuring intellectual level.*

Archives of the History of American Psychology, Henry H. Goddard Papers.

Goddard: traveler in "An Antique Land." One view of an ancient civilization may be obtained from the back of a camel. But a more exalted panorama may evoke more complicated experiences. Below, Goddard contemplates Egypt from the top of the Great Pyramid at Gizeh.

Archives of the History of American Psychology, Henry H. Goddard Papers.

FEEBLE – MINDED CLUB   MAY 27, 1916

This group—also known as "The Gang," "The Boys," or "The Good Fellows"—was socially informal but intellectually serious about the problems of the mentally retarded. As early as 1902, they began meeting semiannually, usually in April and in October, to share ideas and experiences. The group continued to meet for many years, celebrating a golden anniversary in 1952. This picture was taken at the Training School in Vineland, New Jersey, the location of many meetings—most of the members worked in Pennsylvania and New Jersey. Goddard sits at the extreme right in the first row. Other psychologists include Howard C. Warren★ in the front row, second from the left; and Edgar A. Doll★ in the second row, fifth from the left.

Archives of the History of American Psychology, Henry H. Goddard Papers.

Goddard (1910a) compared the level at which the Binet scale classified approximately 400 patients at the Vineland Training School with their ratings by school teachers and staff members. He noted that, even in cases of disagreement, the test results agreed with the opinion of at least one or more of the raters. This concurrence led him to decide that the tests were valid, and for Goddard they stood on their own merits: "We decided that there was no exception to be made to the grouping as determined by the Binet scales" (Goddard, 1910a, p. 19).

Other psychologists soon began to revise the scales and to promote them as measures for all levels of intelligence and for all ages. In 1916, Lewis M. Terman★

published *The Measurement of Intelligence*, the first in a series of manuals that became the most frequently used guides for the administration of Binet-based procedures. The enthusiasm that Binet provoked is documented in the publication of at least 19 papers describing his methods in the interval between Goddard's introduction in 1908 and Terman's landmark 1916 volume. Of the nine authors in addition to Goddard and Terman, five had studied at Clark University and were the most active proponents of the Binet technique, restricting modifications of the scales to details, such as devising additional tasks, clarifying the scoring, and increasing the number of individuals who contributed normative data (McPherson & Popplestone, 1981).

The calling card of William Stern. "Breslau" refers to the University of Breslau where he taught, 1897–1916.

Archives of the History of American Psychology, Henry H. Goddard Papers.

William Stern rides on the top of an open-air bus in Hamburg in 1932. At his left is David Boder,* but the other passengers are not identified. Stern was in his early sixties in 1933 when Hitler came to power, but he was able to emigrate, first to Holland and then to America (Allport, 1968). Stern's contributions to psychology are numerous and varied, including the invention of laboratory equipment, research in child psychology, the organizing of both an institute and a journal of applied psychology, and advocating that the study of the generalized mind be replaced with the study of individual differences or, in Stern's terminology, the study of individuality: "I undertook to give the psychological differences between one human being and another the status of an independent theoretical problem, to be handled with appropriate scientific methods" (Stern, 1930, p. 347).

Archives of the History of American Psychology, David P. Boder Museum Collection.

A break with Binet came in the interpretation of what the tests measure—what constitutes intelligence. A difference first emerged in the terminology used to express the sum of successes on the examination as a whole. For example, Binet would assign a child who passed all tests at 8 years and none at higher ages an *intellectual level* of 8 years, but his successors would assign the child a *mental age* of 8 years. The substitution of the word *mental* for *intellectual* was commonplace during this era and probably not significant, but the substitution of the word *age* for *level* countered Binet's advice. He was aware that age connotes a regular progression, but he did not believe that this regularity had been demonstrated empirically, and, thus, he preferred the more neutral term *level* (Wolf, 1973). The American psychologists did not respect this caution and by their word choice strengthened the idea that intelligence is constant across both ages and tasks.

A second deviation from Binet and one that also suggested immutability of intelligence was introduced in 1912 by William Stern* (Ph.D., Berlin, 1893), a German psychologist. Stern faulted the then-prevailing practice of indicating amount of retardation by subtracting mental age from chronological age because this method does not indicate differences in severity at different ages (A 10-year-old who is one year retarded is much less disabled than a 3-year-old who is one year retarded). Stern proposed a "mental quotient" that could be calculated by dividing the mental age by the chronological age. In opposition to Binet, he asserted that this measure was constant throughout childhood (Stern, 1912/1914). The majority of psychologists accepted Stern's formula even though the numerator is a measure of accuracy and the denominator is a measure of time. Terman suggested multiplying the quotient by 100 and he referred to it as an *intelligence quotient* or *IQ*. This method became so widely recognized that other formulae that are used to calculate IQs are often ignored and the Stern–Terman method is assumed erroneously to be the only one.

The increasing interest in age scaling was concomitant with experimental modifications of the procedure, and among these were tryouts of performance tests, examinations that do not require language either for giving the instructions or for responding. One of the first series of such tests appeared in 1911 when William Healy★ (M.D., Rush, 1900) and Grace Fernald★ (Ph.D., Chicago, 1907) published 22 tests they were using to examine delinquents at the Chicago Juvenile Psychopathic Institute, renamed in 1920 the Institute for Juvenile Research. Healy and Fernald reviewed several single tests that were then being administered and chose ones for their series that they thought would provide information about intellectual and moral judgments as well as ways in which occupational tasks are handled. Because a large number of their examinees came from non-English-speaking homes or had a hearing loss, they selected tasks that could be administered, when necessary, in pantomime. They also heeded "the early advice of a number of eminent American psychologists to avoid mechanical laboratory apparatus" (Healy & Fernald, 1911, p. 3).

Healy and Fernald included some formboards in the test battery. Typically, each of these consists of a frame from which geometric figures have been cut. The number, size, and shape of these pieces vary. The examinee is asked to fit each into its appropriate recess. Formboards were used in the early part of the nineteenth century, first for training a feral boy and later for training both mentally retarded patients and young children. Robert S. Woodworth★ included a "form test" in the examinations that he administered to visitors at the Louisiana Purchase Exposition in St. Louis in 1904 (Woodworth, 1910). Naomi Norsworthy (Ph.D., Columbia, 1904) used a formboard in a testing program for mental retardates that she reported in 1906. Shortly after these introductions, formboards were incorporated into numerous examinations (Sylvester, 1913).

These tests provide an opportunity to assess how an examinee analyzes and understands spatial relationships. This is a necessary intellectual achievement, but it is not significantly related to the comprehension of either abstract or social relationships. Healy and Fernald were among the first to adapt a formboard in ways that allow measurement of the understanding of complex interpersonal and cognitive relationships without the use of language. They constructed devices that they called picture formboards or picture puzzles. Each consists of a drawing of a familiar scene that is mounted on wood or cardboard. Portions of the drawing are removed so that, when selecting replacements, examinees are guided by the content of the picture as well as by the shape of the inset.

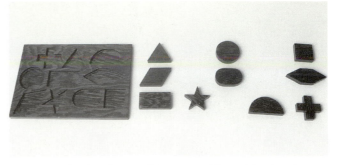

The Seguin formboard—one of the most widely used formboards. This is only one way in which the formboard is presented—the cutouts are placed in different locations in different versions of the test.
Archives of the History of American Psychology Apparatus Collection.

The solution.
Archives of the History of American Psychology Apparatus Collection.

At the 1912 annual meeting of the American Psychological Association, Healy (1914) also described a "Pictorial Completion Test," a modification of the picture puzzle format, and identified it as an addition to the Healy-Fernald series. This test consists of a drawing of an outdoor scene in which ten separate activities are taking place. Small squares have been removed from this drawing, and the examinee must fill these in by selecting the most appropriate inset for each from among several that are available. Some of these extra pieces depict content that is logical but not precise (an alarm clock set for noon instead of early morning), whereas some depict content that is illogical (a bird completing a portion of a flag).

Healy and Fernald presented their tests as more feasible than finished tools. Although they scored each unit, they did not compute a total score, preferring not to reduce an examinee's solutions to a single number. In other words, they promoted the idea of performance tests and left the codifying of them to successors.

A second sequence of performance tests—again ones in which the norms were not completed when the

A picture formboard: an early nonlanguage test. This picture appears in a book for children, Jingleman Jack, A Book of Occupations, written by James O'Dea, illustrated by H. O. Kennedy, and published in 1901 by the Saalfield Publishing Company, Akron, Ohio. A print of the scene that Healy and Fernald selected from Jingleman Jack could not be located, but this one illustrates the complexity and the style of the scene that examinees completed.

Archives of the History of American Psychology, Emily L. Stogdill Papers.

A selection of performance tests. At the back of the picture is one version of the Healy Pictorial Completion Test.

Archives of the History of American Psychology, David P. Boder Museum Collection.

Healy and Fernald used this illustration to show how they employed a Jingleman Jack schoolroom scene. They cut out pieces of it to create the task of "replacing the missing elements in order to complete the picture."

From Healy and Fernald, 1911, p. 15.

tests were introduced—was compiled in response to problems that arose in screening immigrants for admission to the United States. This series was published in 1914 under the authorship of Howard A. Knox (M.D., Dartmouth, 1908). Knox and his colleagues in the Public Health Service on Ellis Island were confronted with perplexing diagnostic problems as they assessed individuals who might be only mildly mentally retarded. An important contributor to the confusion was, of course, the language barrier. Interpreters were generally helpful, but on occasion they were not, usually because they did not translate inept or illogical answers literally but instead tried to interpret them.

In order to systematize procedures, the Public Health Service physicians arranged a number of tasks in successive age levels, from three years to adulthood, based on the number of immigrants who passed and failed each of the tests. Several of these were taken from the Binet scales, and 12 are either formboard or picture puzzles, some adapted from Healy★ and eight devised by Knox and three of his colleagues.

In 1914, the year in which Knox first reported the work on Ellis Island, a second comprehensive method of test construction, point scaling, was introduced. This is more directly linked to modern examination procedures than age scaling. The psychologist who is generally credited for initiating it is Robert M. Yerkes★ (Ph.D., Harvard, 1902). Yerkes would become known for research in comparative psychology, but, at the time he became interested in intelligence testing, he was supplementing an assistant professorship at Harvard with a part-time appointment at the Boston Psychopathic Hospital. In that post, he administered Goddard's version of the Binet scale to patients with various psychiatric disorders, and this experience led him to believe that an examination could be constructed in a manner that would yield more accurate scores than the pass-fail system.

Yerkes credits Edmund B. Huey (Ph.D., Clark, 1899), a member of the Clark group of Binet advocates, with first suggesting point scaling. In this method, tests are grouped not according to age level but according to similarity (for example, vocabulary, memory for digits, drawing). The items within each unit are arranged in the order of difficulty and given to all subjects. Each response is scored by assigning points—that is, numerical scores—that increase with the accuracy of the response, and the total score is the sum of points that an examinee earns.

Yerkes wanted to work with tests that he believed to be satisfactory, so, with the help of James W. Bridges (Ph.D., Harvard, 1915), he chose 20 from the Binet scale to form what was identified as a preadolescent scale, the first of various versions that he, with assistance from several associates, would later compile (Yerkes and Bridges, 1914). Yerkes suggested different ways of scoring the entire test, and the one that is most commonly used today involves dividing the examinee's point score by the mean score for the examinee's age group, a formula that relates only test scores and avoids a mix of test scores and chronology. Yerkes first referred to this as the coefficient of intellectual ability, CIA (Yerkes, Bridges, & Hardwick, 1915). This was soon

Regular mental examination 24 hours after arrival, Ellis Island, 1917. As soon as immigrants landed at Ellis Island by barge from their ships, they were examined to determine their mental and physical status. The average immigrant spent two or three hours at Ellis Island before leaving for his or her destination, but if examiners detected a mental or physical deficit or suspected a history of criminal activity (very broadly defined), they retained the individual for further examination. About 15 to 20 percent of the arrivals were thus reexamined. The mental examination consisted of a series of observations ranging from an informal, global evaluation of the individual's behavior while standing in line and responding to the medical examination to a formal psychological examination. No immigrant was denied admission because of mental deficiency without taking tests administered by at least three different examiners. Typically, a medical examiner with the aid of an interpreter gave the immigrant a series of tasks such as those that appear on the desk in this picture. The woman is probably responding to a four-card color naming test. The examiner is recording her response.
From Mullan, 1917, p. 737.

shortened to the coefficient of intelligence, CI, and then later changed to IQ. This last shift is, of course, misleading because the formula for a point-scale IQ is quite different from the formula for an age-scale IQ! Yet, the two were and still are used interchangeably and generally without reference to this disparity.

Yerkes was expanding the examination when, in 1917, the United States became involved in World War I. The war preempted almost all test construction and Yerkes was put in charge of that enterprise—a comprehensive undertaking described in considerable detail in Chapter 6.

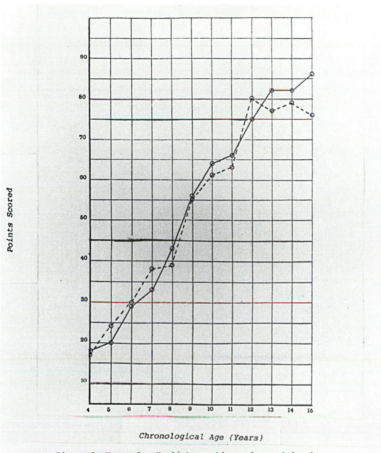

Chronological Age (Years)

Figure 5. Norms for English-speaking males and females.
Solid line (——) indicates scores for males.
Broken line (---) indicates scores for females.

Shown are examples of the normative data that Yerkes and associates established for one of the first versions of a point scale examination. These plots show the average point scores for children from English-speaking homes.

The graph discloses that a boy 7 years and 0 months of age who obtains 35 points would be assigned to a C(oefficient) of I(ntelligence) = 35/33 = 1.06. His M(ental) A(ge) would be 7 years and 2 months (the age of boys whose average point score is 35).

The graph also discloses that a girl 7 years and 0 months of age who obtains a point score of 35 would be assigned CI = 35/38 = .92. Her MA would be 6 years and 7 months (the age of girls whose average point score is 35).

Adapted from Yerkes, Bridges, & Hardwick, 1915, p. 71.

PART 2

Development
–
World War I
Through
World War II

When experimental psychology was taking shape, laboratory personnel tried to demonstrate their scientific credentials by emulating the physical sciences. They were especially enthusiastic about apparatus, one of the most conspicuous emblems of science, and they made numerous efforts to adapt equipment that had been developed for research in physiological and physical laboratories to research that requires the control of psychological stimuli and the measurement and recording of psychological responses. As the pioneers gained more experience, they came to realize that instruments are incapable either of inducing or registering many psychological responses, and they began to design both experimental equipment and procedures that met their own singular research needs. For example, there is no machine that can record or quantify distraction, but its effects can be gauged by changes in behavior. Subjects can be distracted, for example, by reading the names of colors that are printed in incongruous shades, such as the word *red* in green ink or *yellow* in blue. The effects can be quantified by calculating the differences in time and accuracy of reading when the names of the colors are printed in a standard ink color and when they are printed in colors different from the ones they name.

The honing of psychological methods gained such a strong foothold that carefully planned and precisely worked-out procedures became salient features. These innovations began originally in formal laboratories, but the slow pace then in force accelerated markedly when the pressures of World War I induced psychologists to try to meet the immediate and urgent need for techniques for selecting and training military personnel. Since these problems were primarily psychological in nature, there were no guidelines in any science for handling them so psychologists were required to create psychological procedures. Apparently they found this independence gratifying because, after the armistice, their inventiveness increased in both the applied and research domains. The commitment continued at a high level until the beginning of World War II when, once again, military pressures heightened it. The pursuit of experimental know-how still remains a strong force in modern psychology, but, beginning about the middle of the present century, psychologists took on problems so comprehensive and complex that the striving for faultless methodology was at times tempered. Thus, the Era of Development, in which the keynote was procedural refinement, extended during and between two large-scale outbreaks of hostility.

Our account of the attainments in methodology starts with those in experimental settings because these were the matrices out of which applied procedures emerged. We begin the present chapter with a consideration of attempts to use equipment to control stimuli and to record responses. We next turn to some highlights of the supplementing of machines with experimental methods. The discussion is then directed toward the testing movement, outlining the buildup from examinations compiled during World War I through the elaborate technology that came into use in the measurement of intelligence, personality, occupational skills, and academic achievement.

Left to right, front row: Benjamin D. Wood,★ Ralph S. Roberts,[P] Leo J. Brueckner (Ph.D., Iowa, 1919), Calvin P. Stone,★ Wm. S. Foster,★ #, Walter S. Hunter,★ Joseph W. Hayes,★ #, #, Austin S. Edwards (Ph.D., Cornell, 1912), Charles C. Stech,[P] Daniel W. La Rue (Ph.D., Harvard, 1911).

Second row: #, #, Constantine F. Malmberg (Ph.D., Iowa, 1914), Henry T. Moore (Ph.D., Harvard, 1914), John K. Norton (Ph.D., Columbia, 1926), Howard P. Shumway,[U] George F. Arps,★ #, #, Thomas M. Stokes,[P] Edward S. Jones (Ph.D., Chicago, 1917), Lawrence D. Pedrick,[U] Charles H. Toll (Ph.D., Freiburg, 1909).

Third row: Herschel T. Manuel (Ph.D., Illinois, 1917), Robert L. Bates (Ph.D., Johns Hopkins, 1924), Wilford S. Miller (Ph.D., Illinois, 1917), Edwin M. Chamberlain (Ph.D., Harvard, 1917), Gardner C. Basset (Ph.D., Johns Hopkins, 1913),

Arthur H. Estabrook (Ph.D., Johns Hopkins, 1910), Albert T. Poffenberger,★ Charles E. Benson (Ph.D., Columbia, 1922), Marion R. Trabue (Ph.D., Columbia, 1915), Edgar A. Doll,★ Eugene C. Rowe (Ph.D., Clark, 1909), Richard M. Elliott.★

Back row: Donald G. Paterson (A.M., Ohio State, 1916), Karl M. Dallenbach,★ Benjamin F. Pittenger (Ph.D., Chicago, 1916), Edwin G. Boring,★ Harry H. Wylie (Ph.D., Chicago, 1917), John W. Bare (M.A., Ohio Wesleyan, 1908), Horace B. English (Ph.D., Yale, 1916), Reuel H. Sylvester (Ph.D., Pennsylvania, 1912), John J. B. Morgan (Ph.D., Columbia, 1916), John E. Anderson (Ph.D., Harvard, 1917), John D. Houser (M.A., Stanford, 1912). (# = an officer who is not a psychologist; U = career unknown; P = appeared to have remained in personnel work).

Archives of the History of American Psychology Photographic File, Courtesy J. W. Kling, Permission Walter S. Hunter, Laboratory, Brown University.

World War II—the close of the era of development. This is "The Emergency Committee in Psychology," created in 1940 by the Division of Anthropology and Psychology of the National Research Council to coordinate the work of all psychologists in case of a military emergency. At first, the committee focused on preparation, but after 1942, it focused on the actuality of the war. The Committee held 22 meetings from 1940 through 1945. Its composition changed over time; this picture of the original members was taken in September 1942 at the 13th meeting (Dallenbach, 1946). The names in italics designate members who were also in the First Company of Commissioned Psychologists in World War I, shown on page 82. Left to right, front row: Leonard Carmichael (Ph.D., Harvard, 1924); Karl M. Dallenbach,★ Chair; Robert M. Yerkes★; Walter S. Hunter.★ Left to right, back row: Walter R. Miles★; Carroll C. Pratt (Ph.D., Clark, 1921); Robert Brotemarkle (Ph.D., Pennsylvania, 1923); Gordon W. Allport★; Dale L. Wolfle★; Steuart Britt (Ph.D., Yale, 1935).

Archives of the History of American Psychology, Walter and Catharine Cox Miles Papers.

Psychology outgrows any single professor. These books contain notes taken by William A. Hunt (Ph.D., Harvard, 1931) in a four-semester course, taught by Edwin G. Boring★ at Harvard University. The Harvard Catalogue of 1928–29 (when Hunt earned the M.A.) lists the titles as "Psychological Systems and Theories," "Sensation," "Perception," and "Association and Determination". Excerpts from a letter dated January 19, 1968, from Boring to Hunt, provide a perspective:

> For at least 35 years (1874–1911) Wundt kept himself competent in respect of what he regarded as the whole range of psychology, with systematic lectures. . . . It was the great faith in that procedure that Titchener brought to Cornell. . . . The systematic coverage of "all" of psychology for every Ph.D. . . .
>
> My training at Cornell made me feel that instruction of this sort was essential. . . . and to Harvard I insisted that these courses be given. . . . when the spread of knowledge was getting too broad for any one person to handle, [italics added] we tried for a bit splitting up the systematic courses amongst the staff, but it did not work too well. . . . So after that in the 1930s we gave up the systematic courses.

Archives of the History of American Psychology, William A. Hunt Papers, Catalogue Information, Clark A. Elliot. (A copy of this letter is in the papers of E. G. Boring [HUG 4229. 5, Box 80, Folder 1680] and is quoted here by permission, Harvard University Archives.)

1st grade worksheet:

$$\Sigma x = 6599 \checkmark \qquad \Sigma y = 6640 \checkmark$$
$$\Sigma x^2 = 439763 \checkmark \qquad \Sigma y^2 = 445968 \checkmark$$
$$N = 100 \checkmark \qquad N = 100 \checkmark$$
$$(\Sigma x)^2 = 7385583 \checkmark \qquad (\Sigma y)^2 = 7508944 \checkmark$$
$$\Sigma xy = 441395 \checkmark \qquad 44089600$$

$$= \frac{100(441395) - (6599)(6640)}{\sqrt{100(439763) - 7385583}\;\sqrt{100(445968) - 7508944}}$$

$$= \frac{44139500 - 43817360}{\sqrt{43976300 - 7385583}\;\sqrt{44596800 - 7508944}}$$

$$= \frac{322140}{\sqrt{36590717}\;\sqrt{37087856}}$$

$$= \frac{322140}{(6048)(6090)}$$

$$= \frac{322140}{36832320} = .0087 \qquad .69$$

Right worksheet:

$$\Sigma x = 13824 \qquad \Sigma y = 13954$$
$$\Sigma x^2 = 925038 \qquad \Sigma y^2 = 944540$$
$$N = 209 \qquad N = 209$$
$$(\Sigma x)^2 = 191102976 \qquad (\Sigma y)^2 = 194714116$$
$$\Sigma xy = 930870$$

$$= \frac{(209)(930870) - (13824)(13954)}{\sqrt{(209)(925038) - 191102976}\;\sqrt{(209)(944540) - 194714116}}$$

$$= \frac{194551830 - 192900096}{\sqrt{193332942 - 191102976}\;\sqrt{197408860 - 194714116}}$$

$$= \frac{1651734}{\sqrt{2229966}\;\sqrt{2694744}}$$

$$= \frac{1651734}{(1496)(1657)}$$

$$= \frac{1651734}{2478872} = .66$$

Calculators eliminated many of the burdens of calculation. They computed sums, differences, products, quotients, and even square roots—but the results had to be processed manually. These pages are probably work sheets of Dorothy C. Adkins* (Ph.D., Ohio State, 1937). There is no definite identification of what the figures represent. Pages of this sort—typically undated and unlabeled—were commonplace before the advent of computers.

Archives of the History of American Psychology, Dorothy C. Adkins Papers.

The Refining of Experimental Methods

Apparatus

In the late 1910s, scientific instruments were more efficient than the original European equipment; among the most outstanding changes in instruments was the replacement of manually operated devices with powered ones. This improvement, however, was not ideal. The power mechanisms, for example, were frequently slow, both in starting and stopping, as well as incapable of recording many events at the speed in which they occurred.

A glance at some research on just one topic—hearing—brings many of these limitations to light. A different kind of machine had to be used to produce each sound component. The frequency, or pitch, of a tone was generated by various instruments, such as tuning forks and Stern's tone variators. At one time, loudness was generated by acoumeters, instruments that rely on gravity—specifically, on a hand-adjusted height of fall of a lead pellet. Electrically driven audiometers replaced the acoumeters, but the early audiometers were, in retrospect, primitive. A Western Electric model in use in the 1920s, for example, consisted of a phonograph, two records (one of a male voice and one of a female voice), and a radio-type headset. The latter was an advance in that, in contrast to a loudspeaker, it channels the sounds to the ear (Wallin, 1927).

By the end of World War II, acoustical scientists had made striking refinements in equipment suitable for use in laboratories of various disciplines. Many of these pieces supported breakthroughs in psychological research but they are so intricate that many

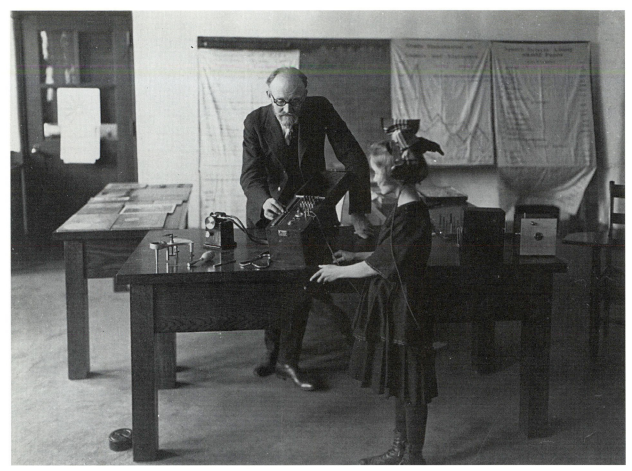

Measuring auditory acuity. This 1920s photograph of J. E. Wallace Wallin* and an unidentified young girl shows various devices used to measure the level of hearing, including tuning forks, the tips of a stethoscope and a Galton whistle. Wallin is testing the child with an audiometer constructed by Carl E. Seashore.*

At the corner of the table is an acoumeter. The subject customarily sits ten meters from the acoumeter with one ear plugged, eyes covered, and mouth closed. The experimenter releases a steel ball, held by forceps, onto a glass plate and asks if the subject hears the sound. The experimenter reduces the height of the steel ball until the sound is inaudible; the height at which the sound disappears marks the hearing level (Whipple, 1910).

Archives of the History of American Psychology, J. E. Wallace Wallin Papers.

The pseudophone, worn by its inventor Paul T. Young (Ph.D., Cornell, 1918). Young constructed the pseudophone in 1928 to control stimulation. Normally, a subject hears a sound coming from the right sooner and louder in the right than in the left ear, and this discrepancy helps the subject locate the source of the sound. The pseudophone picks up sounds in the "trumpets" (taken here from a hearing aid) and delivers auditory stimulation that comes from the right side to the left ear and stimulation from the left side to the right ear. When a subject first wears this equipment, he or she experiences a right-left reversal; that is, the closing of a door on the right is heard as on the left. As experiences continue, the auditory cues become less influential and an object that is in sight is usually localized correctly (Young, 1928). Young conducted this experiment early in his career, when he visited the University of Berlin. He is better known for two books: Motivation of Behavior (1936) and Motivation and Emotion (1961).

Archives of the History of American Psychology, Paul T. Young Papers.

The magic lantern—then. This piece, from the late nineteenth or early twentieth century, is only a remnant but it shows the kerosene reservoir that is reached by the capped fill-hole at the left just above the ring. The three knobs adjust the wick and the chimney carries off heat and smoke. Missing are both the condensing and magnifying lenses as well as the holder for the glass slides and the right angle prism for turning the image upright. Only one slide at a time can be fed into this device.

Archives of the History of American Psychology, University of Michigan, Carl R. Brown Collection.

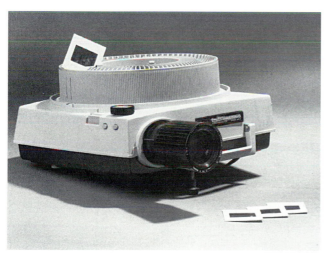

The magic lantern—now. This familiar, modern version of a slide projector is powered by electricity and has an automatic focus. This slide carousel can be prearranged for the presentation of up to 140 slides.

Archives of the History of American Psychology Photographic File.

psychologists are forced into the role of knowledgeable consumers and must restrict their own designs to mechanically simple, but nonetheless serviceable, tools.

Continuing with the example of progress in research on hearing, engineers crafted instruments that could simultaneously and reliably produce and modify all dimensions of sound. Some of these gains in stimulus control are illustrated in "The Perception of Speech," a chapter written shortly after the end of World War II when laboratories were less concerned with military needs but were profiting from research on wartime problems (Licklider & Miller, 1951). That chapter deals with the comprehension of speech, a topic that, in itself, reflects a shift in psychology away from research on the relationship between physical energy and simple sensations toward research on the meaning of experiences. The authors conclude that intelligibility resists distortion—that no single physical dimension is critical and that the interplay of the intensity, frequency, and timing of speech influences comprehension.

Steps Toward the Memory Drum

1. *This kymograph is the basic component of an early memory drum. It consists of a metal drum with a clockwork drive (notice the key at the left) that revolves at a constant speed. The kymograph is designed to record for a variety of responses the rate and amplitude of stylus tracings on paper coated with carbon black (Zimmermann is the name of the manufacturer).*

From Schulze, 1912, p. 168.

3. *Paul Ranschburg (M.D., Budapest, 1894) invented the mnemometer at the right, one of the first instruments that allowed the experimenter to control the speed of the drum. The stimuli that are to be memorized are arranged on the rim of the disc and each becomes visible as it passes through the slit (D) in the rim cover. The mnemometer is a variety of tachistoscope, equipped with electromagnets that regulate the exposure time. The metronome and telegrapher's keys allow the release of the disc at different counts of the beat. This apparatus was used in experiments on perception and association as well as on memory.*

From Schulze, 1912, p. 236.

As automation progressed, psychologists also built laboratory equipment suitable for special research problems. Although many of these specific-to-psychology instruments lacked technological sophistication, they served their purposes admirably. One of the best known examples of a machine that carried out specialized functions in psychological research is the memory drum, an instrument designed for investigations of rote learning. It meets the demand for orderly presentation of material to be memorized

and also regulates the duration of intervals between successive exposures of stimuli and the length of time each stimulus is shown.

The first formal experiments on memory were conducted by Hermann Ebbinghaus (Ph.D., Bonn, 1873), a German psychologist whose work predated sophisticated instrumentation; but, he was so adept at contriving experimental controls that some remarks about his legacy are in order. Ebbinghaus realized that familiar material is easier to memorize than

2. Georg E. Müller* (Ph.D., Göttingen, 1873) and Friedrich Schumann* (Ph.D., Göttingen, 1885) converted a kymograph, a recorder of responses, into a presenter of stimuli. They turned the instrument on its side and attached a strip of paper bearing material to be memorized to the surface of the drum. A screen with a slit in it allows only a single item to be seen at one time.
From Schulze, 1912, p. 238.

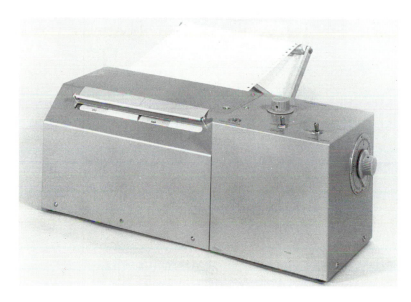

4. Memory drum with built-in programmer, model #23015. This electrically powered memory drum can present stimuli on up to 36" of paper, at four different drum speeds. A pegged drum positions the nonslip perforated paper. There are two automatic and four manual control shutters. This instrument represents the last flowering of the memory drum before it was made obsolete by electronic equipment—nearly 100 years after Müller and Schumann turned a kymograph on its side.

Archives of the History of American Psychology Photographic File. Courtesy Vern Davidson, Lafayette Instrument Company.

unfamiliar material. He invented approximately 2,300 nonsense syllables so as to have units similar in meaning or, more accurately, in non-meaning. Most nonsense syllables consist of a vowel between two consonants in uncommon combinations such as *kaj* and *fuv*. Ebbinghaus, acting as both experimenter and subject, read and reread lists of nonsense syllables until he could recite each list without error. He recognized that the difficulty of memorizing varies with the rate of repetitions, and he tried to monitor his reading by pacing them with a metronome or a watch (Popplestone, 1985).

Ebbinghaus's successors first tried to control the rate by displaying each syllable manually on a separate card. The first component of the memory drum came when experimenters mounted a paper strip bearing a list of nonsense syllables on a horizontal recording drum that rotated at a constant speed. The syllables could be seen only through a slit in a screen at the front of the drum, so the learner, able to see only one syllable at a time, was prevented either from reviewing or previewing the list. This machine was certainly an advance over manual displays, but it, rather than the experimenter, set the speed. As mechanization improved, investigators became able to select both the rotation speed and the exposure interval. Thus, they could increase the number of syllables that could be presented, and they could modify the aperture in which each was exposed so as to enhance legibility. During the 1930s, the noise of the equipment was reduced, its portability improved, and its durability strengthened.

Warden multiple-U maze. Warden's design is found in mazes built both for animals and humans. Since constructing mazes for people is so expensive and cumbersome, substitutes such as this one were developed. The pathways in the maze shown here consist of a series of raised wires; blindfolded human subjects traced the course with their fingers.

Archives of the History of American Psychology, Ohio State University Collection.

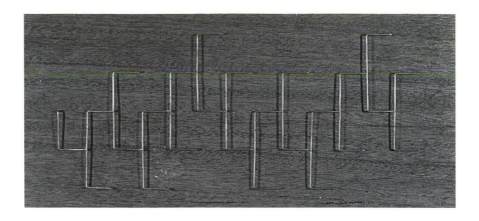

Stylus maze. This maze, also designed for humans, is only 6″ × 9″—it can be held in one hand or placed on a table. The maze consists of a cast metal plate with grooves for pathways. This complex floor plan is similar to but not identical with the living-hedge seventeenth-century labyrinth planted at Hampton Court, shown on page 41.

Archives of the History of American Psychology, Denison University Collection.

A second example of an instrument constructed for a singular purpose is the Warden multiple-U maze. As previously noted, mazes are commonly used to study learning. They consist of a sequence of pathways, some of which are blind alleys and some of which lead to a goal. Because the course through these pathways cannot be seen, it must be discovered. Investigators became aware that some sections of a maze are learned more readily than others—short pathways, for example, are usually easier to master than long ones. Investigators had to eliminate these structural irregularities in order to determine which parts of the sequence are the most and the least difficult to learn. Carl J. Warden★ (Ph.D., Chicago, 1922) obtained this uniformity when he built a maze in which the runways are the same length and the critical points identical (Warden, Jenkins, & Warner, 1935).

Another success in devising equipment for use in specialized problems was achieved by Walter Miles★ who, during World War II, induced dark adaptation by having subjects wear goggles that permit only red light

to reach the eyes (Miller, 1979). Up to this time, sensitivity to faint visual stimuli was customarily obtained by having subjects remain in complete darkness for approximately one-half hour. Personnel working with X rays took one step toward overcoming this interruption when they discovered that the interval could be shortened if they wore dark glasses before entering a darkroom. In the summer of 1941, Miles, connecting this discovery to the relative insensitivity to red light of the receptors that function in night vision, began to observe the effects of red lenses. He determined specifications for the goggles, the lighting conditions, and the timing that sustains "reasonably good vision" and, at the same time, induces adequate dark adaptation. The spectacles relieved flight personnel of the tedium of sitting in darkness before a night flight, and they also eliminated any loss in adaptation from accidental exposure to light and preserved the perception of dim stimuli that comes with sleeping (Miles, 1943). The goggles were first used by British military personnel during World War II.

Walter Miles (Ph.D., Iowa, 1913) was a member of the faculty of Yale University from 1932 to 1953, and this portrait hangs in the Psychology Department. Miles was a dedicated researcher and admirably adept at relating laboratory data to a variety of practical problems. He was elected to the National Academy of Sciences in 1933 and served as president of the American Psychological Association in 1932.

Archives of the History of American Psychology, Walter and Catharine Cox Miles Papers. Courtesy Judith Rodin, Permission of Department of Psychology, Yale University. Photograph by Peter Salovey.

Archives of the History of American Psychology, Walter and Catharine Cox Miles Papers. Courtesy Judith Rodin, Department of Psychology, Permission of Yale University. Photograph by Peter Salovey.

In 1911, Arnold Gesell (Ph.D., Clark, 1906; M.D., Yale, 1915) joined the Yale University faculty as an Assistant Professor of Education, and the Dean of the Medical School appointed him Director of the Juvenile Psycho Clinic. In 1915, the year he earned the M.D. degree, Gesell was promoted to professor in the Yale Graduate School but was required to spend part of his time serving as psychologist to the State Board of Education in Connecticut. This responsibility led to his identification as the first school psychologist. His eminence is, however, based on his contributions to child development. In 1930, the Juvenile Psycho Clinic was renamed the Clinic of Child Development, and this is the facility with which he is most closely identified. In 1950, colleagues founded the Gesell Institute of Human Development for which Gesell, then retired from Yale, served as a consultant (Ames, 1989).

Archives of the History of American Psychology, Louise Bates Ames Gift.

The changes made in the means of recording responses resemble the changes made in equipment that regulate stimuli in that they provided many benefits but not perfection. Since motion pictures, television, and audio transmission are familiar to everyone, they have been chosen to exemplify the advantages and disadvantages of relying on machines to record behavior. The shortcomings may not be immediately apparent, but they do exist.

Researchers take a carefully planned series of motion pictures of phenomena sampling a wide range of complexity from such elementary activities as the movements of discrete sets of muscles to complex interpersonal transactions. One of the relatively simple actions that investigators have tried to capture is that of eyeball movements. These movements have been filmed during experiments on reading, on equilibrium or balance, on scanning by infants, and on reactions to both novel and emotion-arousing stimuli. The original method of observing eyeball movements consisted simply of watching the eyes, either directly or, in some instances, by means of a mirror. Early attempts to obtain permanent records involved attaching intrusive and sometimes pain-inducing equipment directly to the eyes (p. 21). The invention of photography overcame problems of this nature, but a motion picture of eye movements does not provide as direct and obvious a record as first appears; a few of the complications are shown on pages 102–103. Since the eyeball is a sphere and its parts are not differentiated on the surface, a definite, but nonetheless arbitrary, point must be chosen in order to mark and chart the pictures (Thompson, Lindsley, & Eason, 1966).

Gesell's photographic dome. Gesell and his associates carried out much of the cinematography in this shadowless dome. Two camera tracks and one-way vision screens provide an optimal setting for photography. Gesell preferred not to record sound because he believed that it detracted from the visual impact.

Archives of the History of American Psychology, Louise Bates Ames Gift.

Gesell completed several studies of twins. This still of two babies photographed simultaneously illustrates the visual clarity that Gesell so often achieved. The mirror-image phenomenon shown in this one picture says more than many words could about identical twins.

For demonstration purposes—particularly for teaching about twins—Gesell relied on a technique that he called coincident, or simultaneous, projection. In this method, a strip of film is split in the middle and two different original films—for example, one child at two different ages or two children of the same age—are printed together.

Archives of the History of American Psychology, Louise Bates Ames Gift.

Motion pictures of infants and children constitute the data on which much of the information about human growth is based. Arnold Gesell★ was a stellar figure in developing this kind of evidence. He treated motion pictures as laboratory protocols, using them both as documentation of growth and as records that can be analyzed minutely by cinemanalysis, a process that consists of running a film, one frame at a time, through a projector equipped with a lens that throws successive images on a tracing plate. After each image is outlined, the next frame is processed. Analyses of both the stills and the animation allow students of child development to observe minutiae of growth in a variety of skills such as "The Patterning of Prone Progression," "The Conquest of the Spoon," and "Self-Discovery in a Mirror" (Ames, 1989). These motion pictures make overt behavior—as observed—crystal clear, but they do not expose the child's perspective.

The record is not always clear. This poorly defined, indistinct picture illustrates some of the problems in using motion pictures as records. This still is an outtake from films of experiments designed by Kurt Lewin* (Ph.D., Berlin, 1914–1916) and completed by graduate students at the University of Iowa in the late 1930s and early 1940s. These investigations were innovative studies of the reactions of boys to autocratic and democratic leaders as well as to a laissez-faire atmosphere. The leader in this photograph is probably Boyd McCandless (Ph.D., Iowa, 1941).

Ronald Lippitt (Ph.D., Iowa, 1940), one of the experimenters, describes some efforts made to clarify the film:

> *Behind the blankets in the rooms, as you have seen in the motion pictures, were Jack Kounin (Ph.D., Iowa, 1939) and Joan Kalhorn (Lasko) (Ph.D., Ohio State, 1951) and two*

girls taking shorthand notes at one-minute intervals. Ralph White (Ph.D., Stanford, 1937) and I had a tremendous job of marking off everything at one-minute intervals for everybody but they were all synchronized with the group observers, interaction observers, and content observers, all batteried up with a buzzer set with a one-minute shift. Kurt was running around with a camera behind the burlap curtains. Kurt had a little ladder from which he could take pictures.

> *Ralph had $400 research money and this paid for the equipment we needed (Bradford, 1974, p. 9).*

Archives of the History of American Pyschology, Child Development Film Archives, Grace Heider Gift.

Motion pictures of interpersonal activities are less satisfactory than those of individuals. Views of groups constitute a record but it is sometimes as confounding as the original event. Probably the greatest asset is the opportunity for researchers to review the scenes again and again. Psychologists have tried numerous ways of keeping track of all the activity on a film by such means as using multiple observers and taking stenographic notes. Such efforts enrich the ledger but they have yet to make it all inclusive.

Sound recordings and motion pictures transformed both the practice of, and research in, counseling and psychotherapy. Although problems are caused by the intrusion of the equipment into the privacy of both the interviewee and the interviewer, they are countered by impressive returns. The audio- and videotapes allow professionals other than the researcher to see and listen to interviews; this access makes it possible to separate the functions of a therapist, a therapist's supervisor, and an investigator, thereby eliminating distortions that any of these functions can impose on the others. Judges are able to review the proceedings, either independently or as members of a team, to resolve confusion about what did and did not transpire; but, again, there is no record of the private thoughts of the participants (Shakow, 1949).

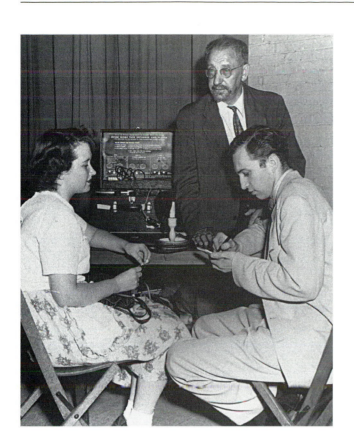

An oral history is a by-product of technology. It is a recorded interview conducted in order to augment and clarify information about past events. Mechanical recording reduces the labor of note taking and thereby fosters spontaneity and elaboration while at the same time securing the accuracy of the record.

Here, David P. Boder* (Ph.D., Northwestern, 1934) appears to be observing a verbal exchange between two people whose identity is not known. A microphone rests on the table between them and in the background—looking like a suitcase—is a reel-to-reel portable tape recorder (weight about 15 pounds). Inside the cover are directions for its use, introduced by means of a well-chosen metaphor: "How to Make 'Snapshots in Sound' with the New Eicor Home Tape Recorder and Player."

From 1927 to 1952, Boder was a member of the faculty of Lewis Institute, now The Illinois Institute of Technology. He was a European refugee, fluent in several languages; and at the end of World War II, he interviewed residents of camps for displaced people in Europe, speaking the language of each interviewee's choice. He translated and published a few of these histories in I Did Not Interview the Dead (1949). Boder recorded these interviews by means of a Peirce Wire Recorder. He is probably the first person to take oral histories, but this priority is generally unknown.

Archives of the History of American Psychology, David P. Boder Museum Collection.

> Glad you referred to the effort of David Boder. He told me on his way to Europe that someone, I think at Ill. Inst. of Technology developed a wire recorder, new type of machine that gave him the idea of using this method of obtaining information —
>
> M. Meenes

An informal and unsolicited confirmation of Boder's role comes from this note from Max Meenes (Ph.D., Clark, 1926), written to one of the authors of this volume as she was reading a paper on oral history at the Annual Convention of the American Psychological Association in August 1973.

Archives of the History of American Psychology Correspondence File.

B. F. Skinner★ speaks to an audience of almost 2,000 people on "What John B. Watson Meant to Me" at a 1979 John Broadus Watson Symposium at Furman University, Greenville, South Carolina. Furman is Watson's★ alma mater.

Archives of the History of American Psychology, Cedric A. Larson/John B. Watson Papers. Identification with the help of Charles Brewer.

The liabilities of equipment are, of course, compensated by the regularity and accuracy of machines. An illustration of complete automation is a box built in 1932 by B. F. Skinner★ (Ph.D., Harvard, 1931) for the purpose of conditioning animals. He designed the box to generate data relevant to the theory that came to be called Skinnerian or operant behaviorism, a modification of earlier forms of behaviorism. Since this device can be appreciated only if one is familiar with this theory, we interrupt our discussion of improvements in apparatus in order to provide some background. Skinner downplays an elaborate theoretical structure and plays up laboratory results, especially operant conditioned responses.

Skinner called this the lever box or the problem box, but many call it the Skinner box. He designed this equipment to yield data which he organized into a system, and it is so integrated into his point of view that it is difficult to think about operant conditioning without this box (Skinner, 1983). The design has undergone various improvements, but has not been altered significantly. Although the rat is the animal most frequently observed, the box can be modified to accommodate a variety of species.

A single animal occupies a uniform area with controlled temperature, noise, and lighting. There is one lever—here made of wire mesh and secured with masking tape—placed at such a height that a rat, in order to manipulate it, must raise its forepaws, put one or both on the lever, and press downward. This response activates the release of a controlled amount of food down the chute into the pan in the rear corner.

Archives of the History of American Psychology Photographic File.

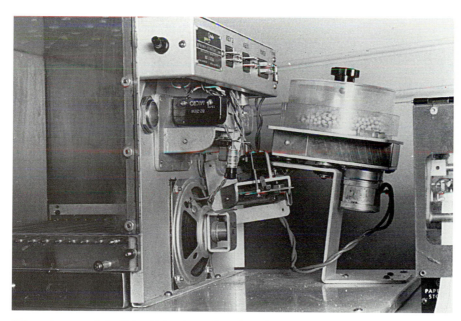

The environmental simplicity of the Skinner box, from the animal's point of view, contrasts with its mechanical complexity. Modern boxes automatically record and tally the animal's manipulations. They also regulate the interval between the push and the reinforcer.

In some experiments, each push is reinforced, whereas in others the reinforcement may be episodic but regular, and in others, it is aperiodic.

Archives of the History of American Psychology Photographic File.

Clark Hull *(Ph.D., Wisconsin, 1918) was a member of the faculty of Yale University from 1929 until his death in 1952. He was one of the most dedicated proponents of the variety of behaviorism that came to be called neobehaviorism. Hull differed from other behaviorists in that he did not reject implicit phenomena, but did disavow using them as explanatory concepts and endeavored to account for them in a behavioral frame of reference. He related behavior to both stimulus and organismic variables, formulated several postulates about the relationships, and from these deduced numerous corollaries. He constructed a formal theory and, whenever feasible, expressed it in equations and formulae. The aura of "hard" science he generated appealed to many psychologists, and for a time he was one of the most frequently cited experimenters, but the theory did not have the staying power of operant behaviorism. Some of the principles were based only on a specific experiment and were so vulnerable to criticism that by the 1950s neobehaviorism had lost much of its appeal (Marx & Cronan-Hillix, 1987).*

Archives of the History of American Psychology Photographic File. Courtesy Judith Rodin, Permission Department of Psychology, Yale University.

The procedures for the formation of operant conditioned responses differ from those used in classical conditioning, and some clarification is required to counteract the suggestion of similarity inherent in the use of the word *conditioning* to refer to both techniques. Both are complicated and can be illustrated more readily than they can be defined. In classical conditioning, stimuli are paired—for example, a tone with food—so repetitively that one stimulus comes to elicit behavior that is similar to that elicited by the other stimulus. In operant conditioning, an effect is sequenced with a stimulus—for example, pressing a lever in the Skinner box is followed by food—repetitively until the sight of the lever elicits depressing it. Skinner chose the label *operant conditioning* because the response *operates on*—that is, has an effect on—the environment. In this example, it provides food. The word *reinforcement* is used to designate an increased probability of an occurrence; *positive reinforcement* is used when the increase comes after a gratifying stimulus (lever pressing—food) and *negative reinforcement* when the increase comes after the withdrawal of an aversive stimulus (lever pressing—termination of an electric shock). In the former instance, food is the effective consequence, and, in the latter, the removal of the shock is the consequence.

This terminology may appear awkward, but it is preferred by operant behaviorists because it plays down the subjectivity implied by reward and punishment. Punishment varies from negative reinforcement in that the latter refers to the likelihood of increasing a response but punishment refers to the likelihood of decreasing a response. Decrements occur when a positive reinforcer is withheld (depriving a child of candy) or a negative reinforcer is imposed (placing a child in isolation). These distinctions frequently fail to

A *"Section of the stage of the Psychological Museum at Lewis Institute, Chicago, showing an assortment of psychological apparatus used in the study of space perception, colour fusion, colour blindness, motor learning, reaction time, etc. There are a number of tests of manual dexterity used in vocational guidance and industrial selection. In the upper right (next to the picture frame) is an oscillograph used in the study of voice qualities, speech and electrical potentials from the brain, nerves, and muscles"* (Encyclopaedia Britannica, *14th edition, s.v. "Experimental Psychology," Plate I*).

Archives of the History of American Psychology, David P. Boder Museum Collection, Permission Encyclopaedia Britannica.

override associations of positive with pleasure and negative with pain, and, as a result, the incidence of misunderstanding is high.

Although operant techniques were initiated and honed in the laboratory, they were applied, beginning in the 1950s, to behavior that occurs in everyday contexts, most noticeably in education, where responses are formed and strengthened, and in clinical practice, where responses are weakened and eradicated. We shall review the uses of conditioning for instructional purposes in Chapter 7 and for therapeutic purposes in Chapter 9.

An account of the Psychological Museum illustrates the support that psychologists found in equipment during this period of cultivation of methodology. This museum was established between 1936 and 1937 in Chicago at the Lewis Institute (later the Illinois Institute of Technology) by David P. Boder.★ Boder was enthusiastic about this project and, for a period of time, it flourished. Many donors offered gifts and encouragement, and there were over 250 items on display, files of tests, donated apparatus, and a library of more than 2,000 books. Boder was an inventor and several of his own publications deal with instruments. His interest is apparent in the museum's

emphasis on the hardware of experimental psychology. Boder also wanted to demonstrate how psychology could benefit society and he included various displays of its applications. Boder retired from the faculty in 1952 and ended all ties with the Museum in 1957. Without the founder's active presence, institutional support weakened and the facility faded (Benjamin, 1979).

During the museum's heyday, special displays were held, symposia were sponsored, and staff were invited to prepare an exhibit for the 1939 New York World's Fair. The Museum provided the *Encyclopaedia Britannica* (14th edition) with photographs that illustrate the article "Experimental Psychology" by Frederic C. Bartlett (A. M. London, 1911; A. M. Cambridge, 1917). The photographs on pages 99–103 are from the holdings of the museum. They do not provide a systematic sample of the apparatus of the era, but they do depict the exploitation of technology in order to increase precision in the laboratory. They also furnish images, for comparison and contrast, of how far psychology traveled from the "Pioneer American Laboratories" described in Chapter 2.

"Experiment in reaction time using a Dunlap chronoscope. The stimulus may be a light, sound, or any other sensory impression. The subject responds with a finger or foot movement or by voice. The chronoscope records the time in milliseconds" (Encyclopaedia Britannica, 14th edition, s.v. "Experimental Psychology," Plate II).

The three icons hanging on the wall behind these two unidentified people show Gustav Fechner (M.D., Leipzig, 1822) on the left, James McKeen Cattell★ in the middle, and Francis Galton★ on the right.

Archives of the History of American Psychology, David P. Boder Museum Collection, Permission Encyclopaedia Britannica.

In the Psychology Department of Cornell University, an unidentified subject with electrodes on her earlobes and forehead sits in an electrically shielded room. The changes in the electrodes are amplified and recorded on a moving strip of paper, creating a record of the electrical activity of the brain called an EEG, or electroencephalograph (literally "electrical brain writing"). The caption of this photograph, which is a pendant of a scene printed in the Encyclopaedia Britannica, informs readers that the EEG will help to understand such varied phenomena as "differences in intelligence, personality traits and mental states such as sleep, hypnosis, frustration, pre-epileptic states, etc. . . . ." (14th edition, s.v. "Experimental Psychology," Plate I).

Archives of the History of American Psychology, David P. Boder Museum Collection. Photograph by George Kreezer.

David P. Boder and two unidentified collaborators demonstrate a homemade polygraph at the Psychological Museum. The man on the right seems to wear on his right arm a sphygmomanometer cuff—for measuring blood pressure—and holds in his left hand a device that probably measures the G(alvanic) S(kin) R(esponse), changes in electrical conductivity of the skin. Changes in both blood pressure and GSRs accompany emotional responses.

Archives of the History of American Psychology, David P. Boder Museum Collection.

Inscriptions on the back of this photograph date it March 1935 and cryptically identify the scene as "Neural Stability Apparatus (Lie Detection)" from the "Driving Research Laboratory" of the Department of Psychology at Iowa State College (later Iowa State University), Ames, Iowa. This equipment registers minute, often involuntary, hand movements, by means of bellows and changes in air pressure. Emotional reactions—including those that accompany telling a lie—induce physiological changes and these changes were interpreted for a period of time as evidence of lying. This research was probably conducted in the Driving Research Laboratory, the only space available for experimentation at the time.

Archives of the History of American Psychology, David P. Boder Museum Collection, Permission Gary L. Wells, and Department of Psychology, Iowa State University. Identification with the help of Daniel C. Edwards. Photograph by John Barry, Jr.

The Darrow photopolygraph, devised by Chester A. Darrow
(Ph.D., Chicago, 1924), is one of several instruments that are called
a "Lie Detector." This particular apparatus "records photographically
changes in electrical skin resistance, blood pressure, pulse, breathing,
as well as voluntary manual and verbal responses under emotional
stress" (Encyclopaedia Britannica, 14th edition, s.v.
"Experimental Psychology," Plate II).

    At the time this demonstration was photographed, many
thought that devices of this kind could determine deception. The
technique was promoted as an "objective" measure of guilt and
innocence that would make police brutality and "third degree"
procedures unnecessary. Disagreement and controversy ensued for a
variety of reasons, but an important one is the similarity of the
physiological changes that accompany various emotional reactions. In
1986, the American Psychological Association concluded that the
polygraph technique does not yield definitive information, and shortly
thereafter the Congress of the United States restricted the use of "lie
detector tests" in the private sector (Bales, 1987).

Archives of the History of American Psychology, David P. Boder Museum Collection,
Courtesy Dorritt S. White, Permission Arthur S. Honneman and Department of
Psychology, University of Kentucky. Permission Encyclopaedia Britannica. Photograph by
John L. Carter.

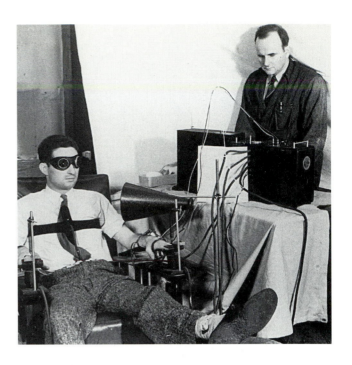

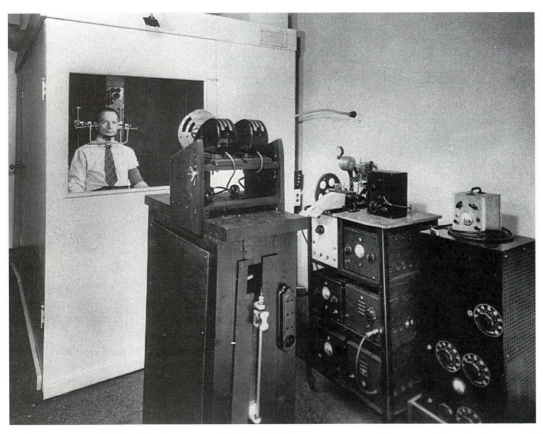

At the University of Chicago in the summer of 1940, Ward C.
Halstead (Ph.D., Northwestern, 1935) records eye movements.
"The subject is placed in an electrically shielded room and electrodes
are placed on the temporal sides of the eyes. The changes in position
of the eyes during movement produce electrical changes which are
recorded on a running strip of paper or photographic film"
(Encyclopaedia Britannica, 14th edition, s.v. "Experimental
Psychology," Plate I).

Archives of the History of American Psychology, David P. Boder Museum Collection.
Permission Encyclopaedia Britannica. Photograph by Ward C. Halstead.

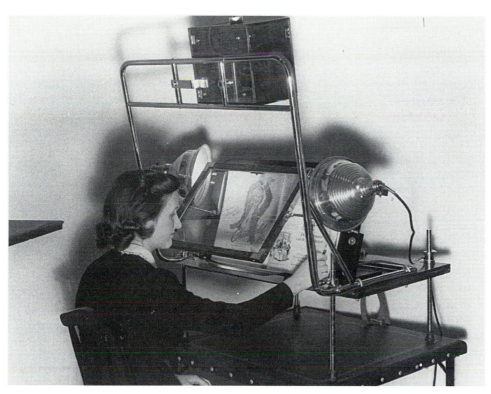

This is the Purdue eye-camera. It furnishes yet another way of observing eye movements. A label attached to the original Psychological Museum photograph identifies it as "an apparatus which is coming into wide use among advertisers and advertising agencies for measuring which advertisements have the most attention power. The device photographs where and how long the reader looks as he [sic] thumbs through a magazine" (from the Laboratory of Applied Psychology, Purdue University). The camera is described in detail by Karslake (1940).

Archives of the History of American Psychology, David P. Boder Museum Collection. Photograph by Swezey, Lafayette, IN.

Instruments that measure eye movements became intricate. This picture shows only the recording equipment of one such device. The subject is in an adjoining room, his or her head is surrounded by a large drum that rotates and induces nystagmus. Laboratory and experiment are unknown.

Archives of the History of American Psychology, David P. Boder Museum Collection.

J. Robert Kantor (Ph.D., Chicago, 1917) formulated interbehavioral psychology, a system that explicitly distinguishes between psychology and other sciences. He identified the subject matter of psychology as the interbehavior of a responding organism and the stimulus field. The psychological ingredients in this interplay are not the physical stimuli and responses but are the meaning and purpose of the stimuli and responses—in Kantor's terms, stimulus functions and response functions. In the case of stimuli, the functions vary even though the physical properties are the same. A book, for example, may elicit reading, purchasing, gift giving, or elevating a flower pot to the level of a window ledge. In the case of responses, the functions of the same action vary in purpose or intent. A person may, for example, open a cupboard door to obtain a dish, to see if an item of food is there, or to inspect the quality of the paint. Stimulus and response functions derive from personal biographies and hence are singular (Kantor & Smith, 1975).

Archives of the History of American Psychology Photographic File.

Experimental Procedures

The experimental method demands altering only one variable at a time and holding others constant. This control is difficult to attain in any science, but it is especially problematic in psychology because of the variability of organisms. Physical matter is relatively inert and predictable, but psychological reactivity is both animate and erratic. Individuals assign different meanings to the stimuli they encounter and thereby transform the physically equivalent into the psychologically nonequivalent. They then respond to this divergence in assorted ways, differing, for example, in what they imagine, remember, and approve. Many of these reactions are implicit but they also modify other responses in elusive and hard-to-trace consequences. As a result, psychologists must contend with numerous irregularities, such as the failures of people who are

suggestible in one situation to display suggestibility in another, discrepancies between a sympathetic attitude and sympathetic behavior, and differences in the rate of food intake by rats—this varies, as expected, with the duration of food deprivation but, as not expected, with the size of the food pellets (Andrews, 1948).

Gradually, psychologists became adept at devising experimental procedures in ways that regulate psychological variables. They succeeded in contriving some conditions in which responses rather than instruments are used to regulate the stimuli and to record behavior. Some of the pioneers used such tactics but these were generally isolated incidents until the period covered by this chapter. Even in the most recent literature, these techniques are partially disguised because reports are still written in the style of the natural sciences. Psychologists are apt to be more explicit about physical than psychological dimensions.

In this painting by a child, the police officer is "larger than life." This is one in a series of slides Kurt Lewin★ used as teaching aids. Lewin elaborated various concepts in psychology, including the importance of the perspective of the person. A German refugee, he was interested in national differences (1936), and it is said that when showing this slide he would comment, "Only a German child would see a policeman as this big."

Archives of the History of American Psychology, Kurt Lewin Collection, Dorwin Cartwright Gift.

In an investigation of fear, for example, most experimenters report the characteristics of the stimuli, but only a few specify the relationship of these measurements to the subjects. They would probably record the distance between the subject and the escape route in feet or yards, but would probably fail to note such psychologically relevant details as the ease of access and probability of escape.

These traditional customs have, however, been replaced in many experiments with psychologically tailored strategies. A few of these strategies are sketched here in order to expose the level of experimental sophistication that psychologists achieved during the second quarter of this century.

One of these accomplishments is the use of responses to measure properties of stimuli. This kind of conversion is illustrated by the calibration of nonsense syllables. Nonsense syllables are not equally nonsensical and systematic information about the number of associations that are made to different syllables was first reported in 1928. In 1951, Ernest R. Hilgard★ collated the associations reported by various researchers, making it possible to identify syllables that range from ones that prompt associations in 100% of the subjects (*cin*) to ones that prompt associations in 0% of the subjects (*cij*).

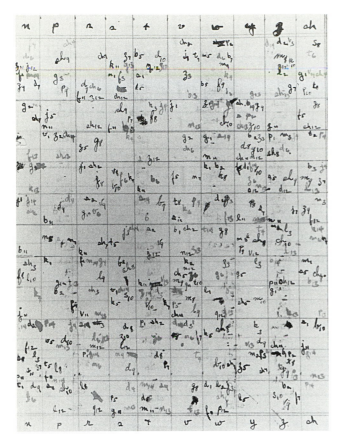

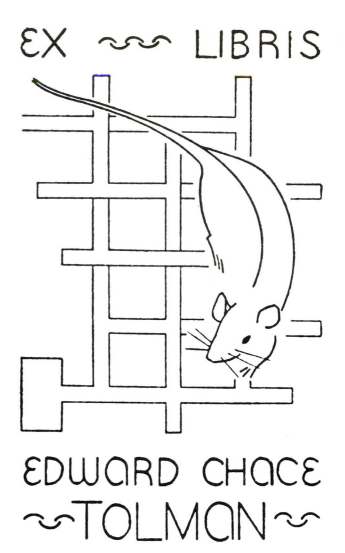

A worksheet from one of eight unpublished notebooks in which Edward C. Tolman★ (Ph.D., Harvard, 1915) created 6,700 nonsense syllables for use in his own research on memory. Tolman made the charts between 1913 and 1918, using ink of different colors. They contain consonant and vowel combinations based on rules devised by Georg Müller★ and Friedrich Schumann.★ The sheets resemble the Periodic Table of Chemistry, Tolman's undergraduate major field and one in which his brother became eminent.

Most modern psychologists, accustomed to prepared lists of nonsense syllables, are surprised to learn how much labor goes into devising them. Tolman seems to have found the task uncongenial. A log of the number of days he worked on nonsense syllables decreased from 80 days during six months of 1916 to complete inactivity by 1919. Tolman's last paper on memory was published in 1919 (Thornton, 1970).

Archives of the History of American Psychology, Edward C. Tolman Papers.

Tolman's bookplate. Tolman was one of the more renowned neobehaviorists and a contemporary of Clark Hull.★ Both of these theorists devoted much of their professional careers to relating "inner psychological dynamics" to the overt behavior of animals. Tolman interpreted the mastery of a maze as evidence that the animal has a "cognitive map," an appreciation of the correct turn at each junction (Tolman, 1932). Tolman's formulations fell out of fashion, but presently they are being seen as forerunners of modern cognitive psychology.

Archives of the History of American Psychology, Edward C. Tolman Papers.

Another technique that helps to regulate psychological variables consists of selecting subjects with similar backgrounds so that their interpretations of the experiment are similar. One of the better known of these designs, called the matched groups method, is one in which groups are formed in ways that make them comparable on such variables as age, sex, education, and socioeconomic status. This homogeneity is then enhanced by measuring the subjects' performance on the behavior that is to be observed during the experiment. Subjects with identical scores are then assigned to pairs, trios, or quartets so as to create samples that not only have a common outlook but are equivalent in respect to the crucial variable. This diluting of diversity helps to bring into clearer focus any differences among the groups in reaction to the experimental procedures (Avery & Cross, 1978). For example, an investigation to determine the length of class periods that is most

This box contains keys, not standard on typewriters, for statistical insignia. When using machines designed for business use, psychologists used these keys to prepare manuscripts.

Archives of the History of American Psychology, David Shakow Papers.

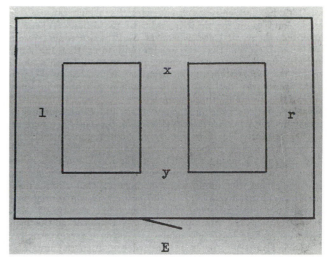

Plan of a temporal maze.

Archives of the History of American Psychology Apparatus Collection.

effective in increasing speed and accuracy of computation might involve three units, each equal in skill at the beginning of the experiment and each treated in the same way except for the duration of the instructional sessions. The control group might attend classes of the customary interval, while one of the experimental groups might attend classes of half the length and another classes of twice the length. Measurements at the end of the term would compare the average speed and accuracy scores of the three groups and estimate the confidence that any differences might be significant and not merely accidental, or due to chance.

A third technique that stabilizes experimental conditions is the inducing of specific experiences during an experiment. This kind of behavioral control is used in various experiments on memory, but its salience is particularly clear in research on reminiscence, the remembering of more material than was previously recalled. For example, a person might recall 90% of a poem on the first recollection after memorizing it and 93% on a second attempt. It is crucial in investigations of reminiscence that there be no opportunity for

practice, neither overt rehearsal nor mulling over of the material. Reviews can be avoided by having subjects perform specific tasks between learning and recall and a number of different kinds of behavior have been relied on to induce this control. In one part of an experiment (Hovland, 1938), subjects memorized a list of 12 nonsense syllables to a level where they could recall seven of them correctly. When this point was reached, the shutter on the memory drum that displays the syllables was closed, a second shutter that exposes colored papers was opened, and the subjects were asked to name each as it appeared. Incidentally, the color naming may have eliminated rehearsal but it did not eliminate reminiscence.

A considerable amount of research experience accumulated before psychologists realized that they could contrive a variety of psychological variables experimentally. They had been quick to recognize that biological deprivation motivates animals and they had rapidly learned how to manipulate hunger and thirst during an experiment, but it was some time before they began to provoke specific kinds of mentation. One of the earlier successes involved using what is known as a temporal maze (above) to determine the ability of different species to master an abstract problem. In one design, the animal was required to run first around pathways on the right half of the maze and second around those on the left—that is, to learn the sequence *rlrl*. In another design, the sequence was *rrll*. Rats learned *rlrl* quite readily, but they did not learn *rrll*. Raccoons learned *rrll*, but they did not extend this to *rrllrrll* (Hunter, 1928). The critical variable appears to be within the organism since the only change is in the immediate past of the animal. This specification is a gain in information, but it falls short of characterizing the change—is it an ability to count, an ability to conceptualize, or something not yet suspected?

In spite of the perplexity of covert variables, some progress has been made in tracing the effects of one kind of response on others. One of the more famous of these endeavors is a 1927 investigation conducted by Bluma Zeigarnik (Ph.D., Berlin, 1927) in order to obtain experimental support for a proposal by Kurt Lewin★ that working toward a goal induces a tension system that is responsible for the continuity of behavior. Subjects were asked to manage 18 to 22 relatively discrete tasks, but half of these assignments were interrupted before they were completed. At the close of the session, the subjects were asked to recount what they had worked on during the session. Even though more time was devoted to the completed than to the uncompleted endeavors, the group recalled approximately twice as many unfinished tasks. This differential in memory is called the Zeigarnik effect. Whether a tension system is the key factor is an interesting matter, but more relevant to this discussion is the demonstration that it is feasible to contrive a specified turn of events and trace some of the sequels.

The successes in building particular responses in the laboratory encouraged the construction of more intricate but, at the time, poorly understood reactions. One of these was the inducing of experimental neuroses, animal analogues of human neuroses. This was done in the belief that learning how to induce disserviceable responses under laboratory conditions might help to understand how they develop in humans in everyday life situations.

An illustration is found in a program of research on frustration that Norman R. F. Maier (Ph.D., Michigan, 1928) started in 1938 and summarized in 1949. In these experiments, rats were thwarted in a number of ways. Initially, the rat was rewarded with food for pushing one of two panels marked with a particular design. Once the animal learned to choose this design, both panels were locked, and when the rat tried to push either of them it landed on a net from a height slightly above its jumping tolerance. After a few of these episodes, the rat simply remained on the jumping stand (above). In order to force it to move, Maier directed a blast of air at the back of the animal. This prompted leaping to the side or above the apparatus, so barriers were installed to prevent escape. These conditions created a situation in which the rat could not obtain a reward, could not leave the field, yet not responding was intolerable. Rats react to this dilemma by replacing differentiated responses with a peculiar mannerism, the pattern of which varies from animal to animal but generally remains the same for any

The rat, the jumping platform, and the air hose (used to provoke responding).

Archives of the History of American Psychology Film Collection, Courtesy Ayesha A. Maier.

one rat. It is repeated whenever the animal is placed in the experimental situation, and it is difficult, but not impossible, to eradicate. Maier's procedures and conclusions drew some severe criticism, but, when viewed from today's vantage point (Dewsbury, 1993), the faults fade and the design comprises an arrangement of experiences that throws light on different facets of frustration.

In the early years of experimental psychology, laboratory workers were typically interested in specific responses (perceiving tones or measuring reaction time, for example), but, as their experimental skills increased, they began to probe such abstract characteristics as honesty, belligerence, and fearfulness. One of the first methods they devised for investigating these reactions was that of looking for a common attribute or theme in numerous specific responses. This kind of scrutiny of behavior is, of course, the basic technique in clinical assessments. But it also came into use in the laboratory; Floyd H. Allport★ was among the first to use this method in formal research. He was interested in learning whether or not "individuality" can be identified. To answer this question, he obtained 630 short themes (nine papers from 70 students) written in the classroom (Allport, Walker, & Lathers, 1934). The

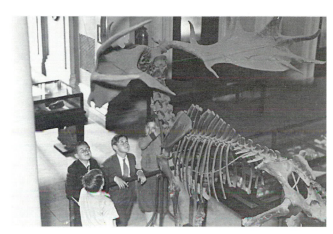

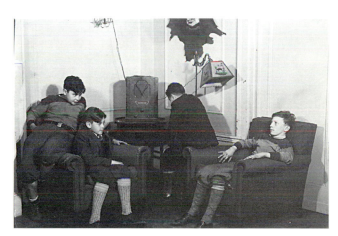

Three social situations pictured in Horowitz's study.
Archives of the History of American Psychology, Eugene L. Hartley Documents.

topics of the themes were assigned because the homogeneity of content would help to make the writing style more conspicuous. Two instructors scrutinized typewritten copies of the papers and attempted to identify those written by the same author. The accuracy of these matchings was 2 1/2 times that of chance and Allport concluded that "individuality" can, to some extent at least, be discerned.

As experimental mastery increased, various other attributes were extracted from behavior, and prejudice is one example. One of the trailblazers in research on racial prejudice is Eugene L. Horowitz (Ph.D., Columbia, 1936). In his dissertation, he interpreted the frequency of particular responses as a measure of prejudice. The experimental design was carefully planned. Horowitz commented that, at that time, racial bias was commonly ascribed to sexual variables, to the

Two Theoreticians—Samples of Their Correspondence

Christine Ladd-Franklin (Ph.D., Johns Hopkins, 1926) completed the requirements for a Ph.D. in mathematics in 1882 at The Johns Hopkins University, but the awarding of the degree was deferred for 44 years until 1926. Her paramount interest in psychology, the study of vision, grew out of an earlier interest in geometric properties of the visual field. Ladd-Franklin formulated a unique theory of color vision, and although it is now obsolete, it merited and attracted acclaim during her lifetime. Her husband's career restricted her academic appointment to lectureships at Johns Hopkins and Columbia, but also expanded her opportunities for professional contact by allowing her to attend classes and work in the laboratories in Germany of three stellar scholars of vision (Notable American Women: 1607–1950).

Archives of the History of American Psychology Photographic File, Permission Science *(AAAS).*

The recipient of this letter from Ladd-Franklin is Harry Helson (Ph.D., Harvard, 1924), an advocate of Gestalt psychology, a system that on occasion relies on the method of phenomenology which is an appreciation of experience just as it occurs. In this letter, Ladd-Franklin elaborates her specialized interest in color vision.

Archives of the History of American Psychology, Harry Helson Papers.

history of blacks, and/or to economic conditions. So he reduced the interference from these factors by including only boys (kindergarten through eighth grade) from specified economic and social levels.

Horowitz observed subjects' reactions to pictures of black and white youths in three different ways. One consisted of showing photographs of 15 social situations, three of which are illustrated on page 109. There are two views of each scene: in one, all the boys are white, and, in a second, a black child is substituted for one member of the original group. Each subject was asked to indicate whether he wanted "to join in with them and do what they are doing along with them" (Horowitz, 1936, p. 11). A response of *yes* was given a score of three, an indecisive answer was marked two, and a response of *no* was counted as one. The scores for the scenes with the all-white cast were tallied separately from the scores for the scenes with a racial mixture. The numerical difference between the scores provided a measure of prejudice that Horowitz used to mark the age of onset of prejudice and the ages at which it changes.

Mary Whiton Calkins (A.M., Smith, 1887) accepted an appointment in 1887 at Wellesley College and remained there until retirement 42 years later. In 1891, she founded the Wellesley psychology laboratory, probably the 13th such facility in the United States. Calkins was the first woman to be president of both the APA (1905) and the American Philosophical Society (1918). Even though all requirements were completed, the Harvard Corporation refused to grant her the Ph.D. degree. Calkins rejected a later offer from Radcliffe College on the grounds that her work had been done at Harvard. She was awarded two honorary doctoral degrees, one by Columbia University in 1909 and the second by Smith College in 1910. The daughter and sister of Protestant clergymen, she was deeply religious and dedicated to the resolution of social problems (Notable American Women: 1607–1950).

Archives of the History of American Psychology Photographic Collection, Courtesy Evan Calkins.

Calkins theorized that "we may define psychology more exactly by naming it science of the self as consciousness" (1911, p. 1). In this letter, she specifies those psychological responses in which she believes "the experiencing individual" is influential. The recipient of this letter is the recipient of the letter from Ladd-Franklin on page 110, Harry Helson.

Archives of the History of American Psychology, Harry Helson Papers.

Another innovative technique emerged in the 1930s when psychiatrists began to treat children's play behavior as a source of information about their emotional difficulties. The support for the validity of this technique had been largely intuitive until Lois B. Murphy* approached the problem in the experimental tradition. She formulated a series of relationships and traced them in the laboratory. She had observed, for example, that youngsters vary in the number of objects they seek in a play situation—those at one extreme use every available toy whereas those at the opposite extreme handle only a single object. Her speculations about the implications of this difference reflect the exploratory or tentative status in which research on this topic was then cast: "This pattern of selectivity in contrast to being dominated by the stimulus will probably be an important one to relate to other aspects of personality, such as the tendency to impose patterns, to carry out one's own purposes in whatever setting one finds oneself, in contrast to the pattern of submitting to real or supposed environmental demands" (Murphy, 1941, pp. 15–16).

Research on the complex topic of personality attracted many psychologists despite formidable problems in methodology. At first, it seemed impossible to measure traits on a psychological scale, although, as early as 1915, the composite judgment of acquaintances was used in a study to define trait strength—that is, an individual was said to be as friendly as acquaintances ranked him/her on friendliness (Cogan, Conklin, &

Gardner Murphy★ (Ph.D., Columbia, 1923) and Lois Barclay Murphy★ (Ph.D., Teachers College, Columbia, 1937) have participated in a number of different areas in psychology, with Gardner's prominence in the role of mentor and author and Lois's in the role of researcher in child development. Their contributions to social psychology are especially pertinent to this discussion. In 1931, they published Experimental Social Psychology, *and their reviews of this research emphasize direct observations. They pay more attention to behavior than to agreement or disagreement with theory. They argue, for example, that it is essential to recognize the social components in each setting and point out that seemingly contradictory responses may, from the subject's point of view, be consistent and that consistent behavior may be inappropriate in particular situations.*

Archives of the History of American Psychology, Gardner and Lois Barclay Murphy Papers.

Hollingworth, 1915). But the advantages of organizing data from the perspective of spectators were not exploited until 1936, when Robert R. Sears★ (Ph.D., Yale, 1932) published a landmark experiment on the psychoanalytic concept of projection, the tendency to see one's own personality traits in others. Sears asked undergraduate male students who knew one another well to rate themselves and their friends on each of four traits of personality: stinginess, obstinacy, disorderliness, and bashfulness. He compared the self ratings with the ratings assigned to each subject and described an individual as insightful if the two judgments were similar and as lacking insight if the two judgments were dissimilar. He then reviewed the ratings made by subjects who have and who do not have insight. He found that those who did not recognize a feature in their own personality tended to rank their acquaintances high on that trait. This demonstration of projection drew some criticisms, and changes in both the experimental design and interpretation of the results have been suggested. These modifications do not, however, defeat the victory of building a gauge that is marked in psychological units.

In brief review, during the approximately 30 years of the Era of Development, psychologists made impressive gains in learning to capitalize on their own subject matter. The present abridged account discloses a few behaviorally based measurements of both stimuli and responses, some ways of stabilizing experimental conditions, and some techniques for developing psychological variables so as to meet specialized experimental needs. The reality of the progress in the laboratory embraces many more accomplishments than are depicted in this chapter.

Field Research

Field research is used to investigate problems that are so dangerous and/or so complicated that they cannot be managed in a laboratory and must be observed in natural settings. Several field investigations were carried out late in the nineteenth century, before laboratory research was commonplace, by naturalists who were seeking evidence of continuity among species. This approach led them to interpret animal behavior in an unrestrained anthropomorphic manner—that is, to read freely and without justification human attributes into animals as in the previously noted example of ascribing the ability to calculate to the horse Clever Hans (page 40). Laboratory standards of evidence were seen as the effective means of preventing anthropomorphism and, as a result, research was consigned to laboratories. This shift produced a mass of objective data but did not clarify numerous intricate psychological phenomena.

In order to unravel the complexity, scientists began to turn again to field observations, but this time around they were armed with a determination to distinguish between facts and interpretations and to base analyses and syntheses only on the former. This caution was appropriate because anthropomorphism was so firmly entrenched that it surfaced at least as late as 1942 and 1943 in a series of articles on ants, published in the *Journal of Comparative Psychology*. The first paper described ants as "following the pattern of human cruelty and sadism" (Lafleur, 1942, p. 36). A prompt and substantive censure (Schneirla, 1942) elicited a defense (Lafleur, 1943) and a second criticism (Schneirla, 1943).

The techniques that are most effective in increasing the merits of field investigations are ones that minimize intrusions into the events that are being probed. In a

Marie Skodak Crissey (Ph.D., Iowa, 1938) and Orlo L. Crissey (Ph.D., Iowa, 1936) at home, Swartz Creek, Michigan, 1988. The Crisseys' contributions include work in industrial, school, and mental health facilities. Their professional relationship is more extended than their 25 years of marriage in that they were both graduate students at Iowa, and after each moved in the late 1930s to Michigan, they lived in the same community and shared several projects, at times in the same organization.

Archives of the History of American Psychology, Orlo and Marie Skodak Crissey Papers.

This photograph was taken in 1933 when Marie Skodak was at Ohio State University where she earned bachelor's and master's degrees. One of her professors was Henry H. Goddard,★ a proponent of constant and inherited intelligence. She personally encountered challenges to this opinion when employed in a service program in liaison with the Iowa Child Welfare Station. In this program, psychological examinations were given to children who had been living in foster homes prior to being adopted. These examinations disclosed a high probability of accelerated intellectual status—a startling conclusion at that time. The data were incorporated into a longitudinal research project for which Skodak was one of the principal researchers in both the original and follow-up studies.

The changes in the theoretical climate converted the initial incredulity about the Iowa findings into acceptance, but they also provoked ill-considered and inflamatory criticisms of the hereditary point of view. Skodak, familiar with both sides of the argument, effectively countered these unwarranted criticisms (Crissey, 1979).

Archives of the History of American Psychology, Orlo and Marie Skodak Crissey Papers.

This photograph was taken in 1927 when Orlo Crissey was an assistant in the YMCA office at the University of Minnesota. His doctoral education and first six years of professional experience were in clinical psychology, but in 1942 he changed this career path by accepting a position at the AC Spark Plug Division of General Motors as the first industrial psychologist at General Motors. He remained with the corporation as Director of Personnel Evaluation Services until his retirement in 1970 from the General Motors Institute. The plural form of the last word in his title is appropriate because of the variety of challenges that arose.

Crissey's tenure coincided with the expansion of the field from industrial psychology into organizational psychology. When Crissey began his career, the focus was on personnel selection, placement, and training; when he retired, the focus was on broader aspects of the employment context, involving such complex tasks as probing patterns of management and underscoring strengths and rectifying weaknesses in personnel utilization. Crissey, far from a passive reactor, used the weight and resources of General Motors to precipitate and implement many of the changes in his specialty.

Archives of the History of American Psychology, Orlo and Marie Skodak Crissey Papers.

John F. Shepard★ (Ph.D., Michigan, 1906) and students viewing ants during a 1912 field trip. Shepard was awarded the first doctorate in psychology at the University of Michigan where he was a member of the faculty from 1906 until retirement in 1951. His strong personality and remarkable intellect influenced a large number of students, including Clark Hull,★ Norman R. F. Maier,★ and T. C. Schneirla.★ Shepard, a comparative psychologist, conducted research on a number of topics, including the behavior of ants. He started this work about 1908, and these pictures illustrate this research and its continuity in both the field and the laboratory (Raphelson, 1980)—in the photo on the right is a maze Shepard constructed for studying learning in ants.

Archives of the History of American Psychology, Z. Pauline Hoakley Papers.

few instances, experimenters are able to collect data in situations in which the ordinary course of events imposes controls, and all they need to do is observe. To illustrate, comparisons were made of the frequency of compliance with a stop sign when a traffic officer was and was not present. A tally of the responses of 100 automobile drivers as they approached an intersection when merely a sign was present revealed that 74 of them stopped, 20 slowed appreciably, 5 reduced the rate a bit, and 1 did not alter speed. When a policeman was on the site, 98 drivers stopped, 1 slowed noticeably, and 1, who was then arrested, slowed only slightly (LaPiere & Farnsworth, 1942).

The everyday world is rarely as considerate of the scientist, and in most investigations experimenters are forced to intrude. In many instances, they confine the interference to the making of measurements. This constraint is exemplified in longitudinal studies of human growth, ones in which development is assessed repeatedly over prolonged periods of time—in some investigations, the children are reared by biological parents (Sontag, Baker, & Nelson, 1958) and, in others, they grow up in institutions or in foster or adoptive homes (Skodak & Skeels, 1949). In these studies, the examinations are both comprehensive and scheduled, but no modifications of the subjects' everyday activities are imposed and the conclusions are based on comparisons of data obtained under different living conditions.

A few problems can be handled after the fact by retrospective analysis; in these cases, investigators do not change the events, but this gain may be countered by the incompleteness of records and recollections. An example is encountered in an account of "a phantom anesthetist" who was blamed for inducing paralysis, anesthesia, gastrointestinal disturbances, and general malaise in residents of a small city during a two-week interval. A researcher interviewed "victims" and

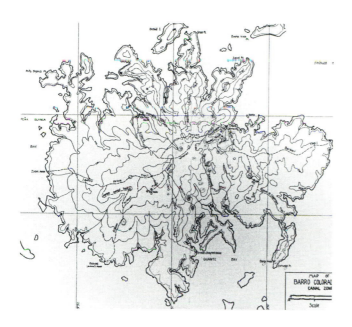

This simplified topographic map illustrates the specific and detailed records developed in field research—it identifies observational sites in a study published in 1940 of ants that was conducted at Barro Colorado Island by Theodore C. Schneirla (Sc.D., Michigan, 1928). Schneirla took the shorthand notes in the margin of the map. He devoted most of his professional life to research on ants, beginning in 1925 with John F. Shepard.★ Schneirla became interested in applying laboratory methods to field research as a means of acquiring more information about the so-called social behavior of ants. He made numerous field observations on Barro Colorado Island between 1932 and 1967 and supplemented them with laboratory work conducted both at New York University and at the American Museum of Natural History (Topoff, 1971).

Archives of the History of American Psychology, T. C. Schneirla Papers.

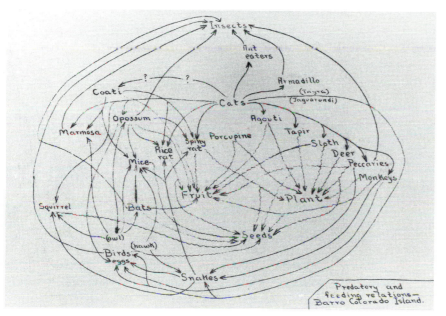

Schneirla believed that it was necessary to understand the field as a whole. This drawing, probably by Schneirla, represents one step in that effort. It indicates the "predatory and feeding relations" among plants and animals in the circumscribed world of Barro Colorado Island. In 1923 the Panamanian government established this island, in Gatun Lake in the Panama Canal Zone, as a nature reserve. Since 1946, the Smithsonian Institution has operated it as a research station.

Archives of the History of American Psychology, T. C. Schneirla Papers.

analyzed police records, including reports of prowlers and other assorted rumors. When put together, these bits and pieces pointed to mass hysteria rather than to the reality of an intruder who eluded detection but who was able to dispense a gas so remarkable that it affected only one or two occupants in a room filled with people and yet was both stable enough to inflict illness and also so unstable that it left no other aftereffects (Johnson, 1945).

When field research makes it necessary to inject some controls, a conservative approach is preferred. One of the more cautious intrusions is the manipulation of ordinary circumstances. One way of doing this is to draft participants in the ongoing activities to serve as observers. This technique is illustrated in an investigation of clothing fads in which the experimenter had seven undergraduates independently and unobtrusively watch the instigation of fads among 279 college women during two successive academic years.

Their accounts were supplemented by records of grades, reports of disciplinary action, and reviews of both participation and leadership in student activities. These various kinds of evidence, when assembled, extended the factual base and in this experiment they disclosed several details about the students who did and did not follow fads (Janney, 1941).

Another guarded maneuver is to introduce merely one variable, most cautiously a familiar, commonplace factor, as, for example, in Arnold Gesell's★ practice of presenting an infant with a cup in order to discover how reaching and grasping develops. In a second example of restraint, the motor skills of twins were compared after the customary amount of exercise of only one twin was increased (McGraw, 1935). These kinds of interventions may appear to be too insignificant to alter the field but they do have the potential to change the normal course of events, particularly when applied repetitively.

Zing-Yang Kuo (Ph.D., California, 1923), a comparative psychologist, was born in China and received his graduate education in the United States. He spent most of his life in China and, although racked by the turmoil of China's history in the twentieth century, he managed to publish important theoretical and empirical papers between 1921 and 1970 in American scientific journals (Gottlieb, 1972). Probably his best known article is "The Genesis of the Cat's Responses to the Rat" (1931), a study that had a strong impact on the continuing controversy concerning the concept of instinct. In this investigation some kittens were raised in isolation and others in cages with rats, with some exposed to cats that destroy rats and others trained to fear rats. These variables had different effects; for example, 85 percent of those raised with cats who kill also annihilated rats, but only 45 percent of those raised in isolation would kill.

This experiment reflects Kuo's conviction that behavior is learned. He insisted upon extensive and thorough observations of development under as natural conditions as possible. This orientation led him to devise a technique that allowed him to watch chick embryos before they hatch, under circumstances that did not disturb the circulatory membrane.

Archives of the History of American Psychology Photographic File, Gilbert Gottlieb Gift.

In some experiments, it is necessary to introduce an artificial and disruptive procedure. This kind of manipulation is exemplified in early investigations of the cues that birds use when "homing," that is, returning to their nests. One of these research procedures consisted of transporting birds in a ship, releasing them at different distances from land, and counting the percent that returned to the nest from various discharge points. The development of air transportation made it possible to track the birds and researchers have taken advantage of this technology, but transportation, either by water or air, deprives the creatures of the experience of flying toward the uncaging point. The effects of this distortion have not yet been demonstrated, but records of the speed and path of flights provide convincing evidence that birds are not guided by an inner sense of direction but appear to explore and look for visual landmarks. The tracking seems not to affect homing ability inasmuch as both the percentage and speed of returns are comparable between birds that are and are not followed (Griffin & Hock, 1948).

The successful application of restrained controls encouraged experimenters to try more intrusive manipulations. Many were experts in contriving experimental procedures, and they began both to apply this laboratory know-how to field situations and to use field tactics in the laboratory. As a result, the differences between a laboratory and a field experiment diminished. The increased similarity is illustrated in a program of research on the sensory cues that visually impaired subjects use to avoid obstacles (Supa, Cotzin, & Dallenbach, 1944). This work included several experiments, but only a few highlights are mentioned

here. The investigation started with assessments of the success of two blind individuals in avoiding obstructions, one made of masonite board and the other of stone, commonplace surfaces that differ in the sound they reflect. The subjects were instructed to walk toward each of these barriers and to signal when it was first perceived and then to go as close as possible to it without touching it. Their accuracy was measured under conditions that alter sensory cues in different ways, some of which replicate daily living conditions, such as walking while wearing shoes on a wooden floor and walking while not wearing shoes on carpets of different thickness. The results indicate that, in the absence of vision, sound is crucial for avoiding obstacles.

Although numerous research problems were clarified, there remain some that are so complex that it is not possible to manage all the relevant variables. Some psychologists react to the impossibility of exerting rigid experimental controls by turning their attention to inquiries that can be dealt with in the traditional manner. Others refuse to relinquish a topic that interests them just because it defies regulation, and they continue to extract as much objective data as possible under natural, or quasi-natural, circumstances. This persistence under less than optimal research conditions has given good, albeit not perfect returns. One illustration of this is the rearing, under the direction of Winthrop N. Kellogg,★ of a young chimpanzee as a member of a human family (Kellogg & Kellogg, 1933/1967). This study produced an impressive amount of information about the chimpanzee—for example, it had an inability to pick up small objects and a brief attention span but a rapid rate of learning and efficiency in recall.

From July 1931 until March 1932, Gua, a female chimpanzee (who was 7 1/2 months of age at the beginning of the experiment), was treated as a human child and lived in the home of Winthrop N. Kellogg (Ph.D., Columbia, 1929), his wife Luella, and their son Donald (10 months of age at the beginning of the experiment). The story of this field research is told in The Ape and the Child *(Kellogg & Kellogg, 1933/1967), a remarkably insightful and sensitive account of both young primates. The authors ask readers to be tolerant of any lack of objectivity on their part in the management of this intricate problem.*

Kellogg, a comparative psychologist, conducted this particular study early in his career. He followed it with a prolific amount of additional research on a number of different species in addition to the chimpanzee including dogs, dolphins, humans, monkeys, porpoises, and snakes. Kellogg's legacy includes many students— both undergraduates and graduates—who regard him with respect and affection.

Archives of the History of American Psychology, Winthrop N. Kellogg Collection. Courtesy of Shirley Kellogg Ingalls and Patricia D. Kellogg.

One field report stands apart from all others both in the gravity of the facts that were acquired and in the conditions under which the researcher worked. This is an investigation published in 1943 by Bruno Bettelheim (Ph.D., Vienna, 1938) of the effects of Nazi concentration camps on both prisoners and guards. This study was not undertaken for the typical purpose of increasing a data bank but was undertaken as a means of self-protection. A prisoner in Dachau and Buchenwald, Bettelheim, a psychologist, believed that if he could maintain his intellectual interests he would be better able to tolerate imprisonment. As a result, he devoted time and energy (then a scarce commodity) to examining the reactions, both overt and covert, of guards as well as prisoners, to the incredible conditions in the camps. The situation could not have been any

An amateur's attempt in 1946 to film the entrance to Dachau Concentration Camp. Delegations representing families, communities, ethnic and religious affiliations, occupational groups, and nationalities continue to bring memorial offerings to Dachau. A large parking lot has been built behind the structure that was the camp administrative building. From there, the groups pass through a modern entrance in the original fence and go to the front of the building which is now a sunken plaza where memorials—hundreds of them—are placed. This picture was taken just a year after the conquest of Europe, which occurred between June 1944 and May 1945.

Archives of the History of American Psychology, David P. Boder Museum Collection. Film by David P. Boder.

Heinz Werner (Ph.D., Vienna, 1914) used this wooden box and several more like it to ship his library out of Germany when he went into exile in the United States. He traded the box for a suitcase and its new owners have used it for mundane moves.

In the United States, Werner held a number of academic and research posts in succession: Visiting Professor at the University of Michigan and at Harvard, Research Psychologist at Wayne County Training School (Michigan), Associate Professor at Brooklyn College, and Professor and Chair of the Department of Psychology at Clark University.

The box is shown open and, in order to evoke its history, four volumes have been put in, not books owned by Werner, but some from the library of another emigré, René Spitz (M.D., Budapest, 1910). The spine of the Internationale Zeitschrift für Psychoanalyse *(The International Journal of Psychoanalysis) Volume X, 1924, is legible.*

Private Collection, Archives of the History of American Psychology, René Spitz Papers.

less favorable and there was no opportunity to control it. Bettelheim and most of the interviewees were underfed, physically injured and/or ill, overworked, and threatened with death. Conversation, one of the main methods of data collection, was forbidden during most of the day. There was no way of recording what was learned, so Bettelheim rehearsed the information in order to fix it in memory.

In spite of these handicaps, Bettelheim was able to gleam a great deal about personality functioning in extreme circumstances. He found, for example, that prisoners were tortured not only as a means of subduing them but also as a means of helping guards to feel superior, especially to those victims from a higher

socioeconomic status. He discovered that the inmates reacted to the cruelty that was inflicted upon them by developing a sense of detachment, feelings that the experience was unreal. Bettelheim discovered that torture was not repeated in dreams but that minor rebukes were reviewed and fantasies of retaliation elaborated. As the duration of imprisonment increased, daydreams became less realistic. With the passage of time, the prisoners began to replace an earlier determination not to allow detention to change their personality with a wish to get along as smoothly as possible. In pursuit of this latter goal, inmates took on many of the values of the Gestapo guards, but their sense of detachment prevented any enthusiasm.

The Burgeoning of Testing

The constructing and administering of psychological examinations was one of psychology's first ventures outside the formal laboratory, and these excursions into the practical realm brought benefits to at least two groups. One was the examinees, with their profits coming from the standardizing and refining of methods of assessing them in ways that sharpened predictions about performance in various extratest contexts. The second group was the psychologists themselves, with their profits growing out of the groundbreaking status of the testing movement. This was such a novel undertaking that psychologists were forced to interrupt their protective imitation of what scientists in other fields were doing in favor of designing procedures for the specialized problems that testing involved. They seem to have flourished under this autonomy inasmuch as the endorsement of tests expanded to such a level that a superabundance of them was created. The many gains that came from this self reliance and the success of the endeavor make it imperative to allot ample space to the history of testing in a treatment of the history of psychology.

Unfortunately, the movement was also tinged with drawbacks, and one of the more important of these is a discrepancy between the reputation of many examinations and their actual validity. There are several reasons for this shortfall and one is the ease of administrating tests. This is generally a straightforward procedure and its simplicity suggests that test interpretation is also straightforward even though it is actually a complicated process that demands sophisticated, astute, and cautiously drawn inferences.

A second weakness is a byproduct of the aspirations of test constructors. Their goal is to impose laboratory standards of precision and accuracy so as to eliminate, or at least regulate, errors of measurement. Psychometrists undertook test construction with enthusiasm but they soon discovered that finesse was not prepackaged and that it had to be learned step by step, and this acquisition was marred at times, misstep by misstep. For many, however, the ideal overwhelmed reality, and faults were minimized and tests assigned an authenticity that not all of them merit. Confidence that they disclose decisive, accurate information helps to obscure the complex and perplexing variables that make up psychological measurement.

The list of tests that have been constructed is extraordinary, with the behavioral spectrum so wide, the purposes so diversified, and the testing methods so different that these instruments can neither be inventoried here nor even all fitted into an organizational outline or logical scheme. Several facets of the history of test construction can be described for two of the most common kinds: first, those that assess attributes that pervade most or all situations in which a

*Worksheets for the first Army Examination—Disarranged Sentences. From June 1 through June 4, 1917, the committee compiled equivalent forms of Examination **a**. Each member was assigned to work on one or two specific tests, and their suggestions were discussed and edited by the entire committee. Haines and Goddard were responsible for assembling tentative items for both the Disarranged Sentences Test and the Test of Practical Judgment (Yerkes, 1921).*

This test is patterned after one that Arthur S. Otis (Ph.D., Stanford, 1920) adapted from Binet. The number above each word probably indicates the order in which the word was to be printed on the examination. The examinee is asked to indicate whether the statement is accurate or inaccurate by underlining either the word true *or the word* false *printed after each statement. Note the corrections in item 9. The incorrect numbering of the words in item 19 is another indication that this is one of the committee's first efforts. The handwriting is probably Goddard's.*

Archives of the History of American Psychology, Henry H. Goddard Papers.

1 A hat is worn on the feet
2 shoes are carried in the hand
3 Everybody has plenty of coal
4 food is plentiful everywhere
5 The Germans will be destroyed
6 by the war
7 We all love to go over the top
8 This war does not amount to much
9 Snow is nice in the trenches
10 Mud makes men much happier
11 Airplanes are no use in war
12 Bottles are sometimes made of glass
13 A good German is a dead German
14 We will win the war
15 Annual rings show how old a tree is.
16 Some plants grow in water
17 Coal is found in the ground
18 Hay is the food of the cow
19 The tanks are useful in war
20 Soldiers do not carry umbrellas

person functions, typically tests of intelligence and personality; and, second, those that assess attributes that are pertinent to a particular setting, typically measures of academic and occupational potential and performance.

Intelligence

The entry of the United States in April 1917 in World War I prompted scientists to offer their services, so a network of committees of the National Research Council and the American Psychological Association began to function. One of the most influential of these was the Committee on the Psychological Examination of Recruits. Robert M. Yerkes[*] chaired this group of six psychologists, three of whom have already been introduced: Henry H. Goddard,[*] the importer of the Binet Scales into America; Lewis M. Terman,[*] the author by that time of two revisions of the Binet scales; and Guy M. Whipple,[*] the author of *Mental and Physical Tests* (1910, 1914, 1915). The others are Frederic L. Wells (Ph.D., Columbia, 1906), then assistant in pathological psychology at the McLean Hospital; Thomas H. Haines (Ph.D., Harvard, 1901, M.D., Ohio State, 1912) at the Boston Psychopathic Hospital at the time Yerkes was compiling a point scale; and Walter Van Dyke Bingham,[*] a pioneer in industrial psychology and apparently the only member of the committee who had prior experience with group tests of adult intelligence (Yerkes, 1921).

When one is ill he sends for a
physician because
    It is pleasant to have company
    a physician can cure one.
    One might be blamed if he did not
    Physicians dress well.

A house is better than a tent because
    it costs more
    it is more comfortable
    it is made of wood
    there are more of them

Shoes are made of leather because
    leather comes from animals
    it is tough, pliable and warm
    it is tanned
    it can be blackened
This is the biggest war the world has
ever seen because
    The Germans started it
    Jerusalem has fallen
    Submarines are used
    The greatest preparations were made
    for it.

Thermometers are useful because
    they tell us how cold or warm it is
    They are made of glass
    They regulate the temperature
    They contain mercury
It is better to fight than to run because
    Cowards are shot
    it is more honorable
    if you run you may get shot in the back
    it is glorious to win.

Worksheets for the first Army Examination—Practical Judgment. This test is an adaptation of a Binet item (Bonser, 1910). It asks examinees to pick from a number of choices the statement that is true. The report that the committee as a whole edited the test items is strengthened by the absence of some of the items in Examination a. The question dealing with shoes appears without modifications on the Army Alpha, Test 3, Form 8 (Yerkes, 1921, p. 229).

Archives of the History of American Psychology, Henry H. Goddard Papers.

The Committee on the Psychological Examination of Recruits, Vineland Training School, Vineland, New Jersey, May 28, 1917. Yerkes, the Chair, is seated in the middle of the back row. Immediately to his left is Bingham, and next is Terman. To Yerkes's immediate right is Whipple, and then next to him is Wells. Directly in front of Yerkes is Goddard, and to Goddard's left is Haines. To Goddard's right is Edgar A. Doll, not a member of the committee but the Assistant Director of the Training School Laboratory.*

These steps are also the site of the photograph of the Feeble-Minded Club on page 74 and the photograph of the Subcommittee on Survey and Planning on page 132. Administrators of the Training School were known for their aspirations to extend the influence of the institution (McCaffrey, 1965).

Permission Robert M. Yerkes Papers, Manuscripts and Archives, Yale University Library. This photograph is also in the Archives of the History of American Psychology, Henry H. Goddard Papers.

This was a civilian committee, not financed by the military; initially, it was given some support by the National Committee on Provision for the Feeble-minded, a group created in 1915 by the Board of Directors of the Training School at Vineland, New Jersey, the institution at which Goddard was then Director of Research. This group invited the Committee on the Psychological Examination of Recruits to meet at Vineland and the members met there for an initial planning session of two weeks. They then traveled to various military installations in order to give the tests a trial run, returning to Vineland for a second two weeks of meetings devoted to evaluating the examinations.

One of the committee's first decisions was to administer an intelligence test to each recruit. The magnitude of this task gave priority to the mechanics of examining—to the procuring of test items that are brief, do not demand complicated equipment, can be administered uniformly, and can be scored objectively. The members specified only a few guidelines for evaluating the content of the test items, but they included the requirement that knowledge of the correct answers should not depend on formal schooling but should be acquired in the culture at large. Members endorsed questions that were thought to be interesting as well as those covering a wide range of ability, but they made practically no specifications about the nature

of the tasks. The committee acknowledged explicitly the dominance of method over content. For example, "Again it was generally agreed that the . . . completion test is a better measure of intelligence than some of the other tests finally accepted. . . . However, the difficulties in securing alternative forms of this test and arranging it for response without writing and objective scoring were too great to be overcome in the time available" (Yerkes, 1921, p. 301).

The National Committee for Mental Hygiene financed a second trial run by sponsoring a program in which examination scores were correlated with both officers' ratings and the educational level of examinees. Enough agreement was found for the measurements to be considered satisfactory, and, in August 1917, the Army assumed responsibility for the testing program. Yerkes was given responsibility for directing the program. Plans were made to measure all company officers, all applicants for officers training, as well as all enlisted and drafted men. The practice of assessing and reassessing examinations was continued and several instruments were evaluated. But only three were in general use: the Group Examination Alpha, a revision of the initial test Examination *a*; the Group Examination Beta, a scale that can be given and responded to without language; and a Performance Scale Examination, given to those who failed both the Alpha and the Beta. By January 31, 1919, examinations

Name of Examiner who is responsible for copy No. ..423

Capt Arps SC

EXAMINER'S GUIDE

FOR

PSYCHOLOGICAL EXAMINING
IN THE ARMY

George F Arps

Prepared especially for military use by the Sub-committee on Methods of Examining Recruits of the Psychology Committee of the National Research Council

▽

Revised by direction of the Surgeon General of the Army and printed by the Medical Department, U. S. A., September, 1917
Second revision, July, 1918

WASHINGTON
GOVERNMENT PRINTING OFFICE
1918

had been given to 1,726,966 men, with more than 83,500 receiving an individual as well as one or two group tests.

An explosion in the measurement of intelligence began right after the war ended. This was multifaceted in that it included both verbal and performance scales, published in single and in revised editions, designed for individuals or groups, some distributed commercially and some used in only a single, specialized investigation. They were intended for infants, children, and adults, both psychiatrically intact and psychiatrically damaged, and for those with sensory impairments as well as with normal sensory equipment. Taking an intelligence test became a routine procedure in school—from admission

This Examiner's Guide, probably the only surviving copy, was issued to George F. Arps★ (Ph.D., Leipzig, 1908), one of the last Americans to receive a doctorate from Wundt. Arps was commissioned captain in February 1918 and major in November 1918; he was discharged in August 1919. After attending the School for Military Psychology, he was assigned to Camp Sherman, Ohio, where he served as Chief Psychological Examiner and later as Chief Morale Officer. He then became Chief Educational Officer at the U.S. General Hospital in Detroit, Michigan, where he was in charge of rehabilitation. The S. C. after his name indicates Sanitary Corps. Psychologists were appointed to this unit because it was the only one for nonmedical personnel in the Army Medical Department (Yerkes, 1921).

Archives of the History of American Psychology, Harold E. Burtt Documents.

Arps at home, on leave, with his family. George Arps spent most of his professional life at Ohio State University. He joined the faculty in 1912 and by 1920 was both Dean of the College of Education and department Chair. During the time Arps held these appointments, the department grew from a teaching staff of two to over 50 and awarded more than 100 doctorates. In 1937, Arps became Dean of the Graduate School (Burtt, 1940).

Archives of the History of American Psychology, Henry H. Goddard Papers.

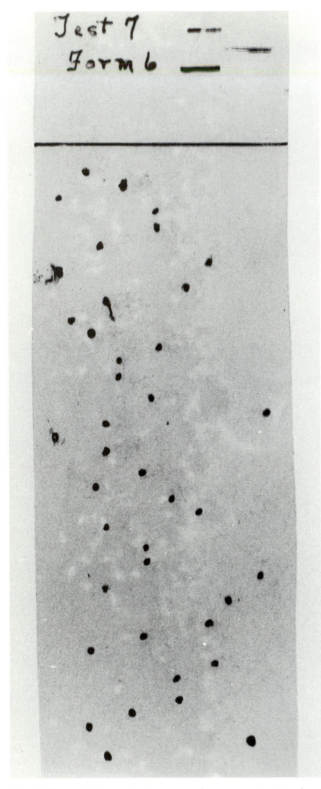

TEST 7

SAMPLES
- sky—blue :: grass— table **green** warm big
- fish—swims :: man— paper time **walks** girl
- day—night :: white— red **black** clear pure

In each of the lines below, the first two words are related to each other in some way. What you are to do in each line is to see what the relation is between the first two words, and underline the word in heavy type that is related in the same way to the third word. Begin with No. 1 and mark as many sets as you can before time is called.

1	dog—bark :: cat— chair **mew** fire house	1
2	foot—man :: hoof— corn tree **cow** hoe	2
3	dog—puppy :: cat— **kitten** dog tiger horse	3
4	wash—face :: sweep— clean broom **floor** straw	4
5	door—house :: gate— swing hinges **yard** latch	5
6	water—fish :: air— spark **man** blame breathe	6
7	white—black :: good— time clothes mother **bad**	7
8	boy—man :: lamb— **sheep** dog shepherd wool	8
9	roof—house :: hat— button shoe straw **head**	9
10	camp—safe :: battle— win **dangerous** field fight	10
11	straw—hat :: leather— **shoe** bark coat soft	11
12	pan—tin :: table— chair **wood** legs dishes	12
13	left—right :: west— south direction **east** north	13
14	floor—ceiling :: ground— earth **sky** hill grass	14
15	cold—ice :: heat— wet cold **steam** stars	15
16	hat—head :: thimble— sew cloth **finger** hand	16
17	Monday—Tuesday :: Friday— week Thursday day **Saturday**	17
18	lead—bullet :: gold— paper **coin** silver copper	18
19	skin—body :: bark— **tree** dog bite leaf	19
20	cannon—large :: rifle— ball **small** bore shoot	20
21	cellar—attic :: bottom— well tub **top** house	21
22	man—arm :: tree— shrub **limb** flower bark	22
23	suitcase—clothing :: purse— purchase **money** string stolen	23
24	knitting—girls :: carpentry— trade houses **boys** lumber	24
25	arteries—body :: railroads— **country** train crossing accident	25
26	ocean—pond :: deep— sea well **shallow** steep	26
27	revolver—man :: sting— gun hurt **bee** hand	27
28	engineer—chauffeur :: locomotive— iron stack engine **auto**	28
29	terrier—dog :: Jersey— City **cow** horse State	29
30	airplane—air :: submarine— dive engine ship **water**	30
31	esteem—friends :: despise— forsake detest **enemies** people	31
32	hospital—patient :: prison— cell **criminal** bar jail	32
33	tears—laughter :: sorrow— **joy** distress funeral sad	33
34	yes—no :: affirmative— win debate deny **negative**	34
35	establish—abol	35
36	order—confusion	
37	education—ignora	
38	10—100 :: 1000	
39	imitate—copy :: ir	
40	historian—facts ::	

This examination sheet is correctly marked and it may well have been used to check the accuracy of the stencil. The tear is not surprising considering the age of the document.

Stencils increased the speed and accuracy of scoring most tests in the Army examinations. A transparent celluloid sheet was superimposed on the examination booklet, and correct answers were those for which the examinee's underlining and a dot, made by india ink on the stencil, marked the same response. The stencils are obviously handmade.

to kindergarten through admission to college. It also became commonplace when seeking employment and when seeking counseling.

When this burgeoning started there was more ambiguity than clarity about the concept of intelligence. The confusion about intelligence and the apparent ease of measuring it fostered a neglect of basic research and favored research on the techniques of intelligence testing. Unfortunately, this imbalance persists even though the concept of intelligence continues to attract controversy (Eysenck & Kamin, 1981; Hunt, 1961).

Many of the instruments that were published shortly after the war were essentially reproductions of the Army Scales and revisions were made until at least mid-century (Wells, 1951). One of the earliest and most popular versions was sponsored in 1919 by the National Research Council as a way of promoting the development of valid methods of measuring the intelligence of school children. The committee responsible for this task was chaired by Robert M. Yerkes★ and its members were four psychologists who

Psychological Tests of Adults

How do our psychological abilities change and develop after college? Little is known actually of the skills and capacities of adults in general from early adulthood to late old age.

THE STANFORD LATER MATURITY STUDY is attempting to fill in the gap. You can help to make this investigation a success, and also obtain information of possibly considerable interest to yourself, if you will go through the mental exercises now being carried on in Booth 107-108. Both men and women of all ages and every profession and occupation may participate. Come yourself and tell your friends conserning this experiment. A total of about 3000 persons ranging in age from 25 to 95 have tried our tests in different parts of the United States.

Any person who completes the set of tests given every afternoon this week at Booth 107-108 will be sent his or her interpreted scores.

WALTER R. MILES
Professor of Psychology
Institute of Human Relations
Yale University
333 Cedar St., New Haven, Conn.

Atlantic City
December, 1932

Measure your imagination on our Kinephantoscope!

This flyer designed by Walter Miles★ was used to recruit subjects for an experiment in a pioneer program of investigations of psychological functions in adulthood. One experiment, published the same year as this announcement, reports correlations between age—from 7 to 94 years—and intelligence (Miles & Miles, 1932). In the paper, the authors comment that they found it difficult to obtain volunteers. Note that the poster makes no mention of intelligence but does refer to "skills" and "capacities." The "Kinephantoscope" is a device that allows the shadow of a turning object to be seen dimly on a screen. Was this included in the experimental design or was it just razzle-dazzle to "get them in the tent"?
Archives of the History of American Psychology, Walter and Catharine Cox Miles Papers.

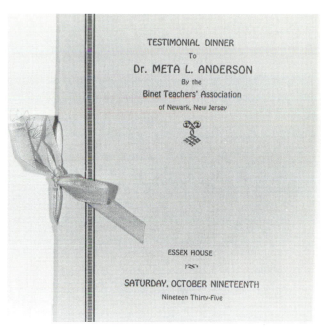

The Binet Teachers' Association was an organization of school personnel responsible for special education. The association published a journal called The Binet Review. *Many of the members, including Meta Anderson (Ph.D., New York, 1922), had received some training at the Vineland Training School. Goddard delivered the testimonial address and, in the correspondence dealing with arrangements for the evening, Goddard was advised not to refer to Dr. Anderson's marriage because of the then current resistance to the employment of married women.*
Archives of the History of American Psychology, Henry H. Goddard Papers.

had participated in military projects, three of whom have already been introduced to readers: Lewis M. Terman,★ Edward L. Thorndike,★ and Guy M. Whipple.★ The fourth member is Melville E. Haggerty (Ph.D., Harvard, 1910) of the University of Minnesota. This roster made it inevitable that the examination would resemble the army tests and, as anticipated, the members decided to design group methods of examining children, adapting them to grades three through eight. They compiled what are called National Intelligence Tests. After conducting preliminary trials of 22 tests, they arranged two scales of 5 tests. There were five alternative forms in the same format or in a minor variation of the army scales (Whipple, 1921). There are reports of sales of 1 1/2 million copies within the first two years of publication (Jonçich, 1968).

The heavy traffic in group examinations—referred to as "apersonal psychometrics" (Wechsler, 1944, p. 47)—was concurrent with a marked increase in the examining of individuals but not in the construction of tests for that purpose. This discrepancy came about because the standardizing of a test designed for the assessment of individuals is a colossal task in that it demands administering examinations individually to a large number of subjects. Immediately after the war, only two tests that received any significant amount of attention were published in America (Herring, 1922; Kuhlmann, 1922), but, during the 1930s, there was some increase in construction in that at least six examinations designed for infants and preschool children were compiled (Goodenough, 1949). This interval also saw the publication of two instruments that, in successive editions, would become the most widely used examinations: in 1937, "The Revised Stanford-Binet Scale" and, in 1939, "The Wechsler-Bellevue Scale for Adolescents and Adults I." The former, constructed by the age-scale method, is a revision of Terman's 1916 "Stanford Revision of the Binet-Simon Tests" and it was processed by Lewis M. Terman★ and Maud A. Merrill.★ The latter, constructed by the point-scale method, was devised by David Wechsler.★

Although Lewis M. Terman★ (Ph.D., Clark, 1905) is probably best known for revisions of the Binet scales, he is also responsible for several other endeavors in psychology. He was among the first to build a scholastic achievement test, he trailblazed investigation of the relationship between occupational and recreational interests and gender, and he initiated and directed a longitudinal study of gifted children, reporting their progress in four volumes during a 25-year span (Seagoe, 1975). After Terman's death, Robert R. Sears★ continued this project.

Archives of the History of American Psychology Photographic File.

From the beginning of her career, Maud A. Merrill (Ph.D., Stanford, 1923) was immersed in milieux dominated by intelligence testing. From 1912 to 1919, she worked at the Minnesota State Bureau of Research where she assisted Fred Kuhlmann (Ph.D., Clark, 1903), a member of the Clark University alumni that first advocated the Binet tests. Merrill, who attended Stanford University as a graduate student in 1919, was appointed instructor in 1920. She remained on the faculty until retirement in 1953 (Seagoe, 1975).

Courtesy Herbert H. Clark, Permission Department of Psychology, Stanford University. This photograph is also in the Archives of the History of American Psychology Photographic Collection.

Both the Stanford-Binet and the Wechsler-Bellevue scales yield scores that are called IQs even though they are computed by different methods and, therefore, offer a high probability that an examinee will earn a different IQ on each test (Hunt, 1961). The widespread assumption that an IQ depends on only the examinee is inaccurate because an IQ depends on both the examinee and the examination. The influence of each test makes it necessary to describe at least a few details of both the age- and point-scale methods of building an intelligence test.

When Terman and Merrill undertook the task of improving Terman's 1916 Stanford Revision of the Binet Scale, they apparently did not question the adequacy of age scaling and intended only to add refinements. They began by assembling available tests and evaluating them for ease and objectivity of scoring, speed of administration, and interest to examinees. The tests that survived this preliminary evaluation were assembled into two equivalent forms, and examinations

were administered to 3,184 subjects, ranging in age from 1 1/2 years to 18 years.

Performance on the test as a whole was summarized as both a mental age and an IQ. Since the former is actually a score on an examination, its upper limit is determined by the length and difficulty of the examination and does not change. Increases in mental age, in contrast, do occur and are variable. Increases are relatively regular during childhood, but they begin to level off during adolescence, flatten out during maturity, and may even decline in later maturity. Chronological age also increases but at a uniform rate throughout the life span. These discrepant courses create serious problems for the calculation of adult IQs by means of the formula in which $IQ = MA/CA \times 100$. Terman and Merrill were so impressed with the concept of mental age and with the ratio of mental age to chronological age that they decided to retain this formula and to accommodate to the difficulties by treating all examinees over 16 years of age as no older

Slide Rules for Calculating the IQ

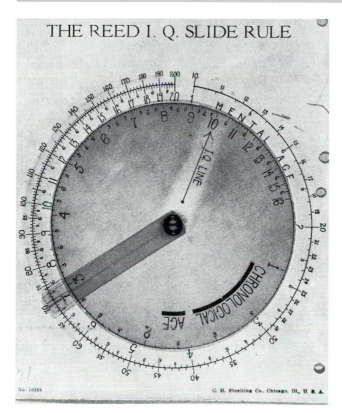

This circular slide rule was invented in 1918 by Samuel Kohs (Ph.D., Stanford, 1918). The word Reed in the title refers to Reed College where Kohs served on the faculty from 1918 to 1923. The rule was distributed by C. H. Stoelting Company at a cost of 90 cents. The catalogue informs would-be purchasers that only three movements are required and that after a bit of practice an IQ can be determined within 15 seconds.

Archives of the History of American Psychology, Henry H. Goddard Papers.

Examining and being examined are considered serious matters, and interruptions are frowned upon because they can "spoil" a test by distracting an examinee, by contaminating a measurement of the time of responding, or by interrupting the instructions. This photograph shows a sign that the Riverside Publishing Company—then the publisher of the Stanford-Binet Scales—included in orders of testing materials. The sign that they distribute at the present time is somewhat different. Such notices, commonplace in clinics and schools, are ignored only by the brazen. In an emergency, the cautious slip a note under the door and the examiner responds to it at the completion of a test item.

Archives of the History of American Psychology Literature Collection, Permission Riverside Publishing Company.

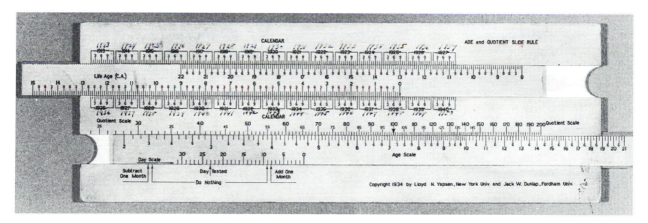

The "Age and Quotient Slide Rule" was devised in 1934 by Lloyd Yepsen (Ph.D., Ohio State, 1931), then of New York University, and Jack W. Dunlap (Ph.D., Columbia, 1931), of Fordham University. It is a refinement of one that Yepsen originally constructed in 1922 when he was on the staff of the Vineland Training School.

Neither the function of the handwritten dates nor their author is known. The model pictured here was distributed by both the Training School and the Psychological Corporation, a company established in 1921 to advance psychology and promote its practical applications.

Archives of the History of American Psychology, Ralph M. Stogdill Papers.

David Wechsler was involved in testing during World War I and World War II. He interrupted the construction of an equivalent form of his first scale in order to complete a test for military use: "The Wechsler Mental Ability Scale-Form B" (Wechsler, 1946).

Archives of the History of American Psychology, David Wechsler Collection.

This is the Preliminary Form of the Picture Completion Test, Army Beta. Each Wechsler Scale includes a Picture Completion Test that consists of a series of sketches similar to these. Binet also used similar drawings on both the 1908 and 1911 scales, and Terman retained them on the various revisions of the Stanford-Binet Scale

From Yerkes, 1921, p. 238.

than 16 years. Many psychologists shared Terman and Merrill's endorsements and they used the scales extensively.

There were numerous criticisms of age scaling but these did not have much effect on individually administered examinations until David Wechsler★ (Ph.D., Columbia, 1925) published a series of point scales, beginning in 1939. Wechsler was younger than the vanguard of test constructors, and this gave him the advantage over his predecessors of being able to acquire considerable experience as an examiner before he began to assemble a scale. Wechsler's career, from the beginning, was saturated with psychometrics. He obtained a master's degree in psychology from Columbia in 1917, and, while induction into the army was impending, he scored and assisted in evaluating tests that were being compiled for military recruits. After induction in May 1918, he attended the School for Military Psychology, and, in his first post, he administered the Yerkes Point Scale, the Stanford

Revision of the Binet and the Performance Scale Examination to individual soldiers. Wechsler's subsequent military duty included an assignment as an army student at the University of London. There he came to know both Charles Spearman★ and Karl Pearson,★ learning about both the statistics of test construction and Spearman's theory of intelligence. After discharge in August 1919, Wechsler won a two-year fellowship to the University of Paris, and, in 1922, returned to New York City where he remained throughout most of his career. In 1932, he was appointed chief psychologist at the Bellevue Psychiatric Hospital (Matarazzo, 1972).

Starting to construct a new scale in 1934, Wechsler tried out a large number of tests including those suitable for the adults with multilingual backgrounds that he encountered at Bellevue. On this and all later versions, Wechsler placed each item in one of 10 to 12 categories, for example, the Picture Arrangement Test (arranging a series of pictures in sequence) and the

This collage shows a section of the score sheet for each of the seven scales that Wechsler compiled personally. The first examination was published in 1939 and an equivalent form in 1946. The former is commonly referred to as the Wechsler-Bellevue I, abbreviated as W-B I, and the latter as Wechsler-Bellevue II, or W-B II. The next tests extended these two scales. The Wechsler Intelligence Scale for Children, the WISC, 1949, is designed for children age 5 through 15 years. The Wechsler Adult Intelligence Scale, the WAIS, 1955, increased the size of the original standardization group and extended the age norms to 75 years and above. The Wechsler Preschool and Primary Scale of Intelligence, the WPSSI, 1963, is intended for children 4 through 6 1/2 years of age. The last two examinations are also revisions of prior scales. The WISC-R(evised), 1974, is suitable for examinees 6 through 16 years of age. The WAIS-R(evised), 1981, is for adults. These revisions update both the test content and the norms. A WPSSI-R(evised) was published posthumously in 1989.

Digit Symbol Test (associating a particular number with a particular symbol). The items within each unit are arranged in the order of difficulty as determined by the percent of subjects in the standardization groups who succeeded with them. The tests are not equal in length, and this inequality is neutralized by transforming the average score that different age groups obtain on each test into a weighted mean score of ten. This conversion makes the tests statistically comparable and equalizes the contribution of each to the total score.

Each separate test is categorized as either verbal or performance depending upon the necessity of language for understanding and complying with the tasks. The scores in each category are combined to yield a Verbal IQ and a performance IQ, and all tests are combined to yield a Full Scale IQ. Each of these three IQs is based on a formula that relates the examinee's score to the mean score for the examinee's age level. There are no mental ages and thus no problems in relating mental and chronological age. The average scores at each age level are scaled to a mean IQ of 100, and IQs at various distances above and below the mean are also comparable. These adjustments led to labeling the IQs as *deviation IQs*.

Point scaling is superior to age scaling in many respects, but it does not remove all irregularities. There is, for example, inequality in the difficulty of the tests. There is also a diversity of content even though the names of the tests suggest homogeneity. This diversity is illustrated in the erratic changes of topics in the

Florence L. Goodenough★ (Ph.D., Stanford, 1924) standardized the Draw-A-Man Test in 1926 as a test of intelligence for children age 4 through 10 years. The examinee is asked to "Make a picture of a man. Make the very best picture that you can" (Goodenough, 1926, p. 85). The score is based not on artistic skill but on the number of details that are depicted. The drawing on the left earns 8 points and the drawing on the right 14 points. Although the drawing on the left is generally less adequate, it is more precise in one scored detail: the portrayal of the fingers as distinct from the hands. A score of eight points is the average score obtained by children age 5 years and 0 months in the Goodenough standardization group; and, 14 points is the average score for those 6 years and 6 months.

Private collection.

Comprehension Test on the Revised Wechsler Intelligence Scale for Children (1974): The first question asks about the management of injury, the second solicits the appropriate action when a wallet is found, the third inquires about strategic behavior in the event of a fire, and the fourth asks about the function of the police.

In spite of some limitations, deviation IQs were received enthusiastically and they set a pattern that persisted, one that eliminated even in the Terman and Merrill series both mental ages and IQs calculated by the traditional formula. This relinquishing was a stepwise process in that the two revisions of the Stanford-Binet following the 1937 version (Terman & Merrill, 1960; Terman & Merrill, 1972) transformed the conventional IQ into a deviation IQ. The most recent edition, published after the deaths of both Terman and Merrill, replaced the arrangement of tests by age levels with tests categorized into four areas. IQs are not computed and the scores are called S(tandard) A(ge) S(cores). These are scaled in a method similar to

that of Wechsler and are calculated for single tests, for each of the area tests, and for the composite (Thorndike, Hagen, & Sattler, 1986).

By the time of World War II, intelligence testing, in contrast to its status at the beginning of World War I, was flourishing. The military was aware of many of the services psychologists could render and their assistance was both solicited and volunteered. One request that spearheaded considerable action came in April 1940 when the Adjutant General's Office asked the National Research Council to appoint a committee to advise them about problems of personnel selection and assignment. The Council complied by forming the Committee on Classification of Military Personnel, chaired by Walter Van Dyke Bingham,★ a member during World War I of the Committee on the Examination of Recruits. The members were first asked to evaluate plans that were already underway for an examination that would measure the level of complexity of military skills that enlistees and Selective Service

Grace Kent (Ph.D., George Washington, 1911). Much of Kent's career was devoted to tests. In the field of intelligence testing, she is best known for the Kent Emergency Tests—the Kent E-G-Y. This is a short examination that provides some preliminary or tentative information about an examinee's level of intelligence. The first version, published in 1932, was followed by three revisions. Each version consists of a series of questions that solicit generally known information about a variety of topics that cover a range of difficulty; for example, "What is candy made of?" and "What is the difference between a cable and a chain?" Various versions of the test were used to screen recruits in World War II (Kent, 1946).

Archives of the History of American Psychology, David Shakow Papers.

inductees might be expected to learn quickly. This was not conceptualized as an intelligence test but as a measure of skills, both those that result from formal instruction and those that people acquire on their own. The assessment was intended to provide a guide in assigning soldiers to appropriate responsibilities and a means of promoting a balanced distribution of proficiency within command units (Bingham, 1952).

The Committee provided technical advice about the structure, content, span of difficulty, and scoring of this test, the first in a series that culminated in the Army General Classification Test, or AGCT, an examination of which the basic structure consists of 150 tasks: 50 vocabulary, 50 arithmetic, and 50 block counting. In accord with the committee's advice, neither mental ages nor IQs were computed, but a single score called the Army Standard Score was devised. This is scaled so that the average raw score equals 100, and scores above and below the mean are related to the spread of scores in the standardization group. Each Army Standard Score is also assigned one of five army grades from a high of I through a low of V. As the war continued, this version of the test was modified and additional sections were added. More than 12,000,000 individuals were examined with its various forms (Staff, 1947). A general classification test was also constructed for the navy, but in that service as well as in the Army Air Forces the emphasis was on tests of specific abilities and aptitudes.

Members of the Subcommittee on Survey and Planning of the Emergency Committee in Psychology of the National Research Council, at the Training School at Vineland, New Jersey, June 1942. Second row, left to right: E. G. Boring,★ C. P. Stone★ (Ph.D., Minnesota, 1921), Edward R. Johnstone (Superintendent of the Training School), E. R. Hilgard.★ Front row, left to right: Richard M. Elliott★ (Ph.D., Harvard, 1913), E. A. Doll,★ Alice I. Bryan (Ph.D., Columbia, 1934), Robert M. Yerkes.★

The impetus for this subcommittee came in 1941 when Edgar A. Doll★ (Ph.D., Princeton, 1920), then Director of Research at Vineland, informed the Emergency Committee in Psychology of the Vineland staff's plans to hold a conference on planning for psychology after the war. After some questions about taking action on a private proposal, Robert M. Yerkes★ was authorized to select six colleagues to attend a meeting. The report of their deliberations was so well received that the group was organized as a subcommittee and charged with submitting proposals for increasing the usefulness of psychology both during and after the war. They held seven additional sessions at Vineland, suggesting a number of courses of action, including many related to the professionalization of the discipline (Dallenbach, 1946).

Archives of the History of American Psychology, Edgar A. and Geraldine Doll Papers.

This 1943 book demonstrates the importance that both would-be and would-not-be soldiers attached to the intelligence testing program in the military services. It describes the responsibilities of personnel officers, reports scores necessary for admission to Officer Candidate School, reproduces questions from the Army Alpha, and exemplifies items on the Army General Classification Test.

Archives of the History of American Psychology, Morris S. Viteles Papers.

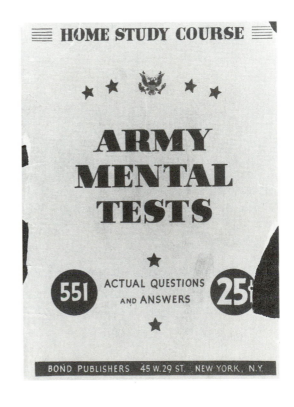

Brothers Floyd and Gordon Allport—Key Figures in the Vanguard of Social Psychology and Personality Theory

In 1924, Floyd H. Allport★ (Ph.D., Harvard, 1919) published Social Psychology, *a book that prompted courses in social psychology in most departments (Hilgard, 1987). Floyd was also working, at the same time, on the measurement of personality. In 1921, he coauthored with Gordon a study entitled "Personality Traits: Their Classification and Measurement." In 1925, he issued "A Systematic Questionnaire for the Study of Personality," an instrument intended to help students increase insight into themselves. In 1928, he and Gordon published a test, "The A(scendence)-S(ubmission) Reaction Study." After completing these early papers, Floyd devoted most of his career to social psychology, contributing research on such topics as social facilitation, attitudes, and prejudice.*
Archives of the History of American Psychology, University of Iowa Libraries Record.

In 1937, Gordon W. Allport★ (Ph.D., Harvard, 1922) published Personality, *a book that prompted courses in personality in most departments (Hilgard, 1987). Gordon was among the first personality theorists and was convinced that traits are the basic unit of personality. Initially, he assembled a list of 4,504 different ones (Allport & Odbert, 1936). This large number of traits he identified not only strengthened the emphasis that Allport placed on them but it also nurtured the spawning of tests to measure them.*
Archives of the History of American Psychology, George S. Klein Papers.

Personality

There are many variations in purpose and method in tests of personality, but the majority are built for one of two reasons: the assessment of emotional disturbances or the investigation of the structure and functioning of the normal personality. The purpose of a test is not linked to any single format, and both maladjustment and personality are evaluated by means of rating scales, self-report inventories or questionnaires, interpretations of ambiguous stimuli, and reactions to circumstances that simulate those in real life. These methods, all commonplace, are generally categorized as either objective or projective. The former designates examinations that are based on directions or questions that are clearly stated and the latter designates examinations that are based on vague, unstructured stimuli. Group-administered paper and pencil inventories and individually administered projective tests are the most popular.

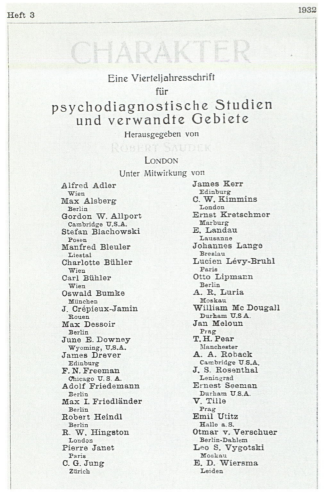

This is the German edition of a periodical, Character and Personality, *that was published in London in 1932. The journal was also printed in Durham, North Carolina, by Duke University Press. On the cover of the German edition the word* Charakter *is printed in red ink on a tan background, but it appears only faintly in the photograph.*

The difference between the German and English titles mirrors the terminology of the era. In the 1930s, the study of individuality or character was just beginning, and for a time the topic was referred to as personology and personalistic psychology and then as personality, the label that ultimately came into standard use.

The journal was innovative in that it was identified as a quarterly review of psychodiagnostic and allied studies. The contributors listed on the cover document the international atmosphere that pervaded psychology at that time.

Archives of the History of American Psychology, René Spitz Collection. Permission Duke University Press, Publisher North American Edition.

Objective Methods

One of the most frequently acknowledged starting points in the modern measurement of emotional status is the 1910 publication of a word association test. This instrument was adopted by researchers, but the compiling of other kinds of tests of adjustment was deferred until 1918 and 1919 when three examinations,

On the Downey Will-Temperament Test, the examinee is requested to copy this specimen of handwriting under three conditions: as quickly as possible, in disguised handwriting, and as exactly as possible. Rapidity is scored in individually administered tests as the number of seconds required to write "United States of America" and in group tests as the number of letters written in 20 seconds. This score was interpreted as a cue to the speed of reactions to life situations. Difficulty in disguising the handwriting was believed to point to a preference for routine and consistency. An accurate reproduction was thought to disclose a respect for details, and probably also, persistence.

Archives of the History of American Psychology, Morris S. Viteles Papers.

each constructed in a different way, appeared: the Downey Will-Temperament Test, the Pressey X-O Test, and the Woodworth Personal Data Blank. The format of these instruments is different; each garnered support for a period of time, but only the Woodworth examination—constructed as a questionnaire—started an uninterrupted sequence of successive revisions.

The two tests in this triad that did *not* start an enduring chain reaction are so frequently mentioned in histories of the measurement of personality that omitting them suggests a violation of tradition and including them helps to call attention to the limited technical base on which the pioneers started. One of these two flashes in the pan, the Will-Temperament Test, was devised by June E. Downey (Ph.D., Chicago, 1907). This test was a derivative of her doctoral dissertation in which she studied the effects of different instructions on handwriting—an examinee-generated record of unique behavior and, thus, an apparently appropriate medium in which to investigate individuality. The word *temperament* reflects Downey's opinion that handwriting is symptomatic of the general activity of a person, and the word *will* refers to the style, such as speed, flexibility, and force, of the activity.

Between 1919 and 1923, Downey issued different versions of the test, adapting them for both individual and group examinations. Although there were some variations, most forms included 12 tests, with writing required in all but three. Each section was scored on a 10-point scale, and these numerically comparable scores were plotted on a "Will-Profile" because Downey thought the pattern of scores offered a more complete and accurate picture than a single score. During that era, it was both unusual and enlightening for a test manual to discuss the meaning of intratest relationships, and merely three variables are used here to illustrate Downey's explanations of what can be discerned from a profile. An examinee who obtained a high score on aggression and speed and a low score on precision was

1. disgust fear sex suspicion aunt.
2. roar divorce dislike sidewalk wiggle.
3. naked snicker wonder spit fight.
4. failure home rotting snake hug.
5. prize gutter thunder breast insult.

Excerpt from the "Pressey X-O Tests for Investigating the Emotions." The examinee is presented with 25 lines of five words each and is requested to cross out each unpleasant word.

1. disgust fear sex suspicion aunt.
2. roar divorce dislike sidewalk wiggle.
3. naked snicker wonder spit fight.
4. failure home rotting snake hug.
5. prize gutter thunder breast insult.

Excerpt from the scoring key. An examiner who suspects flippancy, illiteracy, or impaired comprehension is advised to check for crossing out of the "jokers," words that are not unpleasant. These are arranged in a regular right to left progression throughout the 25 lines of the test. In this scoring key, the jokers are underlined.

1. disgust fear sex suspicion aunt.
2. roar divorce dislike sidewalk wiggle.
3. naked snicker wonder spit fight.
4. failure home rotting snake hug.
5. prize gutter thunder breast insult.

Excerpt from the scoring key. An examiner who wants to inspect responses to sexual content is advised to look at certain critical words, arranged in the same progression as that of the "jokers." The critical words are underlined.

Archives of the History of American Psychology, Frances Perce Papers.

described as enterprising, quick to respond, and prone to inaccuracy. An examinee who obtained a high score on precision and low scores on speed and aggression was said to be accurate but slow, preferring to take things as they came (Downey, 1923).

The test attracted so much attention that a 1928 review of it drew on more than 30 discussions, revisions, or empirical investigations of Downey's technique (Uhrbrock, 1928). This popularity was brief, and, by 1944, the test was dismissed as "now in complete disuse" (Maller, 1944, p. 181). The loss of favor is attributed to the unrealistic claims that were made, indiscriminate applications, and contradictory results.

The second format that did not leave a legacy required the examinee to cross out any item that denoted a specific property, such as *unpleasantness* or *inaccuracy.* Examinations that demand this kind of reply are referred to as "cross-out" tests; they vary from cancellation tests in that a concept rather than a specific structure or form is deleted. This method intrigued Luella W. Pressey (Ph.D., Indiana, 1920) and Sidney Pressey★ because they saw crossing out as a familiar act that does not demand complicated instructions and creates an objective record. In 1919, they described two tests they had designed for group administration in the schools in order to measure "general ability." Most of these examinations required the crossing out of inaccuracies in objects and numerical sequences, but there was also a test of moral judgment and one of emotional control. The two latter units were probably included in response to the evidence then accumulating that intelligence is not, as was originally believed, solely responsible for social, economic, and academic failure or success.

In 1921, Sidney Pressey published both an adult and a children's form of a 100-item "Group Scale for Investigating the Emotions." In this, examinees were asked to draw a line through the one word in lines of five that, in one section, denoted unpleasantness; in a second, impropriety; and in a third, anxiety. The fourth section required the crossing out of words that were associated with a key word. This last unit was an attempt to devise a group-administered version of the Kent-Rosanoff Free Association Test (p. 141) and the words were taken from that list. Examinees were also instructed to encircle the word in each line that was the most extreme—for example, the *most* improper or the *most* similar to the key word.

A small number of other investigators, intrigued by the simplicity and spontaneity of the cross-out method, used it to measure responses other than emotions, particularly attitudes. Establishing both the validity and reliability turned out, however, to be difficult and the technique was only rarely used (Stagner, 1940).

The momentum for personality testing came during World War I from efforts to reduce the incidence of emotional upset in combat. The top level of command asked for professional assistance. One of the results of this request was a questionnaire, the Personal Data Blank, compiled for the purpose of finding, by means of group examination, those draftees with enough neurotic symptoms to warrant individual psychiatric examinations before being accepted for military service (Woodworth, 1919, 1932). The structure and most of the content of this test was put in place by Robert S. Woodworth,★ with the help of a

Personal Data

Answer the questions by underlining "Yes" when you mean yes, and by underlining "No" when you mean no. Try to answer every question.

Name_____   Age_____
Company or Organization_____

DIRECTIONS FOR USE

The Personal Data Blank is scored by counting one point against the subject for each NO and YEs answer marked with green pencil on following pages. If the subject receives above a certain score limit not yet definitely determined, he is subjected to individual neuro-psychiatric examination.

This questionnaire was devised in 1918 to identify emotionally disturbed recruits. There are 116 questions and they are phrased in simple language; for example, "Do you worry too much about little things?" and "Does your heart ever thump in your ears so that you cannot sleep?" This is such an early version that the title given is merely "Personal Data." The test would later be called "The Personal Data Sheet," "The Personal Data Blank," and "The Psychoneurotic Inventory."

Archives of the History of American Psychology, G. Stanley Hall Documents.

This torn sheet of paper is a raw datum in the history of personality testing. It is the first page of the minutes of a joint conference of psychologists and psychiatrists held for the purpose of evaluating the questions Woodworth and Poffenberger devised for the Personal Data Sheet. The participants had access to the results of the administration of the tests to 1,000 military recruits. The committee that sponsored this evaluation began as the American Psychological Association Committee on Problems of Emotional Stability, Fear and Self-Control. In August 1918, it was reorganized as the Subcommittee on Problems of Emotional Fitness of the National Research Council. Woodworth served as Chair of both committees (Yerkes, 1919).

The minutes indicate that Southard and Wills are "neuropsychiatrists," Edwin G. Boring★ examined recruits, and Harry L. Hollingworth★ examined "shell shock" cases. Additional conferees include Robert M. Yerkes,★ Charles S. Berry (Ph.D., Harvard, 1907), Melville E. Haggerty,★ and Joseph W. Hayes★ (Ph.D., Chicago, 1911).

Archives of the History of American Psychology, G. Stanley Hall Documents.

Columbia colleague who was then in the army, Albert T. Poffenberger★ (Ph.D., Columbia, 1912). Psychiatric symptoms were converted into questions to create the first self-report inventory of "emotional fitness." This was the format most frequently adopted in the deluge of personality tests that started right after the war and continues, alive and well, today. Research on this first version was barely underway when the armistice took place, but, soon, numerous editions were prepared for civilian use with children, adolescents, college students, and adults. A sample of these revisions puts the spotlight on both the eagerness and the inexperience of researchers of the era.

As early as 1920, Buford Johnson (Ph.D., Johns Hopkins, 1916) modified some of the original Woodworth items, added new ones, and administered them to enrollees in both regular classes and a special class. Johnson followed the practice of pioneer researchers in intelligence tests of relating the results to measurements obtained with laboratory apparatus, and she determined the agreement between the questionnaires and the results of a steadiness test and dynamometer readings but found no significant agreement.

In 1923, Vernon M. Cady (Ph.D., Stanford, 1925), working under the direction of Lewis M. Terman★ and building on questions that Johnson included, produced a battery of tests intended to pick out children who are apt to become delinquent. Examinees were given opportunities to be dishonest, by, for example, overstating their skills and taking advantage of access to the correct answers to the test questions. The combining of a questionnaire with chances to cheat was due more to optimism than to thoughtful research

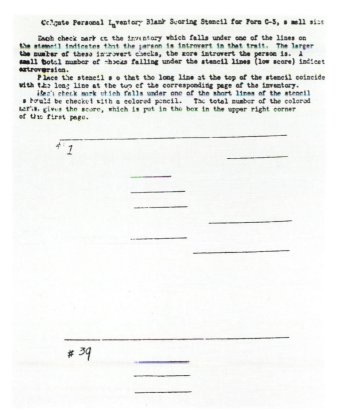

Colgate Personal Inventory Blank Scoring Stencil for Form C-5, a small size

Each check mark on the inventory which falls under one of the lines on the stencil indicates that the person is introvert in that trait. The larger the number of these introvert checks, the more introvert the person is. A small total number of checks falling under the stencil lines (low score) indicat extroversion.

Place the stencil s o that the long line at the top of the stencil coincide with the long line at the top of the corresponding page of the inventory.

Each check mark which falls under one of the short lines of the stencil should be checked with a colored pencil. The total number of the colored marks gives the score, which is put in the box in the upper right corner of the first page.

#1

39

Donald A. Laird (Ph.D., Iowa, 1923) contrived this transparent, homemade stencil for use in scoring a 48-item test of introversion-extroversion. Examinees were directed to check the point on the line that corresponds to the severity or frequency of the complaint during "the past half year" (Laird, 1925, p. 130). The scoring instructions for the examiner are shown in the photograph.

In 1924, Larid began to devise and revise a battery of tests that measure different "emotional outlets" called "The Colgate Personal Inventory Blank," apparently because Laird was on the faculty at Colgate University. Using the Woodworth Personal Data Sheet as a starting point, he was one of the first to broaden the scope of this test but only one of many who constructed an examination that measures introversion-extroversion.

Archives of the History of American Psychology, Ralph M. Stogdill Papers.

design as evidenced by the statement that the questionnaire provided an "opportunity to ask a large number of questions *which might* [italics added], when the answers were tabulated, be found to have something to do with incorrigibility" (Cady, 1923, p. 76). Cady tried to check on the truthfulness of respondents by reversing each statement so that items that ordinarily elicit *yes* would elicit *no*. He measured the agreement between these two forms of the test and found it to be high.

The Woodworth-Mathews Personal Data Sheet, also a children's examination, was published in 1924. This was a derivative of a Columbia University doctoral dissertation, "A Study of Emotional Stability in Children by Means of a Questionnaire," completed by the coauthor of the test, Ellen Mathews (M.D., Pacific College, 1912; Ph.D., Columbia, 1923). There were 75 questions, some from the original test and some adaptations; for example, "Did the teachers in school generally treat you right?" appeared in the Woodworth-Mathews version as "Do your teachers generally treat you right?"

S. Daniel House (Ph.D., Columbia, 1927), one of the first to adapt the Personal Data Sheet to a college population, published "A Mental Hygiene Inventory," designed to identify students who might require assistance with personal problems. House retained some of the original questions and added others that, following Woodworth's practice, he gleaned from the psychiatric literature. House wanted a clinically sensitive instrument and he promoted this in several ways, each an exercise in test technology. To illustrate, he explored the validity of *each* question by calculating a "discriminatory ratio" a quantification of the proportion of healthy and unhealthy answers. He was aware of the growing interest in intervention before complaints became severe, and so he explored the feasibility of assigning *yes* category responses into various gradations of seriousness. He asked a group of college students and a group of veterans, whom he characterized as "declared psychoneurotics," to rate the symptom referred to in each question as *severe, moderate,* or *absent* (House, 1927, p. 13). House, tuned to the then somewhat novel idea that emotional problems originate in childhood, tallied unhealthy reactions reported during childhood.

All these adaptations turned out to be the beginning of the proliferation of pencil and paper tests of personality. The acme of all this productivity is the MMPI (Minnesota Multiphasic Personality Inventory), introduced in the early 1940s. This instrument was created by Starke R. Hathaway★ (Ph.D., Minnesota, 1932), assisted at times by other colleagues. He began the work in the 1930s when he was employed in a neuropsychiatric facility at the University of Minnesota. Hathaway, then among the vanguard of clinical psychologists working in a medical setting, was, in the fashion of the day, eager to standardize interviews. He began to adapt, and in some instances to devise, tests for use in neurological and psychiatric examinations. These steps led him to attempt to build an examination that would include all the symptoms that contribute to diagnoses of psychiatric disabilities (Hathaway, 1978).

Accordingly, he assembled 550 statements that cover a broad range of topics, including a number of physical and psychosomatic complaints; attitudes toward sex, religion, hobbies, politics, superstitions, and interpersonal—as well as intrafamilial relationships; and symptoms of both neurotic and psychotic

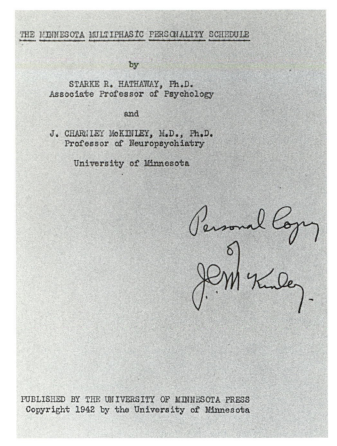

J. Charnley McKinley (M.D., Minnesota, 1919; Ph.D., Minnesota, 1921), a neuropsychiatrist, was Hathaway's principal collaborator on the MMPI. Brief accounts of the test began to appear in 1940, but a manual was not published until 1943. This is McKinley's personal prepublication manual.

Archives of the History of American Psychology, William Schofield Record. The Minnesota Multiphasic Personality Schedule. © University of Minnesota, 1942. Reproduced by permission of the publisher.

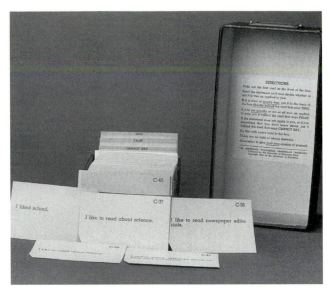

In this form of the MMPI, the examinee finds each item printed on the small card in the box. The task is to make discriminations and file each item-card as TRUE (applies to the examinee), FALSE (does not apply), or CANNOT SAY (the item is an unknown, or the examinee cannot decide).

Archives of the History of American Psychology, William Schofield Record. Card Form Minnesota Multiphasic Personality Inventory. Copyright © the University of Minnesota 1943, renewed 1970. Reproduced by permission of the publisher.

disorders. The agreement and disagreement with each of these statements were obtained from approximately 700 subjects, ranging in age from 16 to 55 years, who were visiting patients in the University hospitals and also from nine groups of psychiatric patients. The data from one of these groups were used to provide a measure of masculinity-femininity, a collection of questions to which the answers of men and of women differ significantly. Each of the other eight groups consisted of patients who manifested particular clinical disorders as defined in the psychiatric classification system then in use—for example, hypochondriasis, depression, hysteria, and schizophrenia. Statements that differentiated, at a statistically significant level, between the normals and the patients in each of these groups furnished the content of separate tests. These tests are, in MMPI terms, called scales—for example, hypochondriasis scale, depression scale.

Hathaway also devised four scales that cue the adequacy of the responses to the clinical scales. These so-called validation scales check on such contaminating factors as carelessness, malingering, illiteracy, and impaired reality contact. To illustrate—the L(ie) scale is a tally of the number of responses that indicate patently untrue answers, such as a response of "False" to the statements "I get angry sometimes" and "I do not read every editorial in the newspaper everyday" (Dahlstrom, Welsh & Dahlstrom, 1972, p. 430).

The MMPI provoked a flood of investigations on both normal and abnormal populations, and the measurements have been extended far beyond the psychiatric domain. They include, for example, personality differences among people pursuing various occupations, changes in personality while acquiring a professional education, suitability for participation in the space program, personality patterns among criminals and predicting parolees who succeed and

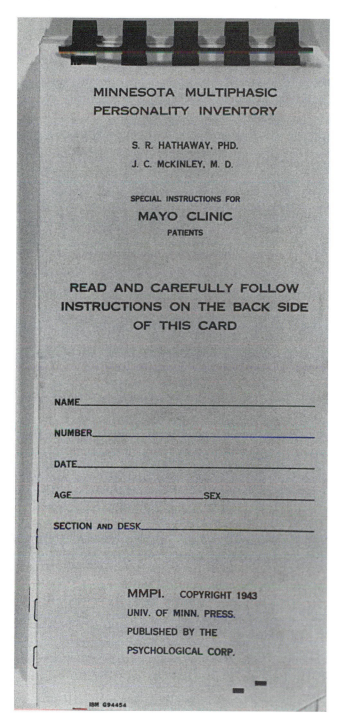

MINNESOTA MULTIPHASIC
PERSONALITY INVENTORY

S. R. HATHAWAY, PHD.

J. C. McKINLEY, M. D.

SPECIAL INSTRUCTIONS FOR

MAYO CLINIC

PATIENTS

READ AND CAREFULLY FOLLOW
INSTRUCTIONS ON THE BACK SIDE
OF THIS CARD

NAME

NUMBER

DATE

AGE   SEX

SECTION AND DESK

MMPI.   COPYRIGHT 1943
UNIV. OF MINN. PRESS.
PUBLISHED BY THE
PSYCHOLOGICAL CORP.

IBM G94454

In the Mayo Clinic form of the MMPI, the test items are printed on cards held in a spiral binding and the examinee marks the response on the card. These responses are machine scored and then a psychological profile is constructed.

Archives of the History of American Psychology, Heinz and Rowena Ansbacher Papers, Mayo Form Minnesota Multiphasic Personality Inventory. © University of Minnesota 1943, renewed 1970. Reproduced by permission of the publisher.

who do not, and on and on and on. The expansion has continued so unabatedly that a 1975 review deals with approximately 6,000 references (Dahlstrom, Welsh & Dahlstrom, 1975).

All this productivity has elicited both endorsements and condemnations, with the latter inflated by the discrediting of the psychiatric diagnostic system in use when the inventory was built. Additional censure is directed at the statistical treatment, the normative sample, and content of some of the questions. The test has, however, withstood this faulting and, in fact, was revised (p. 188) in 1989 (Butcher, Dahlstrom, Graham, Tellegen, & Kaemmer).

One of the strong points of the instrument is the emphasis in interpretation on the configuration of scores. Although constructed scale by scale, the scores were treated statistically so that they are comparable, and a profile analysis similar to that recommended two decades earlier by June Downey is used in both clinical work and in research. A coding system was introduced early (Hathaway, 1947) in order to impose some order on the heterogeneity that comes from the astronomical number of unique profiles. This scheme points out the dominant features of a configuration and provides a system for segregating those that are similar. The patten of scores indicates the probability of the presence, or absence, of particular reactions and portrays each personality as "multiphasic."

Projective Methods

The culture at large has long been aware that ambiguous stimuli prompt people to impose meaning upon them and that what people read into those stimuli varies. Leonardo da Vinci, for example, recognized that stones, cracks in rocks, spots of dampness on walls, and outlines of clouds appear to different artists as faces, battles, and other content. The variations are so striking and provocative, and even entertaining, that, by the latter half of the nineteenth century, inkblots were used as games for both children and adults.

By the late 1890s, inkblots were also in use in research laboratories, most frequently in experiments on imagination but also in investigations of reaction time, discrimination of differences, afterimages, and changes in emotional responses (Hoover & McPherson, 1972). So many experimenters were working with them that, as early as 1910, Guy M. Whipple★ devised a set of 20 and advocated their use so that results obtained in different experiments could be compared.

This 73-page book, published in 1896, contains symmetrical inkblots, one or two to a page, and a bit of verse not unlike that of Lewis Carroll. It also provides directions for playing a parlor game involving blots and rhymes and instructions for making an ink-blot: "Drop a little ink on a sheet of white paper. Fold the sheet in the center and press the ink-spots together with the fingers. All of the pictures in this book were made in this manner—none of them having been touched with a pen or brush. . . . The Gobolink, as his name implies, is a veritable goblin of the ink-blot . . . a self-made eccentric creature of a superior imagination" (p. ix).

Archives of the History of American Psychology Literature Collection.

In the papers of Edmund B. Delabarre,★ there are approximately 100 of these asymmetrical, homemade, blue inkblots, each no longer than 2" square. The documents associated with them do not specify their purposes but Delabarre probably used them around the turn of the century in experiments on the effects of Cannabis indica, hashish, a chemical equivalent of Cannabis sativa, marijuana (Delabarre and Popplestone, 1974). An important goal of psychology at that time was to ascertain the nuances of consciousness. Thus, any changes in consciousness were of particular interest, and some substances that alter consciousness that are now illegal were then legal. Cannabis, for example, was an ingredient in over-the-counter cough syrup. Delabarre and other psychologists consumed the drug in order to observe changes in their own reactions to a number of stimuli (Popplestone & McPherson, 1974).

Archives of the History of American Psychology, Edmund B. Delabarre Papers.

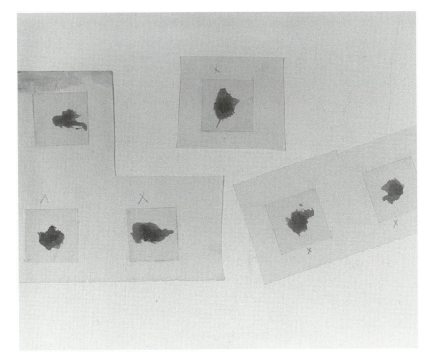

Clouds were also brought into service. In 1902, for example, G. Stanley Hall★ and coauthor J. E. Wallace Wallin★ included questions about what was seen in clouds in an investigation of children's reactions to, and concepts of, various meteorological phenomena. Experiments of this sort were carried out in order to acquire information about various psychological responses, particularly imagination, but the relationship to personality was not explored until Hermann Rorschach (M.D., Zurich, 1912) began to use inkblots. His approach marks the beginning of the projective methods of personality testing, procedures based on the assumption that any meaning that is assigned to a meaningless stimulus comes from within the person.

PSYCHODIAGNOSTIK

METHODIK UND ERGEBNISSE EINES WAHRNEHMUNGSDIAGNOSTISCHEN EXPERIMENTS
(DEUTENLASSEN VON ZUFALLSFORMEN)

VON

Dr. med. HERMANN RORSCHACH

**Mit dem zugehörigen Test
bestehend aus zehn teils farbigen Tafeln**

1921

ERNST BIRCHER VERLAG IN BERN UND LEIPZIG

Archives of the History of American Psychology, Wally Reichenberg-Hackett File.

Since the examinee formulates the replies, his/her characteristics are embedded in those replies and analyses of them can expose his/her personality.

Rorschach found that some responses were reactions to the whole blot but others were reactions to selected areas. Sometimes the color or the form dictated the response and sometimes the blot was seen as either moving or stationary. He discovered that what determines a response is more intimately related to personality than what is seen. This insight helped to move relating the responses away from imagination and toward perception. It also set a course of determining the relationship between the perceptual and organizational properties of the responses and implicit variables such as fears, desires, expectations, and motives. These covert variables were conceptualized as inner dynamics, that is, as predispositions to act in particular ways as mechanisms that underwrite the traits that are measured by objective personality tests.

Rorschach's featuring of the particulars of responses clears the way for a comment on a common but inaccurate treatment of the Kent-Rosanoff Free Association Test in the history of personality testing.

This examination (Kent and Rosanoff, 1910) is categorized by some historians as the first objective test and by others as the first projective test. Unfortunately, it does not fit neatly in either category. The examinee is requested to associate to each word in a series of generally familiar ones. This format complies with the projective scheme in that it gives the examinee the autonomy to choose what is associated, but it also violates that scheme in that it eliminates the ambiguity of the stimulus and reduces the opportunity to respond to selected parts of it.

To return to the main course of events—Rorschach, a psychoanalyst interested in a variety of psychiatric matters, did not pursue systematic research on the diagnostic significance of responses to inkblots until about 1918, but, once he started, his enthusiasm took command. Henri Ellenberger (M.D., Paris, 1934) has written a biography of Rorschach (1954) that is based on extensive primary resources, and it is the source of the inferences in this discussion about what may have set the stage both for Rorschach's attraction to inkblots and his astuteness in interpreting the meaning of the different ways in which they are perceived.

A precursor of his distinction between active and inactive responses may well be his long-standing concern with posture and movement, both in the production and in the appreciation of art. Rorschach is described as personally adept at drawing and as especially skilled in sketching human motion. He was also well-known for a propensity for watching people while they looked at paintings, apparently trying to detect how they felt from their posture and movements during the visual experience.

Another probable antecedent was his knowledge that different kinds of amorphous stimuli prompt familiar interpretations. His wife, for example, told him how, as a child, she and her playmates liked to discern various objects in clouds. He was also personally aware of da Vinci's appreciation of ambiguous stimuli. In one professional paper, Rorschach referred to a patient who recalled looking at a humidity spot on the ceiling and seeing it both as a lake and as a nude woman.

Rorschach also had a few personal contacts with inkblots. He is said to have played with them as a child, and, in 1911, he used them professionally, specifically to acquire some information about fantasy. He also asked a friend, a schoolteacher, to obtain the responses of his students to both a word association test and to inkblots. The friend obliged and Rorschach compared the amount of fantasy that is typical of gifted with that of nongifted children, but he did not publish the results.

Toward the end of 1917, Szymon Hens (M.D., Zurich, 1917) completed a doctoral dissertation that included collecting responses to eight inkblots. This research was extensive in that data were obtained from 1,000 children, 100 normal adults, and 100 psychotics,

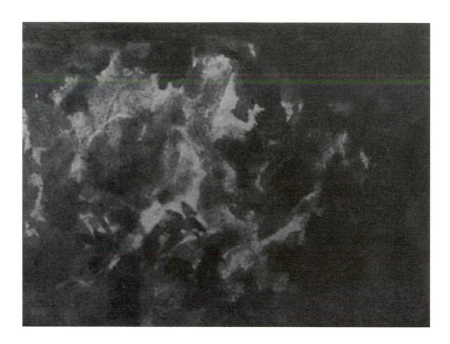

but the analysis was confined to the content of the replies. This experiment prompted Rorschach to devise and try out some inkblots. In December 1918, he reported progress at professional meetings, and, by 1920, he had the manuscript for a book, *Psychodiagnostics,* ready for publication. According to Ellenberger, the manuscript was based on 15 bilaterally symmetrical inkblots. The volume did not appear until 1921 because Rorschach had difficulty locating a publisher. Ernst Bircher, who issued the volume, printed only ten blots. He also reduced their size, modified their colors, and reproduced some of the originally black areas as shaded in ways that suggested different forms. Rorschach reacted to these flaws with more enthusiasm than criticism because he discerned the potential for a high yield from the variations in shading. He began to include this factor in the test scores, but his death nine months later, at age 37, did not allow time to add many details.

At first, the test attracted more destructive than constructive attention. When introduced, it was raw and untried, formulated but not refined. The theoretical basis was inadequate and the procedures for scoring and interpretation were undeveloped. At the time of Rorschach's death, only two or three individuals were struggling with these problems, but a Swiss colleague, Emil Oberholzer (M.D., Zurich, 1910), was effective in promoting the cause in America. Oberholzer had learned the technique from Rorschach and, naming his deceased instructor as coauthor, published a description of it in English (Rorschach & Oberholzer, 1924). David M. Levy (M.D., Chicago, 1918), an American child psychiatrist, was psychoanalyzed by Oberholzer and, upon returning to this country in 1924, spread the word about the test with enough praise to set off a chain of personal contacts that came to include the four

psychologists who would develop variations of Rorschach's basic scheme and become the recognized leaders in the field (Beck, 1969). Each would attract advocates, many of whom would contend that the system they endorsed was *the* best.

One of these pacesetters is Marguerite Hertz (Ph.,D., Western Reserve, 1932). Levy had heard, correctly, in 1930, that Hertz was investigating the potential usefulness of hieroglyphics as well as combinations of pictures in the study of personality. Levy suggested that she try the Rorschach (Hertz, 1985). She took up his suggestion and, in May 1932, completed a dissertation, "Concerning the Reliability and the Validity of the Rorschach Ink-Blot Test."

A second standard-bearer, Samuel J. Beck (Ph.D., Columbia, 1932), who published two papers on the Rorschach in 1930 and in 1932, completed a dissertation on the Rorschach under the direction of Robert S. Woodworth.★ In 1934, he had a fellowship to study in Switzerland with Oberholzer (Beck, 1969).

A third dean is Bruno Klopfer (Ph.D., Munich, 1922). In 1933, he left Germany and accepted an appointment, arranged for him by Carl Jung,★ at the Psychotechnic Institute in Zurich. This position required Klopfer to administer the Rorschach to employees of various businesses. In 1934, he came to Columbia University and soon began to provide instruction in the administration and the interpretation of the Rorschach on a private basis (Exner, 1989).

The fourth forerunner is Zygmunt A. Piotrowski (Ph.D., Poznan, 1927). Piotrowski, then at Columbia University, was one of the earliest and most intent participants in Klopfer's workshops. He was resourceful in designing research and, as early as 1937, formulated and began to use his own scoring system (Exner, 1989).

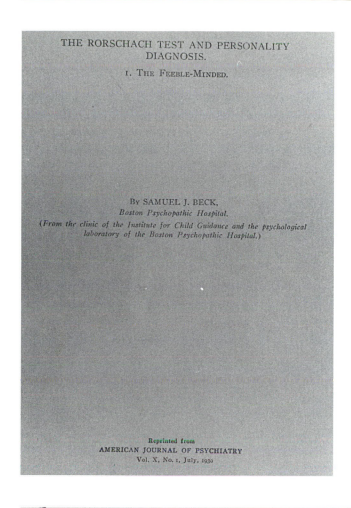

THE RORSCHACH TEST AND PERSONALITY
DIAGNOSIS.

I. THE FEEBLE-MINDED.

By SAMUEL J. BECK,
Boston Psychopathic Hospital.
(From the clinic of the Institute for Child Guidance and the psychological
laboratory of the Boston Psychopathic Hospital.)

Reprinted from
AMERICAN JOURNAL OF PSYCHIATRY
Vol. X, No. 1, July, 1930

Samuel J. Beck describes his research as "the first dissertation on the Rorschach in this country" (1969, p. 4). His description has been transformed and entered into the common wisdom as "the first paper on the Rorschach in English." In fact, the public presentation of Beck's work is not as simple as a single article. In February 1930, he read the paper "Personality Diagnosis by Means of the Rorschach Test" at the seventh annual meeting of the American Orthopsychiatric Association. It was published in October 1930, but in July 1930, Beck had also published the article illustrated here. The doctoral dissertation "The Rorschach Test as Applied to a Feeble-minded Group" was published in May 1932, the same month and year in which Marguerite Hertz completed her dissertation.

American Journal of Psychiatry, (1930) 10, 20–52 (1930). © American Psychiatric Association. Reprinted by Permission.

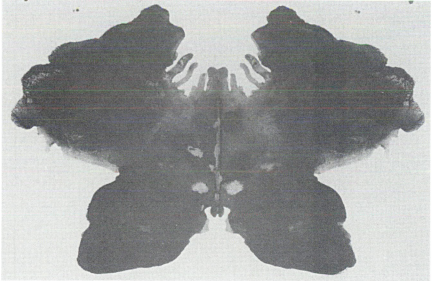

This is Card I in a series of ten inkblots made by Molly Harrower (Ph.D., Smith, 1934). This set of cards is similar to the Rorschach, and is intended for reexaminations so that the examinee would be responding to stimuli comparable to the Rorschach but, in fact, new and unrehearsed (Harrower & Steiner, 1945).

Archives of the History of American Psychology, Molly Harrower Papers.

Approbation of the test was widespread among practitioners but restrained in the academic community. In the 1930s, many researchers still held the opinion that they should deal only with basic psychology, and they rejected endeavors that lacked the precision and theoretical direction of laboratory procedures. As a result, the Rorschach was excluded from university curricula and was taught in workshops, many held off campus and, when on campus, offered only during summer school. The resistance faded slowly so that, at first, university instruction in the Rorschach was frequently restricted to graduate students enrolled in the institution. By the mid-1950s, however, the training of doctoral students in clinical psychology had become so important that instruction in Rorschach and other projective techniques was commonplace.

Henry A. Murray in the mid-1940s, the OSS years.

Archives of the History of American Psychology, Courtesy Caroline F. Murray.

Henry A. Murray in 1985 at the age of 92.

Archives of the History of American Psychology, Courtesy Caroline F. Murray. Photograph by James E. Anderson.

During the interval from 1935 through 1939, interest in the Rorschach intensified and also spread to investigations of other kinds of ambiguous stimuli. There are at least three landmark publications during this period. The first of these is *The Rorschach Research Exchange,* a journal founded in 1936, edited initially by Bruno Klopfer, and one of the direct antecedents of the modern *Journal of Personality Assessment* (Exner, 1989). This periodical was a catalyst for research in that it provided opportunities for investigators to spread, and practitioners to absorb, the growing knowledge.

A second publication, *Explorations in Personality* by Henry A. Murray★ (M.D., Columbia, 1919; Ph.D., Cambridge, 1927), appeared in 1938. In this book, Murray elaborates a method of studying fantasy that was introduced in 1935 (Morgan & Murray) and novel in several respects, including the use of ambiguous pictures rather than inkblots. This technique came to be called the Thematic Apperception Test. It is such a crucial addition both to personality theory and to the roster of examinations that discussion will return to it after comment on the third publication that helped to institutionalize the use of unstructured stimuli.

This last entry is a paper, "Projective Methods for the Study of Personality," published in 1939 and written by Lawrence K. Frank (A.B., Columbia, 1912). Frank

appears to be the first to apply the label "projective methods." In his article, he enumerates various techniques that were then being developed and characterizes the method as an effective way of investigating the "private world." Frank draws analogies between the diagnostic power of projective techniques and such procedures as X rays and the polarization of light and comments that they may function without modifying the domain that they explore. In brief, he succeeded in putting projective tests in perspective and thereby promoted them.

In the 1930s, when Murray started to conduct research on personality, the information available was fragmented and he undertook its enlargement and organization. Motivation, for example, was then explained on the basis of a number of drives, conceptualized as biologically based or biologically derived. Murray sensed that these explanations could not account for the diversity of psychological behavior and he postulated a number of social needs, motives, that are aroused and assuaged by interpersonal relationships—for example, need for affiliation, for autonomy, and for blame avoidance. He assumed that, because these activators direct thoughts and action, they can be inferred from mentation and from behavior. With the assistance of a team of colleagues, he examined the life histories of a group of undergraduate males and extracted the different needs that their behavior indicated.

Murray also devised a scheme for classifying the behavior of others toward the students—for example rejection, deference, and nurturance. He called each of these reactions a press and compiled a roster of the various press or ways in which the environment had reacted to the undergraduates' needs.

The research team decided that the most practical method of studying needs and press is that of analyzing the stories that a subject improvised for a series of ambiguous pictures. The subject was asked to describe each scene and to tell what events preceded it and what events would follow it. The vagueness of the pictures and the freedom to specify any sequence of circumstances fostered projecting the self. This process was brought into sharper focus by centering the analysis of each story around its main character or "hero" and assuming that the needs and press of this "hero" were the same as those of the narrator.

Murray converted this procedure into the Thematic Apperception Test by assembling a series of 20 pictures that depicted the same sex and approximate age of the examinee. He developed criteria for scoring in each story the needs and press, for describing the theme (that is, the way needs and press interact), and for rating the success and quality of the outcomes. *Apperception* is an older term in psychology that refers to a kind of perception. The latter is defined as the integration of sensation and meaning and *apperception* as the integration of perception and impressions about outcomes that come from prior experiences. A difference in apperception is illustrated by a narrator who made up stories in which rejection was followed by nurturance and one who made up stories in which rejection was followed by more rejection. Tallies of needs, press, and themas supplemented by analyses of the patterns they formed and the nature of the apperception disclosed the social motives of the person as well as his/her predictions about consequences. This technique was one of the first available for the study of psychological needs and came into wide use both in the measurement of personality and in research on social motivation (Popplestone & McPherson, 1988).

The enthusiasm for the two prototypical instruments led to the development of a number of additional projective procedures. These include various kinds of visual as well as auditory and kinesthetic stimuli and some require nonverbal responses such as drawing, painting, and arranging toys. A comparison of the chapters on the projective methods in *Theory and Practice of Psychological Testing* (1950) written by Frank S. Freeman (Ed.D., Harvard, 1926) with the two on the same topic in *Theory and Practice of Psychological Testing, Revised Edition* (1955), illustrates the increased attention that projective techniques gained during merely a five-

year period. The single chapter in the first volume consists of 49 pages, documented by 59 footnotes, most of which include literature references, whereas, the two chapters in the second volume consist of 75 pages and 110 footnotes. In the revision, the author added seven tests published between 1948 and 1954 that at the time of the first book were not in existence or had not gained much recognition. Projective testing was on the march!

Personality Assessment

An earlier section of this chapter is concerned with the personality testing that grew out of efforts to assist the armed forces in World War I. World War II did not induce as many changes in that most of the program consisted either of the administration of tests then in general use or of their adaptation for special purposes. There was, however, one project—initiated in 1943 and called personality assessment—that was so much more ambitious and sophisticated than the examinations conducted between 1917 and 1918 that a description of it brings into bold relief some improvements that were attained during a quarter of a century.

The purpose of personality assessment was the selection of individuals who could be expected to be successful in jobs related to intelligence and counterintelligence operations. In this context, the word *assessment* designates a sequence of complicated procedures that were used to screen applicants for these positions. The technique involved teams of examiners who evaluated and integrated the information about each candidate as they obtained it by various means, including interviews; observations of spontaneous, informal responses; objective and projective tests; and situational tests—that is, observations under circumstances that simulate real-life situations.

At the time this unusual selection was undertaken, there were practically no precedents, and the method was developed as work toward the goal progressed. When the suggestion was first made that professionals be asked to take on this task, Robert C. Tryon (Ph.D., Berkeley, 1928) took the initiative in urging the Office of Strategic Services (OSS) to set up a center devoted to personality assessment. The actual planning and conducting of the project was carried out by psychologists and psychiatrists with Henry A. Murray★ identified as the most significant contributor (MacKinnon, 1977).

The charge of OSS to pick out effective operators was handicapped by a number of unusual circumstances. For security reasons, applicants were not given many details about the positions for which they were applying, and the secrecy of the work was emphasized. Both of these conditions are magnets for thrill seekers and those with an unhealthy involvement in danger. These and other difficulties with the candidates were augmented by ambiguities about the problems the

Three OSS staff members, Jacob W. Getzels (Ph.D., Harvard, 1951), David Krech,★ and Charles Davis (a non-psychologist) conducting a stress interview with a candidate who was then using a pseudonym and who remains unknown today. All three interviewers wear civilian dress in order to conceal their military rank, and the candidate wears fatigues also to obscure cues about his status or rank.

Archives of the History of American Psychology, David Krech Papers.

A cryptic label on the back of this photograph identifies it as "David Krech (master sergeant in civilian clothes) in the OSS. San Clemente, CA 1944." Tasks involving maps were used to observe ingenuity, leadership, and the ability to meet unexpected situations. This photograph seems to show a problem entitled "Burma Town." Krech assigns it to the five OSS candidates in fatigues: "You are flying in this direction [pointing toward the mountains on the relief map]. When the plane reaches a point directly over the town, the plane develops motor trouble. . . . crashes into the mountain at this point [indicating the point] and the plane is wrecked and the pilot killed. . . . What do you do?" (OSS Assessment Staff, 1948, p. 345).

Archives of the History of American Psychology, David Krech Papers.

applicants would encounter. There was, for example, no indication of the geographic and cultural environment to which an applicant might be assigned and there was a high probability that abrupt changes in location and responsibilities would occur. There were so many clouds that a decision was made not to assess candidates for specific assignments but to garner knowledge about the personal strengths—such as skill in searching, acuteness in observing, resistance to stress, tolerance for frustration, ingenuity, initiative, and assertiveness—that each would bring, under generally described conditions, to a series of challenges. The program was not designed to test technical skills, such as proficiency as a pilot or competence in a foreign language, but was focused on learning about performance in threatening, complex, and multifaceted settings.

Assessments were made of 5,391 recruits, and the on-site performance of 1,187 of these individuals was rated by both superiors and associates. These evaluations indicated only limited success in selection, but this was a new project and, as the assessors point out (Office of Strategic Services Assessment Staff, 1948), it screened personnel who assume serious risks and heavy

responsibilities so any gain in accuracy is productive, albeit frequently immeasurable.

The military program was followed by the founding of civilian counterparts in some large American companies. These assessment centers have retained the name, but have, of course, modified the original goals and procedures. The programs vary, but typically they are designed to assess the level of development of individual employees and/or their potential for promotion. Small groups of managers and executives are brought together and observed in a number of situations, such as business games, in-basket exercises, and psychodrama, with most of the situations allied to business enterprises. The assessors, drawing on the origin of the technique, pool opinions and decisions. Many of the evaluators are fully trained professionally, but others are managers or people trained for assessment.

Harry L. Hollingworth (Ph.D., Columbia, 1909) was a member of the faculty of Columbia University from 1909 until retirement in 1946. His scholarship covered a range of topics: learning, thinking, neuroses, psychopharmacology, applied psychology, and research on both advertising and vocational guidance. This diversity was more commonplace in the past than it is today and many of the early psychologists were both specialists and generalists. Hollingworth was the 36th president of the American Psychological Association in 1927.

Archives of the History of American Psychology, Harry and Leta Hollingworth Papers.

Harry L. Hollingworth's notes. These comments furnish one example of the numerous struggles involved in the organization of the subject matter of experimental psychology. Reasoning was then believed to follow the rules of formal logic. Hollingworth (1926) suggested that dreaming follows the principle of his adaptation of the philosophical concept of redintegration, the evoking of the psychological consequence of a prior experience when one component is encountered. "Conditioned reaction" appeared to be a special form of redintegration and, therefore, it also had to fit into the framework.

Archives of the History of American Psychology, Harry and Leta Hollingworth Papers.

Occupational Competency

Psychologists became proficient at analyzing the requirements of jobs and workers and devising tests that identify individuals who are most apt to perform efficiently, but their efforts were intermittent and limited prior to World War I. The sparseness is documented in a 1915 paper on "Specialized Vocational Tests and Methods" written by Harry Hollingworth,★ one of the launchers of what was then referred to as vocational or applied psychology. He first comments on the underdevelopment of the field and then points to progress that was underway: "In fact, there are some twenty types of work for which tests have already been proposed, recommended, and more or less tentatively tried out" (1915, p. 919).

This low level of productivity turned into prolific output when the United States entered World War I. The involvement in combat created a personnel emergency in that it became necessary to assign immediately a burdensome number of soldiers to positions that they could handle or could learn rapidly. The gravity of fighting made it crucial that these appointments be judicious, but there were several handicaps. One was the wide range of tasks that are performed in an army—from manual labor through skilled work through scientific research. The roster even includes artists to assist in camouflage. Unfortunately, the skills that are necessary for many of these occupations were not specified, and the demands of

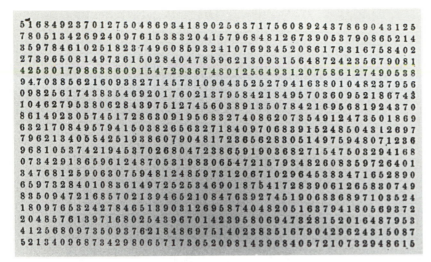

One version of the Cancellation Test. In this test, the examinee is instructed to "cross out every '7' on this slip with a quick dash. . . . Begin at the top line and go across each one, crossing out every '7'. Do this quickly and carefully" (Link, 1919, p. 403). The score is the number of cancellations made in a specified interval.

There are several versions of the cancellation test, and they vary in the number of stimuli, the time allotted, and the item(s) to be crossed out—letter(s), combinations of letter(s), digit(s), word(s), or misspelled word(s). The basic format developed in the 1890s was designed to measure attention, discrimination, distraction, fatigue, and perception.

Henry C. Link (Ph.D., Yale, 1916) was one of the first to use a Cancellation Test in an industrial setting. He was looking for techniques that identify apt employees, and he refrained from speculating about what is measured "because it has been found that such a classification has little practical value, besides being theoretically unsound" (Link, 1919, p. 393). Link reported that the score on the cancellation test predicts the performance level of inspectors of bullet shells.

Archives of the History of American Psychology, Walter and Catharine Cox Miles Papers.

some positions varied with the camp or division. A wagoner, for example, was in many camps responsible for the maintenance of wagons only, but in some he also had to drive them, and in motorized corps he was required to drive vehicles. A "horse shoer" was ordinarily occupied with the care of horses, but in some locations he, like the wagoner, was a chauffeur.

The reasons psychologists were called upon to help bring order into this crisis grew out of research then in progress at the Carnegie Institute of Technology in Pittsburgh. This program started in 1915 when the president of that institution established a Department of Applied Psychology under the directorship of Walter Van Dyke Bingham* (Ph.D., Chicago, 1908). Shortly after Bingham began work at Carnegie, an insurance business executive asked him to provide advice about the selection and training of salesmen. In response, he formed the Bureau of Salesmanship Research and persuaded Walter Dill Scott* (Ph.D., Leipzig, 1900), one of the few psychologists then working in applied psychology, to accept responsibility for the bureau. By 1916, Scott and his assistants had assembled a few tests and had developed a personal history blank, a record of the ability and training of an individual in various occupations (Bingham, 1952).

Scott, confident that the personal history blank could expedite personnel assignments in the army, demonstrated its usefulness at various camps. Newton D. Baker, Secretary of War, was impressed and he instigated a Committee on Classification of Personnel with Scott as Director and Bingham as the Executive Secretary and authorized them to assemble a group of psychologists and business executives to assist them. At first, ten psychologists were included in the group but resignations were followed by replacements and the participation of several other colleagues.

One of the first tasks that the committee undertook was the development of specifications for each position. With a minimum of clerical work, they converted the personal history blank into a CCPQ card (Committee on Classification of Personnel Qualification Card) on which to record the educational and occupational history of each soldier as well as his probable fitness for specific duties. The card was put into immediate use, and by the end of the war it had been used to classify nearly 3,500,000 men (Bingham, 1919a; Napoli, 1981).

The use of a personal history to match man to assignment was supplemented by "trade tests." Because there was not enough time to observe each soldier at work, examinations were devised to indicate whether

RATING SCALE

I. PHYSICAL QUALITIES.		
Physique, bearing, neatness, voice, energy, endurance.	Highest	15
	High	12
Consider how he impresses his command in these respects.	Middle	9
	Low	6
	Lowest	3

II. INTELLIGENCE.		
Accuracy, ease in learning; ability to grasp quickly the point of view of commanding officer, to issue clear and intelligent orders, to estimate a new situation, and to arrive at a sensible decision in a crisis.	Highest	15
	High	12
	Middle	9
	Low	6
	Lowest	3

III. LEADERSHIP.		
Initiative, force, self reliance, decisiveness, tact, ability to inspire men and to command their obedience, loyalty and co-operation.	Highest	15
	High	12
	Middle	9
	Low	6
	Lowest	3

IV. PERSONAL QUALITIES.		
Industry, dependability, loyalty; readiness to shoulder responsibility for his own acts; freedom from conceit and selfishness; readiness and ability to co-operate.	Highest	15
	High	12
	Middle	9
	Low	6
	Lowest	3

V. GENERAL VALUE TO THE SERVICE.		
Professional knowledge, skill and experience; success as administrator and instructor; ability to get results.	Highest	40
	High	32
	Middle	24
	Low	16
	Lowest	8

CCP 1102B 9–18

Walter D. Scott★ designed this rating scale to aid in the assessment of subordinate officers. It provides a standard for comparison because each rater recorded the name of an officer whom he chose as representative of each of the five attributes (on the left of the card) at each of five levels of competency (on the right of the card). Each man was evaluated four times each year and assigned the appropriate numerical scores from the right-hand column. The total score was the sum of these values. The ratings were then reviewed by the rater's superior and recorded on the Officer's Qualification Card (Strong, 1919).

the on-the-job performance would be that of an expert, a journeyman, an apprentice, or a novice. Initially, questions that would disclose the examinee's familiarity with the essential skills of a job were framed, and all those to which novices gave satisfactory answers were eliminated. Thus, each examinee was confronted only with questions that tapped experience. These "oral trade tests" were standardized for 83 positions, and they were supplemented by "picture tests" for 40 occupations. These picture tests consisted of photographs, or drawings, of selected equipment or materials, and the examinee was required to answer a series of questions about the pictured items. "Performance tests" for 30 trades were also developed. These required a sample of actual work—for example, a carpenter might be asked to make a product from a blueprint (Bingham, 1919b).

These large scale projects were augmented by assessments of special, and frequently complex, skills (Yerkes, 1918). These investigations were conducted for several activities, and descriptions of some of the work with aircraft crews is included in this discussion in order to provide an example of how psychologists, starting with very limited experience, learned to measure aptitude for a multifaceted performance. Flying was so new that, in April 1917, there were only 52 trained pilots in the Aviation Section of the Signal Corps, the unit then in charge of aviation. Before the testing program was started, candidates for pilot training were selected by specially created "Examining Boards and Physical Examining Units." These task forces were instructed to be rigorous and they rejected 50% to 60% of the applicants, but their criteria were vague and Ground Schools rejected an additional 15%. Approximately another 6% failed during Flying School. These misjudgments in selection were intolerably costly in terms of human life, man hours of training, and the destruction of airplanes (Henmon, 1919).

The National Research Council Committee on Psychological Problems of Aviation, working in conjunction with personnel from various airfields, attempted "to discover means of prophesying abilities in a school such as had never before existed, in an art which only a few score men in the country had learned, and in a form of warfare which was only three years old and was changing its nature radically every few months" (Thorndike, 1919, p. 58). These research teams collected a body of information, including tests of emotional stability; mental alertness; athletic interest and achievement; skill in the perception of tilt; speed of reaction time, both auditory and visual; stability of equilibrium; ability to sight planes quickly and accurately; and accuracy of judgments of distance, of rate, and of the projected intersection of planes moving at differing rates.

One series of experiments on the changes in psychological functions under conditions of progressively increasing oxygen deprivation was directed by teams led by Knight Dunlap.★ The experimenters measured the changes in efficiency in carrying out tasks under conditions of increasing oxygen deprivation that

Dunlap's method for measuring the interference of anoxia. The subject (in this particular experiment, the "reactor") is endeavoring to respond quickly and accurately to three stimulus changes while breathing on a "rebreathing machine," an instrument that delivers progressively reduced amounts of oxygen, inducing the anoxia that flyers of World War I airplanes encountered at high altitudes. The six other men in the picture manipulate the stimuli, monitor the equipment, measure the reactor's blood pressure and heart rate, and observe his alertness and general well-being.

Archives of the History of American Psychology, Knight Dunlap Papers.

The stimuli as seen by the reactor. The instructions required (1) responding to any flashing of the lamps by touching the corresponding button with a stylus; (2) adjusting the rheostat at the front so that the ammeter (mounted on the arm above the equipment) would remain at a designated marker; and (3) maintaining the motor (mounted at the right side of the table at the rear) at a low speed by depressing a pedal on the floor. When the lights would flash and the ammeter would drop at the same time, the subject was supposed to tend to the lights first.

Archives of the History of American Psychology, Knight Dunlap Papers.

are similar to those in flight. The results appeared at first to indicate that attention and motor coordination remain normal as long as the subject can attend and react. This initial impression was modified when more careful scrutiny disclosed that being observed provoked subjects to mobilize attention, at least for brief spurts, and that this activation masked decrements in functioning. This amendment alerted the researchers to the hazards that are inherent in interpreting laboratory data and pointed to the merits of procuring data under actual flying conditions. This extension was, however, curtailed first by the pressure of other military needs and then by the cessation of hostilities (Dunlap, 1919).

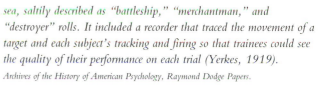

This instrument for teaching the pointing and firing of a gun at sea was designed by Raymond Dodge.★ The complicated apparatus duplicated the aiming and firing of a gun and was used both to train and to select personnel during World War I. This land-based equipment was capable of imitating the rolling movements of a ship at sea, saltily described as "battleship," "merchantman," and "destroyer" rolls. It included a recorder that traced the movement of a target and each subject's tracking and firing so that trainees could see the quality of their performance on each trial (Yerkes, 1919).

Archives of the History of American Psychology, Raymond Dodge Papers.

Raymond Dodge★ (Ph.D., Halle, 1896), the 25th president of the APA, joined the faculty of Wesleyan University as instructor in 1898, and in 1924 he became professor at Yale University. Dodge was elected to both the National Academy of Sciences and the National Research Council. He was honored by the publication in 1936, the year of his retirement, of the "Dodge Commemorative Number" Psychological Monographs. This issue, edited by W. R. Miles,★ incudes "Psychological Studies of Human Variability," written by 55 contributors and "Affectionately Dedicated by His Students, Research Collaborators, and Colleagues" (Miles, 1956).

Archives of the History of American Psychology, Walter and Catharine Cox Miles Papers.

WALTER DILL SCOTT   L. B. HOPKINS   JOSEPH W. HAYES
ROBERT C. CLOTHIER   BEARDSLEY RUML   STANLEY B. MATHEWSON

ANNOUNCE

THE SCOTT COMPANY

ORGANIZED

TO OFFER TO INDUSTRY METHODS

LEADING TO THE SOLUTION OF PROBLEMS

IN THE FIELD OF INDUSTRIAL PERSONNEL

TO SHARE WITH INDUSTRY THE RE-

SULTS OF RESEARCH WHICH MAY PROVIDE

A BETTER UNDERSTANDING OF THE SOCIAL

ECONOMIC AND PSYCHOLOGICAL FACTORS IN

INDUSTRIAL ADJUSTMENT

TO OFFER TO INDUSTRY A CONSULTING

SERVICE WHICH COMBINES THE INDUSTRIAL

AND SCIENTIFIC POINTS OF VIEW

751 DREXEL BUILDING

PHILADELPHIA

The Scott Company is usually identified as the first successful consulting firm in industrial psychology in the United States. The announcement shown must have been issued in 1919, the year Walter Dill Scott★ relinquished the directorship of the Bureau of Salesmanship Research and founded a firm of six consultants, all former members of the Committee on Classification of Personnel. Two other consultants in addition to Scott were psychologists: Joseph W. Hayes★ and Beardsley Ruml (Ph.D., Chicago, 1917). Three of the six consultants would become presidents of institutions of higher learning: Clothier at Rutgers University, Hopkins at Wabash College, and Scott at Northwestern University.

Archives of the History of American Psychology, Walter and Catharine Cox Miles Papers. Career Identification with the help of Edward Skipworth.

Score.....................M

T 12

Write your name here...   Date...................

Make a cross in the square before the best answer to each question—as shown in sample

SAMPLES
1. Cows are useful, because
   ☒ they give milk
   ☐ they are domestic animals
   ☐ they do not require much food
2. Wool is used for clothes, because
   ☐ it comes from sheep
   ☒ it is warm
   ☐ it costs more than cotton

1. We use paper to write on, because
   ☐ it is cheap
   ☐ it tears easily
   ☐ it is made from wood

2. Why are windows made of glass? Because
   ☐ glass breaks easily
   ☐ glass is heavy
   ☐ we can see through glass

3. Why do people buy candy? Because
   ☐ they like sweets
   ☐ they need food
   ☐ sugar is scarce

DO NOT OPEN PAPER UNTIL SO INSTRUCTED

This single page is from a series of tests developed between 1919 and 1922 by Elsie O. Bregman (Ph.D., Columbia, 1922) for selecting personnel at the R. C. Macy Company of New York. Bregman is believed to be the first psychologist employed in the retailing industry. She ascribes her interest in industrial psychology to the encouragement and assistance she received from Harry L. Hollingworth★ (Bregman, 1922). Bregman also published revisions of the Army Alpha in 1925 and 1935.

Archives of the History of American Psychology, Elsie O. Bregman Papers.

The know-how in personnel work that was acquired under military auspices was transferred after the war onto a civilian scene enthusiastic about business and industry and thus responsive to industrial psychology. The widespread expansion that occurred is exemplified in the growth of the Division of Applied Psychology at the Carnegie Institute of Technology. The war had interrupted the projects that Bingham and Scott were directing, but shortly after the armistice the Division was so revitalized that it was divided into two parts: the Division of Cooperative Research and the Bureau of Salesmanship Research. By 1923, seven departments were functioning, involving nine professors, nine instructors, seven statistical and clerical assistants, and a total of 65 graduate students who had enrolled since the

founding. The goal was "practical science," conceptualized as a reciprocal process—the application of experimental psychology to numerous problems and the integration of the information learned in these endeavors into basic psychology (Bingham, 1923).

There were a number of different investigations of occupationally relevant tasks—for example, research in techniques of training people to supervise, probes of the origin and strength of motivation for various careers, and studies of the efficacy of reward systems that differ, such as, the frequency and mode of delivery of reimbursement. The psychologists at Carnegie set much of the agenda for industrial psychology during the Era of Development, and, as a result, many of the later applications are technical refinements rather than

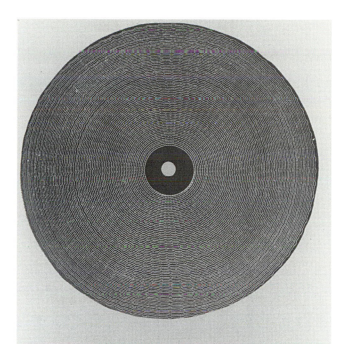

THIS figure illustrates the extraordinary accuracy of the modern phonograph motor. Each wave represents one one hundredth of a second in the motion of the disc. If there were a discrepancy of as much as one-tenth of a wave in two successive circles, that would mean an error of one one-thousandth of a second in the revolution; but there is scarcely any place in this record of a tuning fork in which an error to that extent can be detected. It is this high accuracy of the reproducing machines that has made possible the present "Measures of Musical Talent" in the form of records.

Carl E. Seashore (Ph.D., Yale, 1895) spent most of his career at the University of Iowa serving both on the faculty and in administration. Much of his research was in audition, with an emphasis on both the measurement of musical talent and the analysis of the quality of musical performance. His contributions include the devising and refining of audiometers (p. 86) and the construction of two devices that allow a visual analysis of music. One of these, the tonoscope, produces a visual record of the pitch of tones, allowing the artist, as well as the critic, to see deviations in duration, steadiness, and intensity. In 1937, Seashore, with the aid of two colleagues, constructed the Iowa piano camera, an instrument that registers the nuances of both the loudness and timing of a pianist's performance (Lundin, 1967).

Archives of the History of American Psychology, University of Iowa Libraries Record.

This frontispiece is from the Manual of Instructions and Interpretations of Musical Talent. *The caption in the photograph shows the confidence of the pioneer psychologists in their equipment. The "Measures of Musical Talent" constitute Carl Seashore's 1919 version of a musical aptitude test, the first in a series that he would devise. The test stimuli, recorded on both sides of five phonograph records, consist of pairs of tones that present the components of musical sounds which then were believed to be basic: pitch, intensity, time, consonance, and tonal memory. The phonograph was played at 78 revolutions per minute except for the test of time when it was set for 60 or 65. Examiners were admonished to handwind the player with care, both before starting each record and during an interruption in the middle of each.*

The similarity between the paired stimuli gradually increases and the score is the percent of correct discriminations. Seashore provided scores for a number of adults and children for comparison with those of individual examinees. The number and nature of the basic components are modified in later versions of the examination, and the means of reproducing the stimuli are also improved.

Archives of the History of American Psychology, Morris S. Viteles Papers.

innovations (Strong, 1958). The consistency or reliability of examinations was improved as was the validity—that is, the effectiveness with which the instruments actually measure what they purport to measure. There was a marked increase in the number of vocations for which specialized tests were built. There were also more detailed analyses of occupational skills. For example, the initial attempts to assess the aesthetic sense of students in the Fine Arts College at Carnegie were later broken down by psychologists working in various facilities into measures of such components as the recognition of proportion, sensitivity to light and shade in drawing, the acuity of perception of perspective, and the accuracy of color matching. In brief, much of the progress was the mastery of particulars.

The scores of Henry H. Goddard★ on the Strong Vocational Interest Blank. Edward K. Strong, Jr. (Ph.D., Columbia, 1911), devised this test in 1927. Revisions of it are in use in present-day vocational counseling. It quantifies the agreement between an examinee's interests—as manifested in responses to 400 or more questions about hobbies, recreational preferences, and reading habits—and the interests of people who are successful in a number of professions and specialized occupations. The technique assumes that an examinee who has interests similar to those who enjoy and are adept in a particular vocation will also like the work of that vocation. Strong simplified the interpretation of the scores by assigning letter grades: An A indicates that many of the interests are shared and a C indicates a lack of mutuality (Strong, 1943).

Unfortunately, neither the date on which Goddard took this test nor the revision is indicated. Goddard's grade for a psychologist is superior, but it is not his highest mark. The scores suggest that he would find little in common with an office manager, accountant, or purchasing agent.

Archives of the History of American Psychology, Henry H. Goddard Papers. Reproduced by special permission of the Agent, Consulting Psychologists Press, Inc., Palo Alto, 94303, from the Hankes Report Form from the Strong Vocational Interest Test of the Strong Interest Inventory, Form T325 of the Strong Vocational Interest Blanks ® by Edward K. Strong, Jr. with the permission of the publishers, Stanford University Press. Copyright © 1985 by the Board of Trustees of the Leland Stanford Junior University.

An examiner measures manual dexterity with the Minnesota Rate of Manipulation Test (Betts, 1946). This instrument measures the speed and skill in turning, placing, and moving objects when using one and when using two hands. This aptitude was used most often in assessing candidates for certain occupations where proficiency in coordination and adeptness are crucial and in assessing employees following illness or accident.

The icons on the wall show, from left to right, a session of the Tenth International Congress of Psychology, Copenhagen, 1932, partially obscured; Alfred Binet★; unknown; Lewis Terman★; and registrants at the Copenhagen Congress.

Archives of the History of American Psychology, David P. Boder Museum Collection.

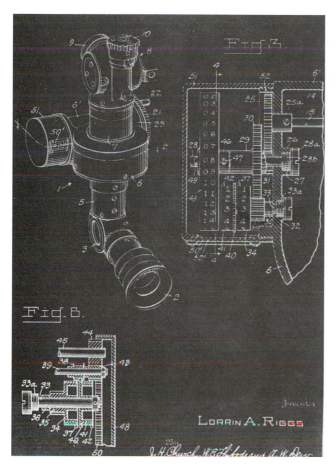

Drawing for a digital readout for the panoramic telescope, a sighting device used to train guns on a target. Lorrin A. Riggs in a personal communication to the authors on June 23, 1989, writes:*

"the instrument makers and engineers up to that time were dismally unaware of human errors resulting from complex indicators. World War II forced the engineering people (and the military establishment) to face the huge costs of faulty human engineering. Walter [Hunter] was ahead of his time in thinking up ways . . . to make military instruments easier to use. . . ."*

"Walter asked me if I could put together a mock-up of a digital readout for the panoramic telescope. . . . [he] procured one of these, and I got hold of a small counter. . . . We had a small machine shop in the basement of the [Brown University] psychology building . . . and I took a few days to mount the counter in such a way as to give a digital reading of the azimuth setting of the panoramic sight. It was definitely a mock-up, rather than a properly engineered production, but it did work. So Walter took it to Field Artillery headquarters, and they arranged to have the drawings made for a more finished product. At that point the war ended."

Archives of the History of American Psychology, Lorrin A. Riggs Papers and Correspondence File.

Walter S. Hunter (Ph.D., Chicago, 1912) served in various capacities in both World Wars I and II. In a 1946 paper, he describes how the digital device at the left counteracts errors. Hunter was a dominant figure on the civilian scene, active in many enterprises, especially in research on learning and on early analyses of what later came to be called cognitive functioning—specifically, the ability to delay responses and to master a temporal maze (Graham, 1958).

Archives of the History of American Psychology, University of Iowa Libraries Record. Photograph by Bachrach, with permission.

World War II reactivated the personnel crisis of World War I in that once again there was an urgent need to transform a civilian population into a fighting force. Several psychologists who assisted during the first conflict participated the second time, and they were equipped with more and better techniques for meeting the challenges that arose (Bingham, 1941).

One of the most troublesome problems came from the advances in military hardware that were forthcoming throughout the entire period of combat. Many of these changes increased both the complexity and speed of human operations, but, initially, attention was restricted to mechanization, with little or no consideration of the capability of human beings to handle the improvements. As a result, many machines were not, or in a few instances could not be, used efficiently, and psychologists were asked to recommend how these instruments might be better adapted to operators. Obtaining the answers to these questions converted much of the research on personnel into research on human engineering or human factors engineering.

Each of the tests on this page was one component in a series developed for the purpose of selecting air crew trainees (pilots, bombardiers, and navigators) in a World War II program in personnel classification in the Army Air Forces School of Aviation (later the U.S. Air Force). John C. Flanagan (Ph.D., Harvard, 1934) directed the project. Each of the tests originated in other contexts and was adapted to allow one examiner to test four or more individuals at the same time (Flanagan, 1948).

In the Discrimination Reaction Time Test shown above, the stimuli consist of a pair of red and/or green lights and a white light. The examinee is required to press, as rapidly as possible, the key that turns off the white light. The appropriate one is determined by the location of the red light in relation to the green light—to the left or right as well as above or below (Melton, 1947).

Archives of the History of American Psychology, Walter and Catharine Cox Miles Papers. Official Photographs of the U.S. Army Air Forces.

In the Two-hand Coordination Test, the examinee tries to keep a small button on top of an irregularly moving target by turning one handle forward and backward with the right hand and a second one laterally with the left hand (Melton, 1947).

Archives of the History of American Psychology, Walter and Catharine Cox Miles Papers. Official Photographs of the U.S. Army Air Forces.

Achieving the best possible fit between a person and a machine demands adjusting both the equipment and the methods of using it. These are lengthy tasks because, typically, a number of different remedies are designed and each must be evaluated. Furthermore, operators have to learn most of these adaptations and, because performance improves with practice, the measurements have to be repeated. Completing these evaluations was handicapped by a shortage of time as well as by the impossibility of testing combat crews in action. Because of these limitations, much of the research on human engineering during the war was relegated to investigations during training rather than during battle (Guilford, 1948).

In spite of these and other obstacles, mechanical properties and human capacities were in several instances successfully aligned. A few specifics about the difficulties that had to be managed are illustrated in the

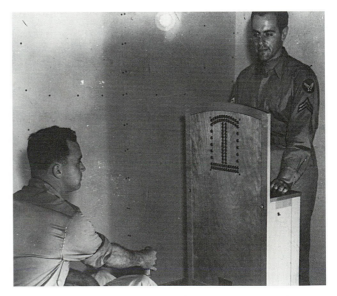

In the Complex Coordination Test, the examinee is required to manipulate controls similar to the rudder and stick controls on an airplane in response to successively presented patterns of visual stimuli (Melton, 1947).

Archives of the History of American Psychology, Walter and Catharine Cox Miles Papers. Official Photographs of the U.S. Army Air Forces.

The Army Specialized Training Program in Personnel Psychology at Stanford University was directed by Paul R. Farnsworth (Ph.D., Ohio State, 1925), here standing in the back wearing civilian clothes. Seated at the tables are students enrolled in the program. The army, in anticipation of a shortage of psychologists, established in the summer of 1943 this educational project in personnel psychology for enlisted men. The courses were offered on eleven college campuses and were taught by regular faculty members, guided by a standard syllabus that focused the instruction on immediate usefulness and required the least possible time. This was the first college training program subsidized by the government. By early 1944, about 1,300 men had completed the curriculum (Napoli, 1981).

Archives of the History of American Psychology, Paul R. Farnsworth Record.

research on the demands made of an aerial gunner operating a flexible machine gun in a bomber during an era when targets were detected by human vision. As soon as he saw an enemy plane, the gunner had to determine the direction of the approach—often without the aid of reference points in the surrounding visual space. Then, keeping the targets in sight, he was required to estimate the movement during the flight time of a bullet, aim the gun, and fire. As the war continued, automated computations of gunsight data came into existence, and, although they increased accuracy, they also complicated the airman's tasks.

An increasing number of complaints from gunners as well as an increase in the number of suicide attacks by the enemy provoked a specialized research project on the "Psychological Factors in the Operation of Flexible Gunnery Equipment." The investigators of this problem were immediately impressed with the number of duties that had to be managed, and enumerating just a few of them should also impress readers and at the same time expose some of the solutions that came out of the experimental work in human engineering. The gunner was required simultaneously to track the elevation of the target and to determine its range by keeping it in contact with marks on visual reference scales. These feats demanded that the gunner turn two knobs, one with each hand, but the movements of the two hands were asymmetrical and not equally paced. This awkwardness was further compounded by some erratic effects. Triggering the gun, for example, induced jerky tracking, and the rates of the hand movements in ranging had to be modified according to the direction and rate of changes in elevation. The researchers concluded, "The task of the B-29 gunner was so complex that its minor components were carried out by the gunner in relative independence of the perceptual situation. The attention of the gunner was so occupied by the tasks of tracking and ranging that he could not make a clear and discriminating choice of the moment at which to fire. In its complexity, the B-29 gunnery taxed the limits of human ability" (Bray, 1948, p. 211).

One outcome of this research was a number of guidelines for the use of engineers in designing equipment. These cover, in addition to optical variables, most aspects of gunnery, including specifications about the most efficient distance between the gunner and the instruments, and plans for the use of powered seating and the arrangement of sighting stations so as to avoid postural stress and distraction. Recommendations include suggestions to design the size, illumination, and shape of controls in ways that reduce errors in using them. The guidelines offer advice to engineer instruments so that the use of controls to obtain one reading would not cause irregularity in a second. They also suggest that the triggering mechanism be constructed so that it could be moved by the foot or by the index finger, thereby freeing the wrist and arm for the task of tracking.

Some of these prescriptions were carried out and found to be useful, but substantiating them required the pursuit of numerous details, and many investigations were still in process when the war ended. There was not enough time to maximize the man-machine fit, but there were convincing demonstrations that the fundamental unit is not a machine but instead a man-machine.

John Dewey, a reformer, educational theorist, philosopher, and psychologist, dealt primarily with psychology for only a short period during his 93 years of life. He was nonetheless influential and was elected the eighth president of the American Psychological Association in 1899.*

Archives of the History of American Psychology Photographic File.

*The National Committee for the
Celebration of the Seventieth Birthday of
John Dewey
invites you to be present at a
Luncheon
at the Hotel Astor
on Saturday, the nineteenth day of October
One thousand nine hundred and twenty-nine
at one o'clock
and at the other meetings in honor of
John Dewey
as described on the following page*

Please reply on the enclosed card

Over

A 131 member committee, about 25 percent of whom were psychologists, arranged this luncheon. The other meetings to honor John Dewey that are referred to were "John Dewey and Education," "The Philosophy of John Dewey," and, "John Dewey and Social Progress"—an impressive array of birthday celebrations!

Archives of the History of American Psychology, Walter and Catharine Cox Miles Papers.

Educational Achievement

Many methods in education were developed long before the discipline of psychology was established, and, as a result, psychologists who became involved in education were more apt to be active in evaluating procedures than in formulating them. When they did suggest educational programs, they were prone to become embroiled in disagreements and to weaken their authority (Hilgard, 1987). One of the more conspicuous disputes centered around the basic function of education. John Dewey★ held that schools should prepare students to participate in a democratic society and, therefore, should focus on the activities, interests, and motivation of the pupils. Edward L. Thorndike★ held that schools should emphasize learning and, therefore, should focus on its promotion, utilizing techniques that are based on experimentally validated evaluations.

Divergent theories about the psychological basis of learning emerged as did opposing opinions about transfer—that is, the amount of aid, if any, that training

in one subject exerts on the acquisition of others. While these debates were going on, quantification became so popular that the assessment of educational skills took precedence over theory. Sporadic attempts to build standardized achievement tests were underway during the first two decades of the twentieth century, but the productivity was minimal until the third decade when, according to one estimate, the number of standardized examinations grew from 19 in 1919 to a total of 227 in 1929. On the latter date, they were available for 38 different academic subjects (DuBois, 1970).

This spurt was merely the beginning of an expansion that encompasses a large number and an extensive variety of instruments. Most achievement tests quantify either the level of knowledge about a specific topic (history, geometry, physics, etc.) or the adequacy of skills in studying and reasoning (speed and comprehension of reading, interpretation of maps, detection of flaws in logic, etc.). Both of these varieties are generally conceptualized as measures of what has been learned and differentiated from aptitude tests which are conceptualized as measures of the potential to

Leta S. Hollingworth (Ph.D., Teachers College, Columbia, 1916) was a professor of education at Teachers College, Columbia University, and the wife of Harry L. Hollingworth.★ Her extensive research includes studies of intellectually subnormal and gifted children with an emphasis on the measurement of academic skills, including the effects of curriculum changes on both "slow" and "rapid" learners (Hollingworth, 1943).

Archives of the History of American Psychology, Kathleen Rutledge Gift. Photograph by Taylor-Sargent, NYC.

In one of E. L. Thorndike's★ first efforts to quantify a scholastic skill, the examinee's handwriting is compared with these selected samples of the handwriting of children in grades five through eight to determine the one that is most like it. Thorndike asked different judges to assign each of more than 1,000 specimens of handwriting to one of several categories of merit. The value of each specimen was determined by calculating the median of the categories to which it had been assigned. The samples in the photograph are those with a value closest to the whole number for each category (Thorndike, 1910).

Archives of the History of American Psychology, Frances Perce Papers. Permission Teachers College Press.

succeed in an occupation or course of study. This difference is not, however, as clear-cut as it first appears, and research soon demonstrated a correlation between the readiness to master and actual mastery. A superior aptitude, for example, promotes the acquisition of facts, and these, in turn, heighten the potential for acquiring more of them. As a result, achievement and aptitude tests may on occasion replace one another as, for example, occurred during World War I when the military relied on "grade tests" (measures of knowledge about particular jobs) to assign recruits to positions for which they appeared to be suited. A more comprehensive assessment practice is, of course, to administer both kinds of tests.

The publication in 1916 of *Educational Measurements* by Daniel Starch (Ph.D., Iowa, 1906) accelerated the measurement of achievement by building a case for the replacement of traditional class or course examinations with "quantitative studies, objective measurements" (1916, p. 2). Starch presents data that disclose

irregularities in teachers' grades. These include divergent marks—in some instances by as many as 35 or 40 points—that different teachers assigned to the same papers. He also assembled figures that demonstrate that numerically small differences in grades, such as between 75 and 76, imply more ability to discriminate than humans possess. Starch ascribed these erraticisms both to variations in the standards that different educators hold and to variations, at different times, in the judgments of the same instructor.

Starch reviewed some standardized examinations and also presented some he had devised. The format of these instruments is generally familiar to modern readers, but some content, such as the following question, has a period flavor: "A girl watching from a window saw 27 automobiles pass a school in an hour. Each auto carried 4 lamps. How many lamps did she see in the hour?" (Starch, 1916, p. 126).

Some of the administrative and scoring techniques differed from present-day tests, and a review of some of these brings to light a few of the early technical shortcomings that have been overcome. Starch's test for

This informal photograph of Edward L. Thorndike★ and Florence Goodenough,★ two prominent figures in the testing movement, was taken at the 1937 meeting of the American Psychological Association, held in Minneapolis. Thorndike's career in psychology was extensive and varied. He was an initiator of animal *experimentation, a learning theorist, a leading educational psychologist diligent about measurement, and a skilled statistician. Florence Goodenough devised the well known Draw-A-Man Test (p. 130). Her 1949 text* Mental Testing *was one of the more comprehensive accounts of the era.*

Archives of the History of American Psychology, Melvin G. Rigg File.

measuring speed and comprehension of reading consists of a passage suitable for each grade, one through nine. The child is asked to read the test at grade level on one day and at the next lower level on the second day. The examinee would read silently and, at the end of 30 seconds, is instructed to mark the last word read, turn the paper over, and write on the back all that he/she could recall. Starch advised supplementing this examination with a test of word knowledge that he compiled by following a method in use at that time of procuring words to be defined by selecting them at regular intervals from the pages of a dictionary. This procedure yielded entries that did not appear suitable for elementary pupils, as, for example, the first three items in Starch's list: "acta, agriculturist, ambulacrum" (Starch, 1916, p. 38).

The scoring methods also varied from present-day techniques in several respects, one of which is the

failure, in some instances, to confirm the examinee's replies. To illustrate—the score for the speed of reading treats the number of words *marked* as read as the number *actually* read. Similarly, in the vocabulary test, the number of words identified as known is considered to be the number that is known.

Starch based several conclusions on the year-end scores of 6,000 pupils in 27 schools. Some are now so well accepted that they would not merit comment, but their presence in a 1916 publication indicates the kind of new information that achievement testing generated. An example is the distribution of scores at various grades. Until the advent of standardized examinations, it was assumed that there is a regular progression in proficiency with grade advancement. However, the tests showed a wider than expected range of scores at each grade as well as considerable overlap of scores between successive grades. These figures were sufficiently

During his first two postdoctoral decades, Daniel Starch★ supplemented research on conventional laboratory topics, such as the localization of sound, and learning with numerous studies in applied psychology—both in education and in industry. In 1926, he founded a firm of business consultants. From then on, his contributions were concerned mainly with the psychology of advertising and the personality of executives (Contemporary Authors).

Archives of the History of American Psychology, University of Iowa Libraries Record.

Ben D. Wood,★ a leader in the testing movement, was active in numerous projects, including the development of methods to expedite the scoring of examinations in large-scale programs (Downey, 1965). Here he is, in 1935, observing an operator running the IBM 805, the first commercially available electronic test scoring machine. This device senses pencil marks on an answer sheet and displays the total score on a dial on the console.

Archives of the History of American Psychology Photographic File, Courtesy Gary Saretzky and Educational Testing Service Archives, Princeton, N.J. Photograph copied by Randall Hagadorn.

startling to provoke plans for forming groups of homogeneous achievement levels within each grade, what would later be known as "tracking."

The adoption of achievement testing at the college level was accelerated by the publication in 1923 of *Measurement in Higher Education* by Ben Wood★ (Ph.D., Columbia, 1923). In this volume, Wood reported a research program at Columbia University that was started in 1919, initially for the purpose of evaluating the adequacy of the Thorndike Intelligence Examination for High School Graduates as a criterion for admission to college. This test was found to be acceptable, but relating the scores obtained on it to academic grades disclosed, as in the grade schools, some erraticisms. Analyses of these led to the devising of a final examination for one course. The results were so satisfactory that the program was extended to several courses and then to tests that were published. Wood ascribed the superiority of these instruments to their length and to the objectivity of scoring.

The examination contains three kinds of questions: one is True or False; another, Completion, requires writing in a missing word; and a third, Recognition, is a 1919–1923 version of the multiple-choice format, one in which the examinee underlines one word or phrase to answer questions such as the following:

> Rural isolation is made unsatisfactory by the instinct of—Gregariousness, Love, Sympathy, Imitation, Reflection
>
> Miserliness or kleptomania are abnormal exaggerations of the instinct of—Hunger, Love, Acquisitiveness, Fear

Wood, 1923, p. 181.

Louis L. Thurstone (Ph.D., Chicago, 1917) carried on research in various areas but is best known for his contributions to factor analysis, particularly the attempts to isolate and measure "primary mental abilities." His work included the construction in 1924 of the first of 24 annual editions of the Psychological Examination for High School Graduates and College Freshmen, *one of the first instruments that yielded more than one score (Hilgard, 1987).*

This is the front of an answer sheet for six separate tests that were assembled into a battery—The Engineering and Physical Science Aptitude Test—for the examination of undergraduate engineering students (Moore, Lapp, & Griffin, 1943). The scores on each of these tests are listed in a format that allows a ready comparison of the level of an examinee's aptness in Mathematics (skills in first-year college physics), Formulation (ability to convert statements into algebraic terms), Physical Science Comprehension (knowledge of physical science), Arithmetic (reasoning), Verbal Comprehension (scientific word knowledge), and Mechanical Comprehension (understanding of mechanical relationships).

The research that grew out of these early assessments of academic proficiency increased the reliability of test scores and also enhanced their precision. Normative groups were enlarged and the representativeness of the population at large improved. Examinations were constructed at extremes of the academic range and tests became available for both preschoolers and doctoral and even postdoctoral students—assessments that range from a readiness to profit from the beginning of instruction through a readiness to profit from advanced, highly specialized education. One of the more productive extensions was the combining of tests of different subjects into a battery with specifications of a composite score as well as one

for each test. This array has the merit of permitting two kinds of evaluations: one compares the overall ranking of examinee with peers, and the second indicates the areas in which the examinee is the most and the least competent. Once initiated, this arrangement was in common and, generally, continuous use in achievement testing and was neither as delayed nor intermittent as it was in tests of intelligence and personality.

The military forces included achievement tests among the numerous examinations they used during World War II, and these served several purposes,

including the somewhat unusual one of helping to regulate instruction. The navy was confronted with so much variation in the skills, as recruits were taught at different training schools, that it became difficult to judge the actual competency of an individual sailor. One remedy was the devising of an achievement testing program as a means of specifying both what instructors should teach and what the students should learn. One of the noticeable differences between this and more traditional curriculum guides was a stress on work-related procedures (Ryans, 1947). The practicality was well received and credited with increased on-the-job efficiency (Porter & Harsh, 1947).

One of the strongest impacts of the achievement testing program was the compilation, beginning in 1942, of the General Educational Development Tests (GED). These were intended originally to assess the educational level that military personnel achieve from various sources, including training programs as well as

self-initiated reading. There are two levels of the tests: one measures proficiency through high school and the second through the first two years of college. The former received a much wider application, and it consists of five sections: general mathematics; the interpretation of reading in the natural sciences and social studies, as well as literary materials; and what was called correctness and effectiveness of expression—that is, proficiency in spelling, as well as the ability to detect errors in capitalization, word order, tense, and sentence structure. Success on the battery gained acceptance in numerous school systems as the equivalent of attainment of a civilian high school education. A 1954 survey of 1,000 secondary schools and 200 colleges indicated that 86% of the high schools were issuing equivalency certificates. "Several hundred business firms" were also accepting them as job applicant's qualifications (American Council on Education, 1956, p. 8).

PART

3

Maturity

–

Third Quarter of
the Twentieth Century

The gains that have been described up to this point are antecedents of a modification that emerged about the middle of the present century as a move away from a concentration on responses that are partitioned artificially for research purposes toward a concentration on intact clusters. Probably the most outstanding example of this progression is the shift away from the study of separate topics such as learning, memory, and perception to cognition, the simultaneous functioning of all these reactions. These changes ushered in numerous investigations of various kinds of integrated behavior, with most so complex that they demanded some relaxation of the entrenched subservience to methodological flawlessness. They also underlined a striking change from the earlier focus on dissections of the substratum of psychology—for example, the breakdown of hearing into pitch, loudness, volume, and timbre—to syntheses of psychological phenomena—for example, the integration of what is heard with such factors as the appreciation of the clarity of the message, the recognition of its power and veracity, as well as the actions that it provokes. Because these probes are much more intricate and relevant to behavior in extralaboratory contexts than previous ones, we refer to this period as the Era of Maturity. We have been unable to discern any displacement of this maturity, and, therefore, refrain from speculating about either the date of termination of the epoch or the nature of its replacement. We also prefer to sustain the historical purpose of this volume and, except for a few references to single experiments and several recent historical papers, we do not deal with publications after 1975, the 100th anniversary of Wundt's appointment at the University of Leipzig.

Once we had outlined the time frame for the last interval, we looked again at the milieu in which the maturity thrived for additional themes and found a dramatic increase in the number of psychologists and the fields in which they specialize. This proliferation was extensive, but the diversity of tasks that psychologists took on was more obvious than any single undertaking, and this plurality survived in spite of the entrance of a disproportionately large number of psychologists into the service sectors. Psychology remained multiform even when most psychologists were practitioners.

The immediate task is to review events during this Era of Maturity. We introduce at this point some illustrations of the broadened scope of psychology.

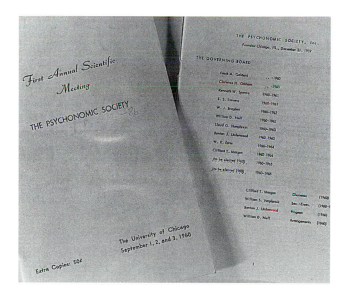

In 1892, there was only one important American publication for scientific psychology, The American Journal of Psychology, *but 100 years later at least 284 English language periodicals report psychological research (American Psychological Association, 1990).*

The Psychonomic Society, represented in this photograph, held its "First Annual Scientific Meeting" in 1959, the year after its organization (Hilgard, 1987). Today, the Psychonomic Society publishes six periodicals devoted to experimental psychology. The Governing Board in 1960: Brogden (Ph.D., Illinois, 1936), Estes (Ph.D., Minnesota, 1943), Geldard (Ph.D., Clark, 1928), Graham (Ph.D., Clark, 1930), Humphreys (Ph.D., Stanford, 1938), Morgan (Ph.D., Rochester, 1939), Neff (Ph.D., Rochester, 1940), Spence (Ph.D., Yale, 1933), Stevens (Ph.D., Harvard, 1933), Underwood (Ph.D., Iowa, 1942), and Verplanck (Ph.D., Brown, 1941).

Archives of the History of American Psychology, William S. Verplanck Papers.

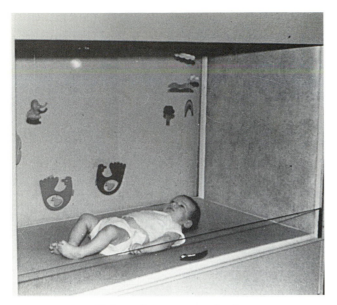

The "air crib" or "baby tender" is an example of an increasing involvement with everyday matters. The prototype for this crib was built in the early 1940s by B. F. Skinner* as both a labor-saving device and an improvement over a conventional crib because it provides a clean, quiet, physically safe, comfortable space. The air is heated, filtered, maintained at a constant temperature, monitored, and warm enough to make any blanket and clothing other than a diaper unnecessary. This allows an infant more than the usual amount of freedom to turn over, kick, and reach. It also eliminates the danger of smothering or strangling. Attempts to manufacture the crib were not successful commercially, but it is estimated that hundreds of babies have been raised in replicas built by enterprising parents. This family friendly refuge was misrepresented (intentionally?) as a place of confinement and isolation in folklore critical of "bringing up baby in a box" (Skinner, 1979).

Archives of the History of American Psychology, Anonymous Gift.

This "Dove of Peace," with an olive branch in its mouth, is the central image on this foot-square broadsheet or poster. A "Vietnam Moratorium," in the language of the time, referred to a stoppage of ordinary activity, such as holding class, for a "teach-in" or some other form of protest against the American presence in the war in Southeast Asia.

The particular focus of the moratorium of October 15–16, 1965, is largely forgotten, but many Americans, and many psychologists, felt very deeply about the events of the Vietnam War.

Archives of the History of American Psychology, William S. Verplanck Papers.

Many psychologists were concerned with the problem of segregation. The United States Supreme Court case Brown v. Board of Education that ended the legality of segregation in schools is reputed to be the first to take into account research in the social sciences. Justice Warren wrote, "Whatever may have been the extent of psychological knowledge at the time of Plessy v. Ferguson [doctrine of separate but equal, 1896], this finding is amply supported by modern authority" (Brown v. Board of Education, 1954, p. 494). The "modern authority" is identified in a footnote as a series of references to research by social scientists.

Archives of the History of American Psychology, H. Rogie Rogosin Papers.

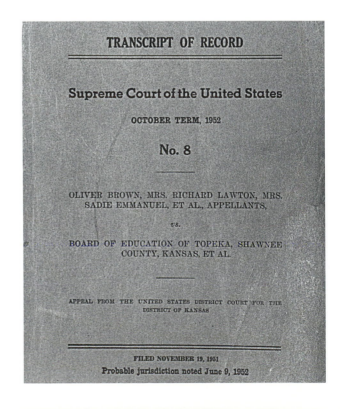

Children: Black & White
by Henry E. Garrett, Ph.D.,Sc.D.

The Court also possessed this Appendix to the Appellants' Briefs, a paper on "The Effects of Segregation and the Consequences of Desegregation: A Social Science Statement." In 1952, Isidor Chein (Ph.D., Columbia, 1939), Kenneth B. Clark,★ and Stuart W. Cook (Ph.D., Minnesota, 1938) drafted this paper, signed by 32 scholars, 20 (63 percent) of whom are psychologists. The psychologists included Floyd H. Allport,★ Gordon W. Allport,★ Jerome S. Bruner (Ph.D., Harvard, 1941), Hadley Cantril (Ph.D., Harvard, 1931), Mamie P. Clark (Ph.D., Columbia, 1943), Bingham Dai (Ph.D., Chicago, 1937), Else Frenkel-Brunswik,★ Daniel Katz (Ph.D., Syracuse, 1928), Otto Klineberg (M.D., McGill, 1925; Ph.D., Columbia, 1927), David Krech,★ Alfred McClung Lee (Ph.D., Yale, 1933), Gardner Murphy,★ Theodore M. Newcomb (Ph.D., Columbia, 1929), Gerhart Saenger (Ph.D., Basel, 1935), R. Nevitt Sanford (Ph.D., Harvard, 1934), S. Stansfeld Sargent (Ph.D., Columbia, 1940), and M. Brewster Smith.★

Archives of the History of American Psychology, H. Rogie Rogosin Papers.

Not all psychologists agreed with the "Social Science Statement." This undated pamphlet, circulated in the early 1970s, offered opposition to desegregation. The author, Henry E. Garrett★ (Ph.D., Columbia, 1923), was a faculty member in the department of psychology at Columbia for 33 years, serving as chair from 1940 until retirement in 1956. In 1946, he served as the 54th president of APA, and during his career he received other honors and recognition. He argued that black Americans are innately—that is, biologically—inferior in intelligence to white Americans and he advocated "separate schools for Negroes and Whites" (p. 30).

Archives of the History of American Psychology, Charles Musser Record.

Henry E. Garrett★ received strong rebuttals from various disciplines. In fact, the Charlottesville Daily Progress *finally declared the debate interminable and closed their* Your Right to Say It *column to the topic.*

This letter to the editor is typical of responses to Garrett, but it is particularly poignant since it was written by faculty members in the department of psychology at the University of Virginia where Garrett, then retired from Columbia University, was serving as Visiting Professor of Educational Psychology.

The signatories are William F. Battig (Ph.D., Wisconsin, 1955), George N. Gerken (Ph.D., Chicago, 1959), John F. Hahn (Ph.D., Chicago, 1952), and L. Starling Reid (Ph.D., Ohio State, 1949).

Archives of the History of American Psychology, William F. Battig Papers. Permission Charlottesville Daily Progress.

From the testimony of Kenneth B. Clark (Ph.D., Columbia, 1940) in Richmond:

> We have developed and used extensively a method of dolls, wherein we present to our children two dolls that are absolutely identical in every respect except skin color. . . . We ask these children certain questions about these dolls. . . . such as 'Which doll do you like best? Which doll is a nice doll? . . . Which doll is like you?' . . . telling us not only how this child reacts to himself but how he reacts to himself in terms of the personal problem of the factor of race. (Davis v. County School Board, 1952, pp. 248–249.)

Archives of the History of American Psychology, Presidential Portraits Series, Kenneth B. Clark Gift.

This picture illustrated a 1952 newspaper story, "Four Experts, in U.S. Court Here, Score Segregation in Schools," in the Richmond Times-Dispatch. *The photograph was captioned, "Social scientists testify in Prince Edward County School Segregation Case. From left, Dr. Isidor Chein,★ Dr. M. Bruster [sic] Smith,★ and Dr. John J. Brooks [an educator]." Kenneth B. Clark★ is the fourth expert who spoke against segregation. Henry E. Garrett★ spoke in favor of segregation.*

This particular case was Dorothy E. Davis et al., Appellants v. County School Board of Prince Edward County, Virginia et al. *It was combined with three other cases and appealed to the Supreme Court as* Brown v. Board of Education of Topeka.

Archives of the History of American Psychology, William F. Battig Papers. Permission Richmond Times-Dispatch. Originally published February 27, 1952.

7

CHAPTER

Some Byproducts of Technology

The unparalleled advances in the physical sciences during the last half of the present century have contributed significantly to advances in psychology, and the equipment that processes quantities of information at high speeds has probably had more effect than any other engineering accomplishment. Progress in this sphere started as early as 1890 when an electromechanical sorting device was devised. This was followed, but only intermittently, by other pieces of congenial apparatus; it was not until the 1950s that self-regulating electronic processors became available (Fleck, 1973). This capability induced changes in the ways in which psychologists viewed their field. There were few, if any, new entries in the subject matter ledger, but there were revisions and fresh perspectives, and many of these were formulated in relation to cognitive psychology.

Cognition is a concept that psychology inherited from philosophy where it had been designated as one of the three categories of the mind: cognition, conation (striving), and affection (feeling). Cognition was conceptualized as a number of different rational responses, for example, perceiving, judging, reasoning, and thinking. But neither the breadth nor the longevity of the concept induced popularity in research prior to the gains in electronics. This limited productivity was originally the result of a conviction that the then so-called higher mental processes are too transient and too complicated to be brought under experimental control. These restraints gained even more force in the 1910s when behaviorism repudiated all mental processes and thereby relegated research on cognition to those responses that can be reported verbally or that have readily observable overt components. This meant, in practice, that experiments pertinent to cognition were generally restricted to perceiving, learning, and memory.

Keen interest in cognitive responses began to develop in the 1950s when behaviorism's "artificial," "dehumanizing" approach was faulted. One of the first indications that psychologists were becoming involved in this issue was their increased use of the word *cognitive* as a modifier—for example, *cognitive dissonance* was coined to designate the reactions that occur when contradictory information is encountered (Festinger, 1957). Gradually, the practice spread, and psychologists recommended modification of the names of numerous psychological concepts—for example, replacement of the term *ability* with *cognitive ability* and *discrimination* with *cognitive discrimination* (Kinkade, 1974).

The acknowledgement of cognition was transformed into fascination when the engineering achievements in data processing demonstrated that a focus on processing per se was fruitful. For some theorists, this orientation had the additional merit of bypassing the failure to discover the biological basis of cognition. As a result, many psychologists adopted electronic data processing, the performance of equipment, as a model or metaphor for the performance of living organisms. Analogies between inanimate and animate functioning began to circulate. A few terms customarily applied to organic phenomena were applied to inorganic referents—machines, for example, were said to be endowed with memory and afflicted with viruses. Several words previously used to describe inorganic subject matter were also related to organic events; psychologists began to employ previously alien words such as display, filter, input, message, program, resource, allocation, retrieval, screen, stage, and storage.

Electronic processing is an active phenomenon and adopting this perspective in psychology helped to change the emphasis on the role of a person from recipient of stimulation to interpreter and organizer. This orientation called attention to covert tactics that had previously been slighted, such as the way subjects comprehend and how they identify the meaning of stimuli. This interest led to explanations of additional linkages, both among responses and between stimuli and responses. To illustrate—the longstanding idea that the amount that a person remembers depends on the associative strength of what he/she memorizes was questioned as a result of demonstrations that the amount varies with how the person organizes the material when memorizing it (Tulving & Thomson, 1973). Interest was also aroused in the ways imagery facilitates the forming of associations (Pate & Newsom, 1983) and in the way the simultaneous presentation of stimuli interferes with their recognition (Duncan, 1980).

The study of implicit maneuvering became so popular that it was investigated even in subjects who do not have speech—the customary source of information about reactions that are not manifest overtly. Since these reactions cannot be observed directly, they must be inferred, and modern experimenters appear more willing than their immediately past predecessors to make such inferences. This readiness is illustrated in the use of visual behavior as an indication of the nature of an infant's psychological reactions. A baby shifting its eyes back and forth from one object to another came to be taken as a demonstration that the infant is *comparing* the objects, but visual fixations per se are construed as evidence of *discrimination* and/or the *perception* of various stimulus attributes, such as novelty, similarity, and coherence (Bertenthal, Proffitt, Kramer, & Spetner, 1987; Kellman & Spelke, 1983; Meltzoff & Borton, 1979). Interpretations of this nature are replacing the earlier opinion that infantile comprehension consists only of fragmented experiences that are gradually combined experientially with the belief that children quite quickly come to perceive their surroundings as somewhat stable and coherent (Mandler, 1990).

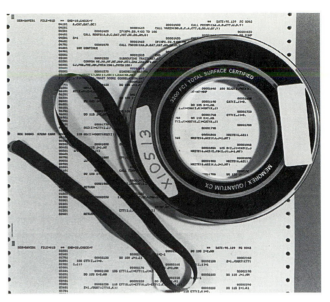

This tape represents a startling increase in efficiency over the calculation sheets, also from the Adkins collection, shown on page 84. A printout dated 90.129 indicates that the tape contains a program for "partialing item—trait characteristics."
Archives of the History of American Psychology, Dorothy C. Adkins Papers.

The research on cognitive functioning in animals commonly relies on operant conditioned responses as behavioral evidence of covert activity. For example, pigeons are presented with different sequences of stimuli, such as exposure to a red light followed first by a delay interval and then by a second light, and reinforced when the latter is the same as the original (red light) but not reinforced when it is different (green light). The complexity of the stimulation is increased by adding horizontal and vertical lines, tones of different frequencies, or variations in the duration of the delay interval. The stimulus patterns that facilitate mastery are seen as disclosing the importance to the pigeon of particular sensory cues as well as the difficulty of learning single and combined stimuli (Bowers & Richards, 1990). The discussions of these laboratory results refer to attention, even divided attention, memory and "prospective processing"—an astounding contrast with the objectivity of the customary terminology of the behaviorists.

Although experimental designs that are based on analogies are welcomed by many psychologists, they also draw fire. The critics point to differences between machines and living organisms. They observe that computer memory is intentionally activated and terminated, but the memory of an organism is activated variously and falters, fails, and succeeds unpredictably. They note that equipment adheres without deviation to a program whereas thinking is selective and flexible. Technicians have not been able to program this variability; they have yet to learn, for example, how to replicate the compensations that humans make for

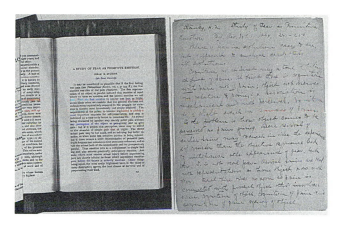

Prior to the invention of rapid, inexpensive techniques for duplicating documents, scholars could acquire professional literature by purchasing it, obtaining a reprint from the authors, taking handwritten notes (usually in a library reading room), or making typewritten copies, a tedious process. G. Stanley Hall★ took these written notes on an unspecified date from an article in the Psychological Review, *1894.*

Archives of the History of American Psychology, G. Stanley Hall Documents.

This is the first page of a 23-page, single-spaced typescript. It falls short of being an exact copy. Neither the typist nor the date of the typing is indicated.

Archives of the History of American Psychology, David Shakow Papers.

limited information or the techniques they use to predict differential outcomes (Denning, 1986; Estes, 1980; Henle, 1962).

Some theorists see analogies as a step away from direct contacts with the topic under investigation (Kantor, 1971; Skinner, 1984). These critics argue that direct observations are responsible for impressive advances in science, such as the increase in knowledge that came when anatomists were allowed to work with cadavers, when oceanographers were able to explore the ocean floor, and when biologists were able to see microscopic phenomena. Simulations, in contrast, must be evaluated indirectly—by inferences, such as the

suppositions noted just a little earlier in the discussions of infant and animal research, or by comparisons between predicted and actual measurements (Posner & Mitchell, 1967). Only an oracle could disclose the outcome of these arguments, but many psychologists began to deal with responses that are important even though the experimental treatment is based on reaching for, rather than an actual achievement of, methodological precision and interpretative caution.

Although the impact of modern technology on psychology seems to be concentrated in research on cognitive psychology, it also extends to the use of self-regulating machines for both assessment and

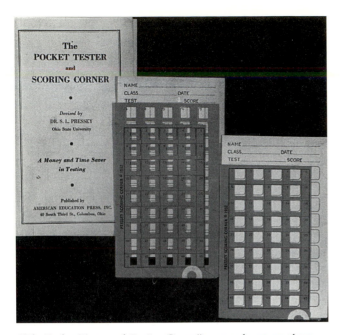

"The Pocket Tester and Scoring Corner"—an early answer sheet. This "answer card" allows the recording of responses to 100 questions (45 on front and 55 on back). Devised by Sidney L. Pressey★ to save paper as well as time and labor in scoring examinations (Pressey, 1932), the answer card was also innovative because the same test blanks could be reused. Each answer card is 3"× 5" and can easily be slipped into a coat pocket or filed in a standard size drawer, thus eliminating the need to copy the test results. For each question, the examinee writes either T(rue) or F(alse) or, if alternatives are present, the letter of the correct alternative. The card is slipped into a "Scoring Corner," a cardboard frame solid on both the bottom and the left side so that it can be held in a fixed position. The corner bears the correct letters and the examiner needs merely to mark and count the incorrect responses.

Archives of the History of American Psychology, Morris S. Viteles Papers. Courtesy of Ohio State University Archives.

This piece differs from the other machines that Sidney Pressey★ constructed in that it has five rather than four keys. It was used in a dissertation completed at Ohio State University (Little, 1934) in which mastery of a course in educational psychology was compared among groups of students learning under various conditions. The machine exposes a new question only after a correct choice is made. It also tallies the total number of responses. Students can repeat the entire series of questions until answering each without error. A final course examination indicated that this method was superior to both conventional classroom instruction and to a procedure in which the instructor discussed topics pertinent to questions frequently failed.

Archives of the History of American Psychology, Ohio State University Collection.

instructional purposes. One of the first steps in the alignment of machinery and applied psychology predated the Era of Maturity. It was taken by Sidney L. Pressey★ (Ph.D., Harvard, 1917), a psychologist who devoted much of his career to discovering ways of reducing the labor of administering and scoring tests. He displayed a machine he had constructed at the 1924 meeting of the American Psychological Association and a second mechanically improved one at the 1925 meeting. Both of these instruments could be used either for testing or for teaching. They exposed a series of questions in an aperture of a drum and the subject recorded the answer to each by pressing a key that corresponded to the alternative that was believed to be correct. When the machine was serving as an examination, a count of the correct number of choices was made, but when the machine was serving as a "mechanical instructor," it informed the learner

immediately about the accuracy of the reply inasmuch as a correct selection was followed by the exposure of another question and an incorrect one left the drum motionless. The facilitation of learning by promptly delivered information about accuracy was augmented by the release of a piece of candy when the number of correct responses equaled a number that the experimenter had set. The machine also provided opportunities for practice in that all the questions could be repeated again and again.

Pressey constructed other machines and modified them in various ways (Pressey, 1926, 1967), but most of the interest in the instrumental support of learning at that time came from Pressey and his graduate students. The reasons for this limit are obscured, but probably important among them was the economic climate of the depression and the surplus of teachers (Benjamin, 1988).

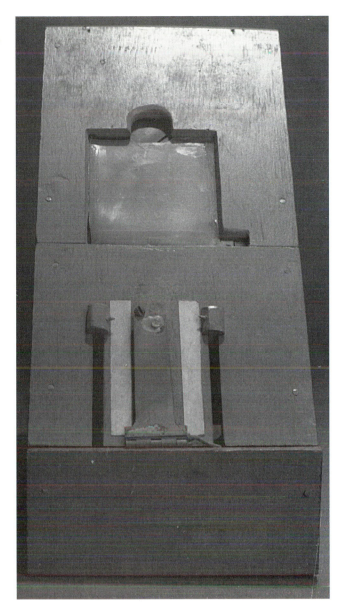

B. F. Skinner's★ *inscription on the back of this equipment is "1st T.M." This teaching machine, built in 1953, was prompted by Skinner's dissatisfaction with the instruction he observed while visiting his daughter's fourth-grade arithmetic class. He was at the time unaware of Pressey's machines. In this initial device, a problem in arithmetic is placed in the square at the top. By moving levers at the bottom, the student can expose a two-digit number in the smaller square above. Pressing the brass strip between the levers causes a light above the problem to flash if the answer is correct.*

Archives of the History of American Psychology, B. F. Skinner Gift. Identification with the help of B. F. Skinner.

The dilution of interest turned out to be merely a hiatus inasmuch as B. F. Skinner,★ the master of operant conditioning, in 1953 devised the first in a series of machines that he programmed to accelerate learning in accord with the principles of operant behaviorism. Skinner's inventions differ from Pressey's in at least three respects. First, they emphasize new material while

Pressey's dealt with subject matter to which the student had previously been exposed. Second, the Skinner technique demands that the learner construct answers, whereas the earlier procedure demanded only the choice of an answer. Third, while Pressey's information varied in scope, Skinner machines present at any one time only specific, fragmented bits of information. If the material demands more than rote learning, the units are presented in a step-by-step format so that they accrete into coherent, even abstract, knowledge.

During the 1960s, the Skinner machine caught the attention of psychologists, educators, and journalists. Personnel involved in education took them seriously, some suggesting that they constructively supported teachers and others making fearful predictions that teachers would be replaced. Some believed that the technology was impersonal, and was not educating students but training them to act as robots.

For elusive reasons, teaching machines dropped in popularity, and, by the 1970s, their function had been taken over in some circles by computer-assisted instruction and by microcomputers (Benjamin, 1988). The impact and fate of these most recent versions of technological aids to education are beyond the scope of this volume. In fact, many resemble teaching machines only because they are mechanized. They are dissimilar because they lack the systematic, prearranged, and controlled reinforcement of what is to be learned (Atkinson, 1968).

Automatic devices have also been adapted to the administration, scoring, and interpretation of psychological examinations. Computers are used to present test items, identify the accuracy or inaccuracy of the replies, tally both sub- and total scores, convert raw to scaled scores, compute IQs as well as similar measures, and indicate the sections of a test on which the scores are significantly discrepant. When large numbers of examinations are processed, the savings in personnel time can be substantial. These computerized operations do not make computational errors and they have an additional advantage in that, unlike humans, they do not have lapses in memory or attention, and, thus, they do not inadvertently overlook details that should be taken into account (Fowler & Butcher, 1986).

There are, however, some important differences between personal and impersonal reports. The latter are restricted to quantified scores, and as yet they do not have the capability of integrating singular, idiosyncratic items. In other words, automated reports present a series of statements that are based on probabilities. These constraints contrast with the scope and flexibility of a well-trained, experienced examiner. A human interpreter is able to deal with unique behavior, to relate demeanor during the examination to the manner in which the test content is handled, to integrate all

Improvements in biochemical techniques contributed to the design of this experimental cage. The efforts to relate changes in brain anatomy and physiology to behavior met with some success in the 1950s when technical advances made it possible to discover small but stable changes in the cortex. The investigators responsible for this research represent various disciplines and among them are two psychologists: David Krech★ (Ph.D., California, 1933) and Mark R. Rosenzweig (Ph.D., Harvard, 1949). These researchers discovered increases in enzyme activity and in cortical weight and thickness in the brains of rats following certain psychological experiences. The most effective of these experiences consisted of being caged, generally for a period of at least 30 days, with other rats in an enclosure similar to the one in this picture. The animals must have at least moderate periods of exposure to and must interact with the objects. Many nuances of both the sources and nature of the brain modifications have yet to be delineated, but the experiment made the task of understanding appear attainable (Rosenzweig, Bennett, & Diamond, 1972).

Archives of the History of American Psychology, David Krech Collection.

these observations with the examinee's life history, and to assess the conclusions by reference to the strength of the research substantiation. This is a complicated process, an interpretive exercise, and the psychologist stamps the report with his/her credentials by signing it.

This openness contrasts with the customary failures of computers to identify either the personnel responsible for their accounts or the validity of the interpretations that are contained in the reports (Matarazzo, 1986). The latter are nonetheless written in impressive style. Indications of their packaged, technological sources are minimal, and repetitiveness is reduced by phrasing the same or similar conclusions in different ways (O'Dell, 1972). They often contain "Barnum effect" statements—that is, they state what is true of everyone. To illustrate—"At times she fails to show consideration of others," "He is capable of becoming angry." Items of this nature are obviously

accurate and cannot be faulted on that basis, but for the purposes of clinical assessment they are "pseudo-successful" (Meehl, 1956, p. 266).

Computer-originated reports may be constructive when they are explained to the examinee by personnel trained in psychology, experts who understand the limitations of tests and who are familiar with the differing amounts of experimental support of various inferences. Unfortunately, machine-generated accounts may be delivered to professionals who are educated in disciplines other than psychology, and, under these circumstances, the best interests of examinees may not be served. As early as 1966, the American Psychological Association began to issue warnings about these shortcomings (Newman, 1966), but the advice is not yet in control and some of the electronic-dependent psychological service currently offered is not maximally beneficial.

8

C H A P T E R

Experimental Excursions into Psychological Reality

The improvements in instrumentation that occurred during the Era of Maturity were augmented by experiments designed to approximate commonplace responses more closely than those previously in use. Once again the productivity of psychology blocks a comprehensive review and forces the use of illustrations to call attention to these gains in realism. Following are descriptions of five investigations that feature different kinds of extralaboratory authenticity: one uses dynamic, multidimensional physical stimuli; a second measures over a 50-year period; a third observes intricate emotional responses both within and between generations; a fourth scrutinizes the anomalous reactions of members of a religious cult; and the fifth deals with the enigma of suspending moral judgments so as to comply with authority.

The first of these examples relies on a visual field that stimulates everyday conditions. The equipment was devised for a series of experiments that were carried out at Cornell University (Gibson & Walk, 1960). Eleanor J. Gibson (Ph.D., Yale, 1938), the central figure in this work, investigated the role that experience plays in the depth perception of human infants as well as of a variety of both young and adult animals including chickens, dogs, kittens, kids, lambs, rats, pigs, and turtles. The laboratory equipment, a visual cliff, consists of a flat surface painted like a checkerboard. On top of this rests a thick, level sheet made of glass, one section of which rests directly on the board and another is suspended a foot or more above the floor. The visual cues from the plaid are varied so that they resemble changes that occur as the rate and motion of the perceiver and the distance from the viewed object changes. Subjects are usually placed above the board and observations are made of their approach to the section above the floor. They disclose a strong dependence on vision and—in the case of human babies—a resistance to crossing the deep side even when they pat the glass and apparently sense it to be solid. Gibson concluded that human infants probably discriminate depth by the time they are able to crawl and before they acquire the motor ability to keep from falling, whereas young animals probably discriminate depth as soon as they are mobile.

Examples of intricate visual equipment: A monocular distorted room. The actual proportions of this room are shown in the sketch at the right and the way it is perceived is shown in the photograph at the bottom. The back wall recedes so that the right-hand corner is almost twice as far from the viewer (or the camera) as the left-hand corner. The ceiling is higher on the left than on the right. In spite of these irregularities, the area, when viewed with one eye, appears as it does in the photograph to be an ordinary room, although the two individuals appear to vary in size.

One explanation holds that people are so accustomed to regularity in an enclosed space that they may not perceive distortions in a room, but they may perceive irregularities in what is in the room. In this instance, the psychologist at the left, Ross Stagner (Ph.D., Wisconsin, 1932), seems to be smaller than the psychologist at the right, Edwin D. Lawson (Ph.D., Illinois, 1954). These distortions are facilitated by common knowledge that people do vary in size and by the fact that the image at the left is smaller than what is expected at that apparent distance.

Adalbert Ames, Jr., an attorney and painter, constructed this room. When functioning in the latter capacity, Ames became interested in what was called transactualism—the effects of experience upon vision—and he devised various ways of demonstrating just what is and is not seen (Ittelson, 1952). Psychologists, long interested in illusions, did not have access to large, intricate demonstrations until the relatively recent past and, thus, much of the early research was based on drawings and photographs.

Archives of the History of American Psychology Literature Collection, Paul T. Young Papers. Courtesy Ross Stagner and Edwin D. Lawson.

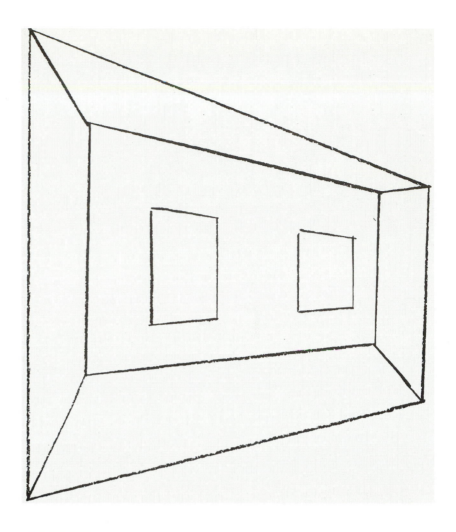

Examples of intricate visual equipment: a room that may be tilted. This photograph and the one below show two pieces of apparatus that Herman Witkin (Ph.D., New York, 1939), with the assistance of several collaborators, used in a series of experiments that began with studies of the perception of the upright. The researchers discovered that some people rely more on visual cues and some more on postural ones. The former are described as "field dependent" and the latter as "field independent." The preference for particular cues suggested that personality plays a role in the perception of space and alerted the research team to examine the differences between the responses of field dependent and field independent individuals to a number of different kinds of stimuli. These experiments disclosed numerous differences including variations in cognitive style, sensitivity to social cues, and tendency to assertiveness (Witkin, Lewis, Hertzman, Machover, Meissner, & Wapner, 1972), but not all the conclusions have been confirmed (Kurtz, 1969; Wachtel, 1972).

Archives of the History of American Psychology, S. Howard Bartley Papers.

A chair that may also be tilted inside the tilting room. The occupant may experience changes in both the position of the room and the chair.

Archives of the History of American Psychology, Cecil and Helene Mann Gift. Permission of Jefferson A. Sulzer and Department of Psychology, Tulane University.

Psychologists studied memory only over brief intervals until the mid-1970s when Harry P. Bahrick (Ph.D., Ohio State, 1950) determined the amount of material that is retained for five decades. He measured the retention of names and faces (Bahrick, Bahrick, & Wittlinger, 1975), the recall of a cognitive map of a city (Bahrick, 1983), and the retention of Spanish learned in a classroom (Bahrick, 1984). Data that cover such protracted periods are distorted by more than the usual methodological irregularities, and the measurement of Spanish may well have been deflected by changes in teaching methods, inflation of school grades, and differences among students' attracted to coursework in Spanish. These distortions are probably also compounded by errors that subjects make when they retrieve from their remote past the number of courses taken, completion dates, and grades.

Bahrick relied on large numbers of subjects and statistical analyses to control, or at least to monitor, contaminants. Examinations covering Spanish vocabulary, grammar, word order, and idioms were given to 733 subjects who had enrolled in formal classes and to an additional 40 who had had no instruction and who, thus, provided information about the amount of Spanish that is casually acquired or is a product of guesses on the test. The subjects were separated into groups representing different amounts of coursework as well as different intervals since enrollment.

Bahrick's method of measuring the errors in the subjects' accounts of their academic history illustrates one of the ways he estimated the extent to which the experimental results may have been skewed. It was possible to obtain school records for 14% of the sample, and these disclosed that 81% of these subjects reported the number of courses they had taken accurately, that 78% of the marks that were reported were correct, and that there was a tendency to overestimate rather than underestimate grades.

In spite of some vagaries, there is enough consistency in the results as a whole to command attention. First, several findings agree with well-established experimental results. To illustrate—the recognition of what is learned is, over the decades as well as during shorter intervals, superior to the recall of what is learned. Further, the amount that is remembered appears to be the highest among subjects who have the most instruction and earn the best grades.

The new information about memory is in the long term curve of forgetting. The amount people remember declines during the first five or six years after learning, then stabilizes for up to 30 years, and then the amount again declines. These results have provoked

Jean Piaget (Ph.D., Neuchatel, 1918), an explorer of the complex cognitive world of the normal child. Piaget's doctorate is in biology but his postdoctoral education and professional appointments are in psychology with a concentration in child development. Piaget's first publication was written when he was 10 years old. A native and resident of Switzerland, he enjoyed an international reputation and his writings are widely translated.

Piaget has concentrated on the development of thinking in children, tracing stages from early animism to logic. His first publications coincided with the rise of behaviorism and, because of his non-behavioral emphasis, he received only limited attention. The amount of attention began to change with the rise of cognitive psychology and its respect for complex, implicit responses. Although Piaget modified and refined his ideas during the course of his career, his elevation to the status of a leading theorist may be due more to a change in the intellectual climate than to revisions of his theory (Hilgard, 1987).

Archives of the History of American Psychology, Gardner and Lois Barclay Murphy Papers. Photograph by Lois Barclay Murphy.

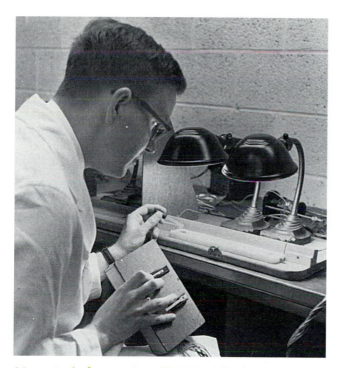

Memory in the flatworm. James V. McConnell (Ph.D., Texas, 1956) was interested in a variety of aspects of psychology. He was a master teacher, receiving the Distinguished Contribution to Education in Psychology Award from the American Psychological Foundation in 1976. Here he demonstrates the classical conditioning of a planarian, a flat worm that, when mutilated, regenerates parts of its body. Planarians do not at first react to a light flash, but do react after the light has been paired repetitively with discharges of electricity into the water. McConnell found that conditioning required fewer pairings in planarians fed bits of a previously conditioned planarian and in planarians with regenerated heads. These results startled many traditional, orthodox scientists (Dewsbury, 1991).

Archives of the History of American Psychology, James V. McConnell Papers.

questions as to why the curve takes this form, but it does not appear to be strongly influenced by opportunities to rehearse. Various explanations are proposed (Neisser, 1984).

What is particularly noteworthy for this discussion is Bahrick's safari into a complicated and methodologically perplexing arena. Although the age span of these data is impressive, it falls short of observing the entire memory span in that subjects still retain an impressive amount of Spanish at the end of 50 years.

A research program on some cognitive and emotional reactions of monkeys, in progress for at least 40 years at the University of Wisconsin under the direction of Harry F. Harlow (Ph.D., Stanford, 1930), succeeded in manipulating animal contacts both within

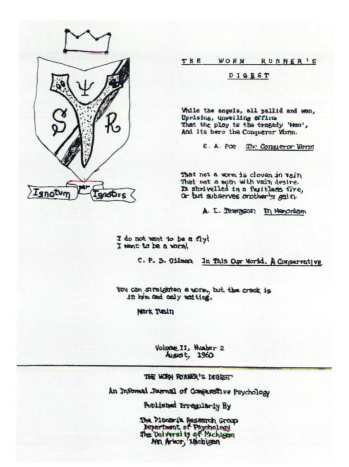

The Worm Runner's Digest was introduced by James V. McConnell in 1959 as a simple, dittoed pamphlet, but after 1967, it became The Journal of Biological Psychology/The Worm Runner's Digest, *a more polished, professionally produced publication. The magazine was titled* The Journal of Biological Psychology *and its cover was followed by serious, scientific matter. Turning the magazine over and upside down exposed the cover of* The Worm Runner's Digest, *followed by less formal material, parodies, satire, and cartoons. The last issue appeared in 1979. The stationery for the two journals was similarly adaptable. A single sheet of paper had the letterhead for* The Worm Runner's Digest *at one end and the letterhead of* The Journal of Biological Psychology *at the other end. The purpose of the letter determined which heading was at the top (Dewsbury, 1991).*

Archives of the History of American Psychology, James V. McConnell Papers.

and between generations in ways that are psychologically intricate; effective in altering behavior; and informative about the precursors, consequences, and treatment of behaviorally caused psychological problems (Harlow, Harlow, & Suomi, 1971). The enterprise *started* as an investigation of learning in monkeys, one that included a study of the mal-effects of

The coat of arms of The Worm Runner's Digest *is surely unrecognized by any college of heralds. The initials* S *and* R *represent the commonplace paradigm of "stimulus-response." The Greek letter* Ψ *(PSI) is a frequently used symbol for psychology. The two-headed worm, looking downwards, represents a planarian. The Latin motto "Ignotum per Ignotius" is a cold warning about trying to clarify the unexplained by means of something even less clearly understood. The "coronet" over the shield represents the "cell-assembly" or "alternating" reverberation suggested by Donald O. Hebb (Ph.D., Harvard, 1936) as the basic unit of perception and thought (Hebb, 1949).*

Archives of the History of American Psychology, James V. McConnell Papers.

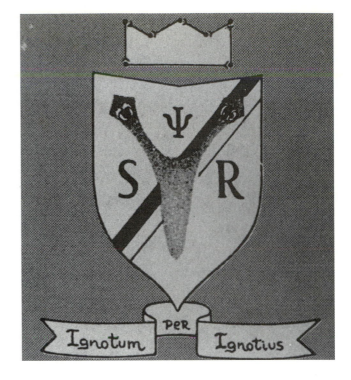

cortical lesions. Since it was essential to distinguish the errors that come from these disorders from erraticisms that occur in normal growth, it became necessary to chart the development of the ability of monkeys to perform various tasks. This goal led to the establishing of an animal colony in which the young were, for reasons of cleanliness, raised in individual cages and cared for by humans. These practical measures produced infants that displayed unrelenting attachments to cloth that was intended to be worn as diapers. They persisted in keeping pieces on their heads and grasping and fondling them.

This attachment prompted a study of whether infant monkeys have a stronger preference for gratification of nutritional or of tactual needs. In order to determine this, Harlow devised two so-called surrogate mothers, one built of wire but providing milk and one built of soft fabric but not delivering milk. The results disclosed, as expected, that the infants spent more time in contact with the cushiony mother than with the hard substitute, but also, as was not expected, that the absence of this soft surrogate provoked intense reactions, ones that resembled terror.

These outbursts prompted a series of experiments to evaluate the influence on young infants of such variables, both individually and in combinations, as the effects of temperature and texture of the caretaker, growing up without contacts with other animals, having access to playmates but not to a living mother, and being subjected to unpredictable episodes of distress and even pain inflicted by primate mothers.

The sequelae of some of these experimental treatments appear in infancy, but others are delayed until adulthood. Some of the conditions increase cognitive skills, but, in some instances, only those of the highest level. Other experiences induce minimal and transitory emotional and cognitive problems, and still others are followed by emotional symptoms that are both disabling and seemingly immutable. Various kinds of treatment were tried, but, since the antecedents are psychological relationships, the emphasis was on contacts with animals. One effective interanimal manipulation involved putting monkeys that had been raised in isolation in a cage with healthy, young animals. At first, the isolates merely huddled in a corner where the socially normal monkeys sought them out and clung to them. Gradually, the isolates began to cling back, and cautiously they started to indulge in a few restrained responses. By degrees, their reactivity increased and, after a few weeks, the two—normal and abnormal—played with one another.

This research program put together a base of comprehensive information about the relationship between various patterns of early experiences and later behavior. This unusual yield is due to a variety of factors, but important among them is the choice of monkeys as subjects. For many psychologists, the target of research of emotional disability is the young, psychologically damaged human, but infantile monkeys reveal more about themselves than human babies because they are able to move about and thereby offer cues about their likes and dislikes.

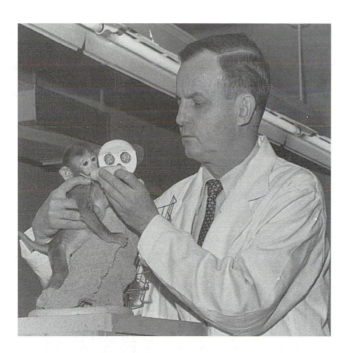

A real monkey with both a genuine psychologist, Harry Harlow, and a fake but soft comfortable mother.

Archives of the History of American Psychology Photographic File, Permission Harlow Primate Laboratory, University of Wisconsin.

Harlow, a couple of decades later, still pursuing the complex mysteries of monkey relationships.

Archives of the History of American Psychology Photographic File, Permission Harlow Primate Laboratory, University of Wisconsin.

Conflict may not be inevitable. When the cat and the rat "cooperate," that is, step simultaneously on plates on the floor, the gate drops and they can obtain food. This apparatus is an adaptation of equipment designed by Loh Seng Tsai (Ph.D., Chicago, 1928) for research on cooperation. The Soviet Union's setting off of an atomic bomb in 1949 prompted Tsai to find out if "natural enemies" could be trained to work as a team. He found that cats and rats can learn to act in concert, but the plates must be relatively large and close enough to the food to be seen and smelled (Tsai, 1951).

Archives of the History of American Psychology, Paul T. Young Papers. Courtesy Loh Seng Tsai.

Abraham Maslow (Ph.D., Wisconsin, 1934) is one of the foremost proponents of humanistic psychology. He labelled this approach the "third force" in psychology to differentiate it from two prior and more conventional systems. He dubbed behaviorism the "first force" and criticized it because it offers only dehumanized explanations. He tagged psychoanalysis the "second force" and faulted it because it stresses pathology and analysis rather than wholeness (Maslow, 1954/1970).

Humanistic psychology emphasizes integrated functioning, a state achieved in personal growth by the management of an ascending sequence of needs, beginning with biological requirements and progressing through desires for affection and affiliation to needs for esteem and recognition. The sequence may culminate in self-actualization, a condition that generates needs for investment in the interests of others (Maslow, 1967).

Archives of the History of American Psychology, Abraham Maslow Papers.

Leon Festinger (Ph.D., Iowa, 1942), Henry W. Riecken (Ph.D., Harvard, 1950), and Stanley Schacter (Ph.D., Michigan, 1950) succeeded in uncovering the psychological coherence of an unworldly ideology. When they were members of the staff of the Laboratory for Research in Social Relations of the University of Minnesota, they found it tenable to hypothesize that contradictory evidence might *strengthen* rather than *weaken* a belief. When first pursuing this riddle, they had access only to written accounts of reactions to anticipated but nonoccurring momentous episodes, such as the second coming of Christ or the destruction of the earth. They heard, quite by chance, about a contemporary group in the United States that was forecasting that on a specific date nearly three months in the future a flood would develop and spread so as to create an inland sea between the Arctic Circle and the Gulf of Mexico and that this disaster would be mitigated since the faithful would be picked up by flying saucers, taken to a planet beyond the solar system, indoctrinated, and then returned to repopulate a cleansed earth.

Preliminary inquiry indicated that this sect embodied five conditions that the researchers thought necessary for a faith to be nourished rather than depleted. First, several in the coterie held firm convictions. Second, they had acted in accord with this

trust by carrying out such bridge-burning acts as leaving employment and discarding material possessions. They also met the third and fourth demands: because specific events had been predicted, a failure would be apparent to all and would force acknowledgment, even by the faithful. The fifth condition calls for a social support system available to the prophets at the time the forecast fails to materialize. Circumstances offered, albeit unwittingly, some built-in control of this factor in that some of the believers were students residing in a college community. Since the crucial event was expected on December 21st some members would be at home for the winter break. Thus, one sample would be able to discuss the defeated expectations with others in the inner circle—a support group—but a second sample would not have access to this kind of social support—an isolated group. Festinger, Riecken, and Schachter (1956) saw a study of this sect as a chance to move away from the limitations of historical records and to investigate real rather than experimentally induced behavior.

The raw data of this experiment were observations made by participant observers, experimenters who joined the fellowship. This in itself was a difficult role in that it was critical that the observers alter neither the group's responses nor plans, but, at the same time, appear to agree with its tenets. They had to compile a log of activities, evaluate the staunchness of the faith of each follower, keep track of the amount of proselytizing, and note any expressions of doubts about the validity of the creed. The number of observers that would be needed was not clear at first since there was only limited information about the number of disciples as well as the frequency, amount, and nature of their activities. Learning more about the group did not simplify the planning. The members, for instance, believed that their directives came from extraterrestrial sources and the observers learned that orders came at erratic, unpredicted, and inconvenient times. In the authors' own words, "Problems of rigor and systematization in observation took a back seat in the hurly burly of simply trying to keep up with a movement that often seemed to be ruled by whimsy" (Festinger, Riecken, & Schachter, 1956, p. 248).

The observers watched events for 29 days in the college group and for 31 days in the second. The recording of information was difficult. The most accurate procedure would have been to dictate what had been observed as soon as possible after each contact, but this was rarely feasible. Sometimes it was possible for the observers to appear to take an outdoor walk or rest break, but only infrequently so that suspicion was not aroused. In spite of the handicaps, the team managed to dictate 65 reels of one-hour auditory tapes (nearly a 1,000 page transcript) and procure verbatim recordings of the many incoming telephone calls that the members kept because they expected to receive calls from supernatural agents.

These records disclosed that the members who had contacts with fellow believers when the flood did not occur did, as predicted, actually intensify their attempts to convert others. They manifested a heightened desire to publicize their views in various ways but, most clearly, in a dramatic increase in willingness to talk with media personnel. There is ample evidence that the nonfulfillment of the prophecy caused a great deal of distress, and that conversations with fellow adherents produced various rationalizations, such as a decision that the date was incorrect or that there had been a failure to realize beforehand that the failure was scheduled as a test of readiness and faith. These explanations appear to reduce discomfort and to provoke additional alleviating actions, one of which is to try to persuade others because the larger the number who concurred the higher the probability that the trust is well founded.

These results are based on data that are much more frequently qualitative than quantitative. Both the subjects and the subject matter are extraordinary. The number of subjects, originally small, was reduced by the failure to acquire more than fragmented bits of information about five of the fifteen most deeply committed college students. The certainty of convictions fluctuated throughout the study. There is no substantial evidence that the level of commitment was equal in the groups with different opportunities to socialize.

These, as well as other irregularities, cause some to dismiss this project as methodologically too unsound and topically too unimportant to merit consideration. There are, in contrast, those who commend the research team for tolerating the ambiguity and for not retreating to the haven of a topic that can be rigorously controlled. These supporters see coalescence of data as evidence of authenticity and they were able to point to various cohesive and complementary results in the Festinger, Riecken, and Schachter study. For example, the only member of the isolated group who continued to proselytize was not really alone in that she happened to have a house guest who was a member of the support group. Further, the two members of the communal group whose faith was reduced were the only two in that sample who were denied an opportunity to socialize.

There are innumerable additional illustrations of the buttressing of experimental findings by a neat meshing of the results. One of the better known of these is the research on subservience that Stanley Milgram (Ph.D., Harvard, 1960) began in 1960. This investigation gained much of its significance from its clarification of the perplexing willingness of some people, when directed by superiors, to commit acts which they know are wrong—for example, in the cases of the Nazi persecution of Jews, the My Lai massacre, and the destruction of the American Indian population (Milgram, 1974).

Milgram told participants in this experiment that he was concerned with the effects of punishment on learning. He designed the setting and instructions so as to lead subjects to believe that they were administering a genuine electric shock to a learner. The "shock" was delivered by depressing switches on an instrument panel that disclosed progressively increasing voltage strengths. Each subject, functioning as a teacher, was instructed to apply the next higher voltage whenever a student made a mistake when learning a series of paired words. The "student" or "victim" (a confederate) looked as if he were strapped in the chair and unable to escape. He reacted to each shock with apparent discomfort that increased to a level at which he declared that the pain was intolerable and demanded to be released from the equipment. The experimenter was not swayed and persisted in ordering the "teacher" to continue. The measure of obedience was the maximum amount of shock administered before the subject refused to continue to deliver more.

The Milgram shock generator. This is the equipment the subject uses to "shock" a victim whenever the latter makes an error. Depressing a switch illuminates a bright red light directly above it, makes a blue light (top row, second from left) flash, activates an electric buzzer as well as a series of relay clicks, and moves the dial on the voltage meter (on the right).

Archives of the History of American Psychology, The Milgram Gift.

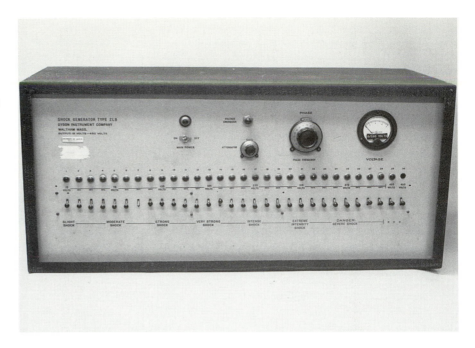

Scores were obtained under a variety of conditions, such as differences in the audibility, visibility, and proximity of the "victim"; conducting the experiment in both prestigious and mundane locations; and informing some subjects that the learner has some cardiac impairment. These scores were supplemented with information obtained in interviews held with each participant at the end of the session. These debriefings allowed learning more about each subject as well as clarifying the actual purpose and conditions of the experiment. At that time, each subject also met the unharmed "victim."

Milgram reports that nearly one-half of the "teachers" continued to follow orders in spite of the learner's suffering. A closer look at this unexpectedly large amount of compliance also uncovered some instances of defiance. Some subjects made unauthorized reductions in voltage when the experimenter was out of the room. Some even challenged the experimenter. Physical contacts also appear to have had some braking power in that orders to hold the victim's hand forcefully on the shock plate increased refusals to comply.

The data also offer persuasive evidence that authority stands a good chance of overwhelming attempts at resistance. In one design, for example, the victim, although seemingly in pain, ordered the subject to increase the voltage, giving as the reason a desire to equal the performance of a friend who had endured the entire sequence of shocks. The experimenter continued to indicate that the shock was to be administered in the usual sequence and not one of the subjects complied with the would-be martyr's directives.

Milgram's attempts to understand why people carry out acts that they know are wrong led him to the formulation of the concept of what he calls an agentic state, one in which an individual relinquishes the sense of personal autonomy and thinks of him/herself as an agent for another person. This is a *covert reaction*, one of openness to regulation, whereas obedience is an *overt response*. Although the two are usually related, in unusual circumstances authority may not demand action and there may be merely an agentic attitude. Whether action is or is not taken, the individual perceives him/herself as regulated by someone in a higher status. Subjection is, of course, learned during childhood dependence on authority, when servitude and compliance are expected and reinforced. This early and repetitive practice in subordination builds acquiescence into the behavioral repertoire of everyone.

Milgram's interpretation reconciles contradictory behavior. It explains, for example, why the disapproved may be carried out, why there may be a sensitivity to orders from superiors but not to those from other sources. Undoubtedly, there are variables that are not managed in Milgram's scheme, but his analysis nonetheless moves responses that on occasion are menacing and even dangerous from a category of unexplained into a category of explanation-in-progress.

Magda Arnold (Ph.D., Toronto, 1942). Although emotion is an important psychological response, there was only a limited amount of interest in the topic and confusion exceeded understanding until at least the middle of the twentieth century. Much of the controversy was about whether the physiological changes that are characteristic of emotion are the instigators or the result of emotional response.

Magda Arnold in the spirit of her era chose to pursue the quandry: "She became for a number of years the most persistent contributor to the literature of emotion, early introducing a cognitive approach through insisting that the first step in emotion is an appraisal of the situation. Such an appraisal makes knowledge, not reaction, the first step in differentiating the emotional response" (Hilgard, 1987, p. 333).

Archives of the History of American Psychology, Magda Arnold Papers.

Arnold accounts for this picture in a letter of October 23, 1990, to the authors:

My name in lights was done on the occasion of my retirement from Spring Hill College [Mobile, Alabama] in 1975. On that occasion I also received three framed documents: one a Certificate of Appreciation signed by the president of Spring Hills College, one a commendation for my contributions to the city of Mobile, signed by the city fathers who also declared a 'Day of Magda Arnold.' . . . And the third one really amused me: an appointment as Lieutenant-Colonel Aide-de-Camp in the Alabama State Militia, signed by Governor George C. Wallace. Yes, Alabama really honors its educators.

Archives of the History of American Psychology, Magda Arnold Papers and Correspondence File.

9

C H A P T E R

Psychological Services

Testing

The improvements in instrumentation and research designs during the Era of Maturity were supplemented by an expansion of the kinds of services that psychologists perform. The most conspicuous of these was the devising and applying of techniques of intervention, but these functions were additions, not alternatives, to assessment.

The administration and interpretation of tests continue to figure among the major responsibilities of psychologists even though psychological examinations are receiving an increasing amount of criticism. A few comments about this censure are in order before proceeding to an account of therapeutic endeavors. At least three different kinds of condemnation of tests are repeated, with each exerting a different amount and kind of influence.

The criticism that appears to be the least effective in causing changes is also the oldest. It consists of attacks on both the validity and the reliability of examinations. Tests have in the past and still continue to be faulted because of failures to measure what they purport to measure and variations in retest scores. Although these shortcomings have summoned improvements in both validity and reliability, weaknesses persist, but practitioners tolerate them and continue to value tests (Wade & Baker, 1977).

This photograph of Starke R. Hathaway was taken when the momentum for the MMPI was just beginning. The first Inventory was published in 1940 and revised in 1989 as the Minnesota Multiphasic Personality Inventory–2 (MMPI–2). This second version is based on improvements in the normative group, on the addition of new scales, and on refinements in the statistical processing of scores. The original format is retained but outdated content has been eliminated. The Inventory now consists of 567 items, but only 370 are scored, leaving the remainder available for research (Butcher, Dahlstrom, Graham, Tellegen, & Kaemmer, 1989).*

Archives of the History of American Psychology Photographic File. Permission University of Minnesota Archives.

Scoring Services

MICROTEST Assessment Software

MICROTEST assessment software offers the flexibility to administer, score and generate reports in minutes—on site. It provides you with easy access to objective reports. You can choose in-depth interpretive reports or profile reports that provide results at-a-glance. MICROTEST software operates on an IBM or IBM-compatible microcomputer. A base package must be purchased by first-time users. The base package includes a user's guide, a ScorBox® interface to facilitate scoring and toll-free telephone support from our technical support staff.

Arion II Teleprocessing

Arion II teleprocessing links you directly to the NCS central computer, which is ready to process tests any time day or night. In addition to a telephone, the only equipment needed to process tests is a microcomputer with communications software, a printer and a modem. (Arion teleprocessing operates with virtually any microcomputer or data communications terminal.)

Mail-in Scoring

NCS' mail-in scoring service offers you a convenient, reliable way to obtain test results. Test answer sheets are processed within 24 hours after receipt at our office then mailed back to you. Although mail-in scoring doesn't provide you with results as quickly as MICROTEST software or Arion teleprocessing, you will receive your results back in a matter of days.

If you require results faster than regular mail allows, expedited service is available through Federal Express or Express Mail. This service is billed back to the customer.

Hand Scoring

Materials for hand scoring are available for both hardcover and softcover test booklet formats.

The profile obtained by hand scoring yields the ten Basic Clinical scales and three Validity scales. (Cannot Say is reported as a raw score.)

In addition, sets of hand-scoring materials are available for several special scales. These include the MMPI-2 Content scales; Supplementary scales (Anxiety; Repression; Ego Strength; MacAndrew Alcoholism-Revised; Back F; True Response Inconsistency; Variable Response Inconsistency; Overcontrolled Hostility; Dominance; Social Responsibility; College Maladjustment; Gender Role-Masculine; Gender Role-Feminine; Post-Traumatic Stress Disorder-Keane; Post-Traumatic Stress Disorder-Schlenger; Social Introversion subscales [Shyness/Self-Consciousness, Social Avoidance, and Alienation-Self and Others]); Harris-Lingoes subscales, and the Wiener-Harmon Subtle-Obvious subscales.

Excerpts from a 1989 announcement of the scoring services available for the MMPI–2. This notice documents the tremendous gains that have been made in scoring examinations.

Archives of the History of American Psychology Literature Collection. Permission National Computer Systems.

"Which girl is starting the best way to put in the new light bulb?" This is one question in the Davis-Eells Games, a test for grades 1 and 6, in which all content is restricted to material familiar to urban American children at the time the test was standardized. This restriction is one of several ways of minimizing distortions of intelligence tests that are due to lack of information rather than to lack of intelligence. A second technique, also used in the Davis-Eells

Games, requires the examiner to ask each question so that the examinee's reading skill does not influence the score. The test items highlight problem solving, and the authors suggest computing an Index of Problem Solving Ability (IPSA) rather than an IQ (Davis & Eells, 1953).

A second kind of censure, the result of the modernizing of theory, sets the stage for, but has not yet induced, radical alterations in testing. As psychology increased the distance from its philosophical origins, examining behavior became more important than trying to examine postulated internal forces, and as a result the attractiveness of hypothesized variables lessened. In the field of personality, many tests of traits were displaced by assessments of overt behavior, preferably in naturalistic, real-life situations (Goldfried & Kent, 1972). The effect of updated theory on the assessment of intelligence may, in the long run, be even more sweeping since intelligence conceptualized as an immutable attribute-of-the-individaul is being renounced in favor of intelligence conceptualized as a mutable attribute-of-behavior or, in popular terms, limited mental capacity may not exist, but skills do exist and they can be modified (Popplestone & McPherson, 1988).

This formulation could convert in actual practice into tests of behavioral *competence* (Hunt, 1961; McClelland, 1973), but, to date, not many examinations have been compiled for this purpose, in part because new and unfamiliar methods have to overcome longstanding convictions that intelligence is unitary and constant in amount. Progress in setting aside this tradition is coming from the currently popular practice

of designing experiments as metaphors for information processing (Sternberg, Ketron, & Powell, 1982). This procedure interprets familiar unitary "powers" such as ability, talent, and capability as cognitive strategies such as retrieving, decision making, and planning. Furthermore, efforts to improve these strategies are meeting with some success. As a result, statements that were considered untenable prior to the middle or latter part of the twentieth century are, at its close, in circulation—for example, "*Ability* [italics added] is attained through experience over time and consolidated through exercise" (Snow, 1982, p. 18).

A third variety of fault finding has succeeded in inducing some changes in testing, but these are restrictive in that they exclude the use, for purposes of educational and occupational placement, of examinations in which there are ethnic differences in the percent of successful subjects (Ash & Kroeker, 1975; Carpignano, 1987). Throughout the history of psychometrics, differences among groups in averages of test scores have been reported, but the general assumption has been that the range of scores among all groups was and is equal. The ideal of social equality elevated this belief into a fact, and tests that do not yield equal averages are contested (Campbell, 1969; Cronbach, 1975).

Scenes from a Meeting Sponsored by the National Training Laboratory

Collaboration

Archives of the History of American Psychology, National Training Laboratory Archives.
Photograph by Mort Kaye Studios.

Conflict. In the 1960s, there was an "increasing lessening in cognitive input via general lectures, skill exercises, and research . . . until a great number of labs put their emphasis almost entirely on self-awareness and interpersonal learning" (Bradford, 1974, p. 128).

Archives of the History of American Psychology, National Training Laboratory Archives.
Photograph by Mort Kaye Studios.

Therapy

The psychologists who became involved in remediation and prevention took on a multiplicity of problems for people who present a spectrum of economic, educational, ethnic, and social differences. These undertakings contributed significantly to the choice of the label *Era of Maturity* but they also nourished the previously noted softening of respect for the authority of the laboratory. Many psychologists still defer to traditional scientific standards and endorse upgraded credentials for therapists and more rigid standards for clinical techniques. In contrast, others place more credence in social vectors, endorsing, for example, the educational mainstreaming of atypical children, the

deinstitutionalization of psychiatric populations, and, most relevant to this discussion, similitude between the therapist and the patient.

The popularity of support groups led by lay members testifies to the current appeal of a nontechnical background. The patronage of these groups is enormous and the vicissitudes they seek to manage form a lengthy and assorted roster including, but certainly not limited to, adoptive status, alcoholism, anorexia, bereavement, bulimia, caring for aged or ill parents, child abuse, divorce, drug abuse, gambling, obesity, sexual transgressions, shoplifting, single parenting, smoking, as well as a large number of phobias, physical illnesses, and surgical treatments.

Many of these efforts are evidently successful, but the bases of these victories have yet to be clarified. A frequently voiced explanation is the lifting of feelings of loneliness, but a second and probably stronger factor is the opportunity to talk about and learn what alleviates and what increases distress. The acquisition of this information may account for the research conclusion that "Misery doesn't love just any kind of company, it loves only miserable company" (Schachter, 1959, p. 24).

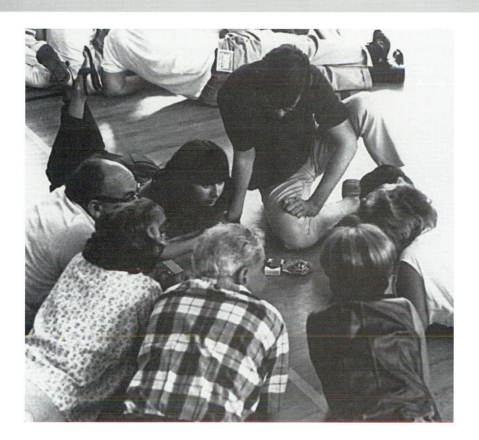

Communication

Archives of the History of American Psychology, National Training Laboratory Archives. Photograph by Mort Kaye Studios.

Carl R. Rogers (Ph.D., Teachers College, Columbia, 1931) and Alfred J. Marrow (Ph.D., New York, 1937) at the "First Presidents Conference" (National Training Laboratories) held in 1965 at the La Coquille Club, Palm Beach, Florida (Bradford, 1974).

Rogers conceptualized a system of psychotherapy, first called nondirective and later client-centered therapy, *that assumes that the* client (not the patient) *possesses inner strengths and resources. He perceives the task of therapy as assisting the client to become aware of and to use the assets already at hand (Rogers, 1967). This concern with wellness would be elaborated later by the human potential movement. The emphasis on the present as a stepping stone to fulfillment harks back to the ahistoric orientation of Kurt Lewin.★*

The APA awarded Rogers the Distinguished Scientific Contribution Award in 1956 and the Distinguished Professional Contribution Award in 1972.

Much of Marrow's interest centered on the relevance of scientific information to social behavior, and he participated in studies of industrial conflict and group dynamics. He is the author of the frequently cited biography of Kurt Lewin,★ The Practical Theorist (1969). Marrow met Lewin in 1934 when he sought Lewin's advice regarding his dissertation which involved the Zeigarnik effect, the higher recall of uncompleted than completed tasks, a phenomenon first investigated by one of Lewin's students.

Archives of the History of American Psychology, National Training Laboratory Archives. Photograph by Mort Kaye Studios.

In this house at 855 Ardmore Avenue in Akron, Ohio, on June 10, 1935, Dr. Bob began sustained abstinence from alcohol with the help of his wife Anne Smith and Bill Wilson. This date is considered the founding of Alcoholics Anonymous. Here the principles of AA were first articulated and many of the first members, whose stories are told in the AA "Big Book," began their recovery. Although there are other sites in Akron important in the origins of this international mutual support movement, Dr. Bob's House is the preeminent place because of its rich associations. It is a National Historical Landmark and is open to the public.

Archives of the History of American Psychology Photographic File, Courtesy of Founders Foundation, AA.

On the modern scene, both individual psychotherapy and group therapy are conducted by people whose preparation ranges from merely enthusiastic reading about psychotherapy to graduate education in the case of a professional practitioner with a doctoral degree that has been supplemented by an extended period of practice under the supervision of experienced clinicians. This discussion—from here on—is confined to therapy that is carried out by trained professionals.

Psychotherapeutic procedures originated in the medical speciality of psychiatry, and, initially, the principal practitioners were psychoanalysts. For a time, this was considered to be the most effective and prestigious kind of treatment, but, by the mid 1970s, this reputation was so weakened that some authorities described classical psychoanalysis as more historic than operational (Burnham, 1978; Garfield, 1981). As indicated in Chapter 3, psychology's faulting of psychoanalysis came from the depicting of psychological phenomena as the unfolding of predetermined, inevitable courses of psychic or ethereal powers, forces outside the jurisdiction of science. Psychologists could not condone this but neither could they find many directives for psychotherapy in their own disciplines. As a result, they were confronted with the dilemma of how to maintain a commitment to science while retaining a model based on unacceptable assumptions (Hathaway, 1958).

The career of Neal E. Miller (Ph.D., Yale, 1935) from 1932 to 1966 was at Yale University, but it was interrupted by a Fellowship at the Psychoanalytic Institute in Vienna from 1935 to 1936 and by a military assignment during World War II. In 1966, Miller became professor at the Rockefeller University.

Miller's contributions are abundant and sterling. His experimental work, covering a range of topics including the genesis of secondary drives, frustration, learning, and motivation, was honored in 1959 when the American Psychological Association gave him the Distinguished Scientific Contribution Award. Miller also excels in synthesizing the information acquired in the laboratory with that acquired in the pursuit of practical problems, such as those related to health: for example, the utility of avoidance learning in the measurement of psychopharmacological effects, the reduction of stress by means of biofeedback, and the relationship between acquisition of emotional problems and their dissolution by psychotherapy. The relatively recent interest in the influence of behavior on illness has prompted the emergence of what is called behavioral medicine (Miller, 1983). The American Psychological Association presented Miller with the Distinguished Professional Contribution Award in 1983 and the Award for Outstanding Lifetime Contribution to Psychology in 1991.

Archives of the History of American Psychology, Presidential Portraits Series.

Early attempts to convert psychoanalytic propositions into a behavioral framework are reported in *Personality and Psychotherapy* (1950) by John Dollard (Ph.D., Chicago, 1931) and Neal E. Miller.★ Transference is one example of these changes. Freud construed transference—the patient's feelings toward the psychotherapist, conscious and unconscious, positive and negative, instinctive and inborn—as a discharge of intense emotions that the patient has harbored for a long time. For Freud transference was a product more of prior conditions than of immediate external stimulation. Dollard and Miller presented transference as an instance of generalization; in this case, due to the similarity between stimuli: the therapist directs and controls behavior, reassures, criticizes, and withholds and offers

rewards and punishment in ways that resemble the actions of authority figures the patient has known previously. This similarity provokes the patient to react to the psychotherapist as he did to predecessors. Thus, the responses that comprise the transference are learned and stimulated in the same way as other psychological responses.

It is impossible to capture in the laboratory the psychic forces that abound in psychoanalytic concepts, but it is possible to measure success in predicting actual behavior. Robert R. Sears★ in 1943 reviewed experiments in the psychological and psychiatric literature that evaluated psychoanalytic formulations. For example, he described how researchers identified a core of emotional problems for a number of neurotic

David Shakow (Ph.D., Harvard, 1942) preferred to integrate, rather than segregate, the functions of researcher and clinician. Excerpts from his Curriculum Vitae display this duality:

> Chief psychologist and Director of Psychological Research, Worcester State Hospital *(1928–1946)*
>
> Professor of Psychology, University of Chicago *(1948–1954)*
>
> Chief, Laboratory of Psychology, National Institute of Mental Health *(1954–1966)*
>
> Author of Clinical Psychology as Science and Profession: A Forty-year Odyssey *(1969)*
>
> Fellow of the American Psychological Association, the American Orthopsychiatric Association, and (Honorary) American Psychiatric Association
>
> *Editorial Boards:*
>
> Psychological Review *(1954–1958)*
>
> Journal of Abnormal and Social Psychology *(1950–1955)*
>
> Psychological Monographs *(1961–1966)*
>
> Psychoanalytic Review *(1966–[1981?])*
>
> Journal of Personality *(1948–1954)*
>
> American Journal of Orthopsychiatry *(1949–1957)*

Archives of the History of American Psychology, David Shakow Papers.

and psychotic patients. They then exposed briefly a picture relevant to each patient's problem and asked that it be described immediately from memory. On the following morning, the patients were asked to recall dreams of the previous night, and their accounts revealed that items that had been omitted from the descriptions of pictures appeared in the dreams— corroborating Freud's observation that items apparently neglected or unnoticed may have emotional force and durability.

Laboratory support for many of the predicted responses was found, but the confirmation was not sufficiently solid to silence the skeptics, and this weakness embarrassed the defenders. The response was a quickening of research, and the issue was of such

importance that Ernest R. Hilgard,★ in his 1949 presidential address to the American Psychological Association, recommended increasing experimental facilities for investigating hypotheses about psychodynamic processes. Confirmation is still in progress, and, paradoxically, some failures to obtain laboratory substantiation had the effect of a backlash in the form of dissatisfaction with research procedures. Critics pointed out that, in spite of ingenuity, experimenters are not able to simulate in laboratory work all attributes of psychoanalytic variables (Jahoda, 1963; Pumpian-Mindlin, 1952). These criticisms differ from the more recent denigration of experimental work in that they were not generalized but were directed at specific research targets.

American Psychological Association
Distinguished Scientific Contribution Award
1975
presented to

David Shakow

For his seminal contributions to research and theory
that have pioneered the development of an experimental psychopathology of schizophrenia. His research studies, spanning four decades, have fused clinical
insight with experimental precision to enhance our
understanding of psychological processes in schizophrenia.
His work modified the concept of 'deterioration', enlarged knowledge of the depth and dimensions of
psychological deficits in schizophrenia, and assayed the
qualities of set and motivation that generate them. In
so doing, he has rendered an extraordinarily complex
mental disorder more comprehensible. This generativity
and dedication to experimental inquiry in psychopathology
have profoundly influenced a generation of experimental
psychopathologists and clinical psychologists.

Archives of the History of American Psychology, David Shakow Papers.

American Psychological Association
Distinguished Professional Contribution Award
1976
to

David Shakow

In a career that spans almost five decades, his
activities reflect his abiding concern with psychology's
historical antecedents, his leadership in creating a
training model for clinical psychology that would retain
the unique quality that characterizes a psychologist,
and his research contributions in the psychological
study of schizophrenia. David Shakow by his imagination, by his influence on his many students - graduate
and postdoctoral - as teacher and mentor, by his
dedication to important scientific studies, by his
advocacy of the coordinate role of researcher and
practitioner for the clinical psychologist, and by his
broad knowledge and commitment to humanistic
values has indeed made a distinguished contribution
to professional psychology.

Archives of the History of American Psychology, David Shakow Papers.

*Ernest R. Hilgard (Ph.D., Yale, 1930). Some psychologists achieve
fame because of research productivity, others because of author skills,
and others because of effective leadership. "Jack" Hilgard excels in all
three arenas.*

*He has received many honors for research. He concentrated
initially on learning and was awarded the Warren Medal of the
Society of Experimental Psychologists. Stellar productivity in research
on hypnosis earned him the Morton Prince Award of the Society for
Clinical and Experimental Hypnosis and the Benjamin Franklin
Gold Medal of the International Society of Hypnosis. These
accomplishments helped to clear up the clouded reputation of research
on hypnosis and to open the door for graduate students to conduct
experiments on the topic (Hilgard, 1974).*

*Hilgard is a preeminent author. His reviews of the scientific
literature earned him the J. Murray Luck award of the National
Academy of Sciences. His introduction to psychology and learning
textbooks are classics, and his volumes on hypnosis, psychoanalysis
and science, and the history of psychology are substantive,
authoritative references.*

*Hilgard's professional activities are also weighty. His presidency
in 1949 is but a single entry in a series of responsibilities he has
carried out for the American Psychological Association. He also
represents psychology in numerous other professional organizations
including the National Research Council, the Social Science Research
Council, the National Health Council, and the National Institute of
Mental Health.*

Archives of the History of American Psychology, Presidential Portraits Series.

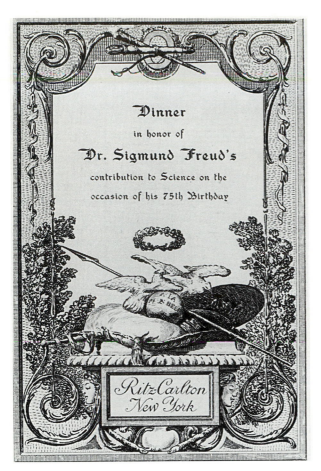

Sigmund Freud★ was 75 years old on May 6, 1931. He returned home on May 4, 1931, from surgery on his cancerous jaw. The combination of age, surgical trauma, pneumonia, and starvation—from an inability to swallow—had taken such a toll that he was too ill to participate in any of the numerous birthday celebrations (Jones, 1937). The dinner referred to in this announcement was attended by 200 guests and was reported in The New York Times. There were several speakers and a cablegram was sent to Freud. The committee in charge of the affair included three men who were sometime members of the American Psychological Association: John Dewey,★ Jerome Frank (Ph.D., Harvard, 1934; M.D., Harvard, 1939), and Adolf Meyer (M.D., Zurich, 1892).

Archives of the History of American Psychology, Walter and Catharine Cox Miles Papers.

Anna Freud and Gardner Murphy★ at the Menninger Foundation in Topeka, Kansas, about 1962. Anna Freud (Graduate, Cottage Lyceum, 1912), the youngest child of Sigmund Freud,★ became a child psychoanalyst. Her earned degree was complimented by five honorary doctorates. She is the author of several books including the important volume The Ego and Mechanisms of Defense (1937). During World War II, her concern about the problems that children experience when removed from their homes and when threatened by air raids led her to organize a residential facility on their behalf.

Apparently Sigmund Freud did not like the United States, and he declined invitations to visit in the years after he attended the Clark University Conference in 1909. But his daughter came to this country several times and had a number of American friends (Young-Bruehl, 1988).

Archives of the History of American Psychology, Gardner and Lois Barclay Murphy Papers.

Sanitizing theory, accumulating experimental support, and justifying the failures to accomplish these goals both weakened the resistance to psychoanalysis and modified many of its propositions. As a result, psychologists accepted several concepts that are psychoanalytical in origin, and several varieties of psychotherapy, with different amounts of psychoanalytical tinge, came into being. Many of the principles spread and left clearly discernible influences on various areas of psychology, such as personality, developmental, and industrial psychology (Shakow & Rapaport, 1964).

The influence of psychoanalysis was never extensive enough to overwhelm the service sector, and several

kinds of treatments quite devoid of its influence came into existence. One of the best known of these is behavior modification, a technique for strengthening appropriate responses and weakening inappropriate ones by means of procedures derived from operant behaviorism, a system of psychology that asserts that behavior is determined by its consequences—that is, by the reinforcement that it elicits. Since behavior modification ascribes change to the environment, it bypasses probes of personality and deals directly with responses. The technique has been used for a variety of purposes, for example, alleviating emotional symptoms, improving scholastic skills and decreasing ineffectual classroom behavior, increasing occupational efficiency,

promoting adherence to medical regimes, and fostering compliancy in prisoners.

When the goal is to develop a new response (learning to add or to dress oneself), positive reinforcement (typically, food, praise, or money) is applied when the target response is made. When the goal is to eradicate a response (eliminate temper tantrums or fighting), an aversive stimulus (typically, a monetary fine or loud noise) is applied when the target response is made. The success of these procedures demands precision and regularity in their presentation: reinforcing only a clearly defined response (differentiating screaming from swearing); ascertaining the exact circumstances that elicit the complaint (is the screaming directed at everyone or only at some specified group, such as young or smaller people?); making certain that the target response is not inadvertently reinforced (reassuring an angry person could reinforce the response of anger); adhering to a planned schedule of reinforcement; and measuring the frequency of the target response in order to have a baseline for measuring the changes.

Behavior modification is criticized for a number of drawbacks and condemned for being dehumanizing, punitive, manipulative, and "mind controlling." When it is applied to captive subjects (prisoners or hospitalized patients), the denunciation escalates, even though the purpose of incarceration is frequently control and the purpose of behavior modification is to improve the behavioral repertoire, either by developing new and useful skills or by eliminating disserviceable ones. The use of strong aversive stimuli (typically, brief and a nondangerous amount of electric shock or nausea-inducing drugs) elicits accusations of torture, sadism, and the like with little or no consideration of the restrictions governing their use—for example, applying them only after other measures have been found to be ineffective and when the disorder is physically injurious or life threatening (head banging or drug consumption).

It is impossible to measure precisely the success of behavior modification because outcomes are, as in the case of all methods of treatment, altered by many variables besides the therapy per se. Some of the extraneous factors that play a role include the severity of the problem, the amount of intervention, the stability of the results, and the extent to which improvement transfers to contexts other than the treatment setting. In general, behavior modification appears to be beneficial for the management of complaints that can be characterized unambiguously and for which reinforcers are known and are amenable to manipulation. The list of problems for which improvement is reported includes phobias, anxiety, destructive behavior both of self and others, the lack of self-care skills, and obesity. The technique has not yet been able to alter abstract convictions or generalized attitudes about the self: "For many persons, it is highly reinforcing to resist attempts to alter their behavior and highly aversive to succumb to external control. . . . [We] may not find any

Both the questions and the answers remain the same. Teaching is one of the responsibilities that many psychologists assume, and in fact, in the early years it was essentially the only source of income for a psychologist. The nature of rewards that are appropriate for responsibilities outside the classroom is a long-standing issue.

These undated and unsigned, worn sheets are included among the notes that G. Stanley Hall* took while reading literature published between 1908 and 1917. Hall devised numerous questionnaires, possibly even the one that provoked these remarks. Cal, Cath, Columb, and Corn probably refer to the university with which the respondent is identified and P might designate a professor and D a dean. Modern answers do not vary markedly from these.

Archives of the History of American Psychology,
G. Stanley Hall Documents.

consequence strong enough to compete with the individual's desire to remain unchanged" (Stolz, Wienckowski, & Brown, 1975, pp. 1037–1038).

Behavior therapy is a remedial procedure that warrants special attention because it has come to serve as a bridge between contrasting kinds of treatment, those that in the past were directed primarily to the modification of covert difficulties and those that were directed to the modification of overt responses. Behavior therapy began with a procedure called systematic desensitization, a method designed to dissipate unpleasant subjective experiences. In the case of fear, for example, the patient is asked to rank feared stimuli in a hierarchy from the least to the most distressing (Wolpe & Lang, 1964). The individual is taught to relax and instructed to imagine the least disturbing stimulus while remaining relaxed. This achievement is followed by a directive to move on to the next feared stimulus and so on through the list, without sacrificing the relaxation. There are various modifications of this procedure—for example, dealing with actual exposure to the feared stimulus rather than images—but the mark of all behavior therapy is twofold: a patient-therapist relationship and a focus on changing a response.

Thus, behavior therapy involves the pursuit of subjective experiences, the subject matter that behaviorism has struggled, since the first of the twentieth century, to remove from the psychological agenda. It also prompts therapists who feature the role of personal background in psychopathology to come into closer contact with immediate, ongoing behavior. These steps toward a common ground have the potential to replace the theory-induced bipolarity of an "either" depth "or" behavior orientation with an integration of the influence that each exerts. The conquest of this endeavor, although underway, is still in the future (Messer & Winokur, 1980).

Colleagueship

Psychologists have not confined their assistance to the laity but have developed a commendable record of assisting both students and colleagues. The beneficiaries are too numerous and the benefits too varied to be listed here, and this text ends, as it began, with incidentals. One of these is an exercise of such consequence that it merits a description before we proceed with more traditional kinds of help.

Prestigious professors. On the left, Mary Henle★ (Ph.D., Bryn Mawr, 1939) and, on the right, Edna Heidbreder (Ph.D., Columbia, 1924) at the 1978 meeting, in Wellesley, Massachusetts, of the Cheiron Society, formerly the International Society for the History of the Social and Behavioral Sciences, an interdisciplinary group founded in 1969.

Heidbreder is the author of one of the classics in psychology: Seven Psychologies, *a volume published in 1933 that reviews the various systems of psychology then extant. She was professor at Wellesley College from 1934 until retirement in 1955.*

Many psychologists cast Mary Henle as "a psychologists' psychologist" and all who know her cast her as a learned, articulate interpreter of Gestalt psychology. She is the editor of The Selected Papers of Wolfgang Köhler★ *(1971) and the author of several books, the most recent of which is* 1879 and All That *(1986), a collection of her astute penetrations of psychological theory. She was professor of psychology on the Graduate Faculty of Political and Social Sciences, at the New School for Social Research from 1954 until retirement in 1983.*

Archives of the History of American Psychology, Mary Henle Papers. Photograph by Nicholas Pastore.

This course list describes the offerings of the last summer school for English-speaking students that was held at the University of Vienna Psychological Institute before Hitler entered Austria in March 1938. Of the seven instructors listed in this announcement, five came to the United States after the Anschluss: Egon Brunswik (Ph.D., Vienna, 1927), Charlotte Bühler (Ph.D., Munich, 1918), Karl Bühler (M. D., Freiburg, 1903; Ph. D., Strassburg, 1904), Else Frenkel (-Brunswik),★ and Käthe [Katherine M. T.] Wolf (Ph.D., Vienna, 1930).

Archives of the History of American Psychology Literature Collection. Identification with the help of Mitchell Ash.

University of Vienna
Psychological Institute

July 12 — August 7, 1937

Sixth Annual Summer School in Psychology

Eight courses for English-speaking students

(1) HUMAN PERSONALITY (Karl Bühler)
A survey of different means of determining personality and character. — **(6 hours lectures.)**

(2) SPEECH AND LANGUAGE (Karl Bühler)
An analysis of the structure of language: speech in its three aspects: expression, representation, appeal. — **(6 hours lectures.)**

(3) CHILDHOOD AND ADOLESCENCE (Charlotte Bühler)
A survey of the most important recent experimental and observational studies on children and adolescents, tracing the entire development of the individual from birth to maturity through its five principal phases. — **(10 hours lectures, 4 hours demonstrations.)**

(4) BIOGRAPHICAL METHODS (Charlotte Bühler, Else Frenkel)
An analysis of those attitudes towards life that are common to and typical of all individuals in certain periods of life. A new methodology, based on a detailed psychological examination of biographies and case histories. — **(10 hours lectures.)**

(5) EXPERIMENTAL PSYCHOLOGY (Egon Brunswik)
Demonstration and theoretical discussion of outstanding recent European investigations in experimental psychology, including: object-constancy in perception, Gestalt, eidetic imagery, perception-types, psychology of thinking. — **(12 hours lectures with demonstrations.)**

(6) VIENNESE TESTS FOR CHILDREN (Lotte Danzinger, Liselotte Frankl)
A discussion, with demonstrations, of the Viennese Developmental Tests and of the technique of testing young children. — **(6 hours lectures, 10 hours demonstrations.)**

(7) CASES OF PROBLEM CHILDREN (Charlotte Bühler)
Discussion of the application of the Viennese Tests in cases of different developmental and character problems. Profiles of normal children and of borderline cases. — **(10 hours lectures.)**

(8) PSYCHOLOGY OF EXPRESSION (Käthe Wolf)
A historical survey of the theories of expression; the expressive values of the human voice, face and hands; an inventory of the expressions of the motion picture actor; modes of expression in the film, novel and drama; the film contrasted with speech; indirect interpretation of expression by means of the environmental situation; expression in insanity. — **(10 hours lectures.)**

All Courses taught in English.

Further Information
regarding courses, tuition fees, registration, certificates, examinations, credit, living arrangements in Vienna

may be obtained from:
Psychological Institute
University of Vienna
1. Liebiggasse 5, Vienna, Austria
(Phone A-21-0-74)

or from:
Dr. Henry Beaumont
Dep. of Psychology
University of Kentucky
Lexington, Ky.

This memorandum was considered sensitive because it reported the educational and occupational histories of more than 100 professionals. Readers were cautioned not to expose details that would cause problems for individuals who had not yet been able to migrate or for relatives still residing in Europe.

Committee members who have not been introduced previously in this volume are Luton Ackerson (Ph.D., Columbia, 1927), William E. Blatz (Ph.D., Chicago, 1924), David B. Klein (Ph.D., Columbia, 1930), and George D. Stoddard (Ph.D., Iowa, 1925). The German coordinator Guenther Stern is a philosopher, then residing in the United States.

Archives of the History of American Psychology, Gardner and Lois Barclay Murphy Papers.

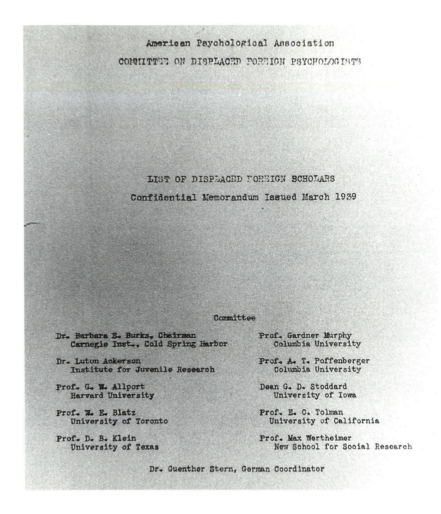

American Psychological Association
COMMITTEE ON DISPLACED FOREIGN PSYCHOLOGISTS

LIST OF DISPLACED FOREIGN SCHOLARS
Confidential Memorandum Issued March 1939

Committee

Dr. Barbara S. Burks, Chairman
Carnegie Inst., Cold Spring Harbor

Dr. Luton Ackerson
Institute for Juvenile Research

Prof. G. W. Allport
Harvard University

Prof. W. E. Blatz
University of Toronto

Prof. D. B. Klein
University of Texas

Prof. Gardner Murphy
Columbia University

Prof. A. T. Poffenberger
Columbia University

Dean G. D. Stoddard
University of Iowa

Prof. E. C. Tolman
University of California

Prof. Max Wertheimer
New School for Social Research

Dr. Guenther Stern, German Coordinator

When Hitler came to power, ideologues tried to destroy scholarship—they burned books, dismissed professors, and purged the staffs of clinics and hospitals. American psychologists, acting both individually and cooperatively, took what actions they could to protect their German colleagues. In 1936, Barbara Burks (Ph.D., Stanford, 1929) toured Europe, and when she returned she circulated a lengthy, private memorandum among professional friends about the state of psychology in England and on the Continent. Her observations of German activity under Nazi control depicted the then only dimly perceived devasting sacrifice of intellectual resources. One of the reactions to this oppression came in the form of a Committee on Displaced Foreign Psychologists, formed by the American Psychological Association in 1938, with Burks as Chair. This ad hoc team had a light budget and a heavy program of advising professionals who were hoping to emigrate as well as helping arrivals to master the peculiarities of American ways and to secure appropriate professional employment. America had not yet recovered from the depression and many native born psychologists were unemployed. The Committee,

therefore, took on the goal of developing new positions "rather than increasing competitive pressure through partiality toward refugees" (Burks, 1940, p. 717). In order to accomplish this, they searched for situations in which psychology was understaffed and pushed for the creation of nonacademic posts. Their 1940 report reviewed contacts with 269 displaced scholars, 134 of whom were then in the United States (Burks, 1940).

The exact number of psychologists who immigrated is elusive, but an accurate count is not as important as is the depth and quality of their knowledge and the esteem they were awarded by the psychological community. Accounts abound about strong personalities with fresh perspectives presenting ideas that modified several aspects of American psychology. The impact was particularly strong on Gestalt psychology (Mandler & Mandler, 1968) as well as on psychopathology and personality, with an emphasis in the latter on prejudice and conformity (Adorno, 1968).

A second illustration of psychologists taking responsibility for the well-being of other psychologists is their creation and maintenance of two elaborate networks of professional communication—journals and

The Winter Holiday Meeting of "The Topological Group" at Bryn Mawr in 1935. From left to right, William Stern,★ Eugenia Hanfmann (Ph.D., Jena, 1927), Kurt Lewin,★ Edward Tolman,★ and Kurt Koffka★ joke for the photographer. David Krech★(?) and Wally Reichenberg-Hackett (Ph.D., Vienna, 1935) pose with two unidentified children. Donald MacKinnon (Ph.D., Harvard, 1933) stands at the right.

The Topological Group was founded in 1933 by Kurt Lewin★ and disbanded in 1965, nearly 20 years after his death. The meetings were informal, usually restricted to 35 or 40 participants, and characterized by the eminence of the members, the high quality of the discussions, and an atmosphere of informal, cooperative exchange of opinions. Lewin, a refugee, was a charming, entertaining figure, attracting both students and colleagues, many of whom were also refugees (Marrow, 1969).

Archives of the History of American Psychology, Donald K. Adams Papers.

```
        Program of the Meeting of Topological Psychologists

      Northampton, Massachusetts, September 4-6, 1948


Saturday, September 4  Morning    Reports from the Research
                                  Center for Group Dynamics
                                  (Massachusetts Institute
                                  of Technology)

                       Afternoon  Jerome D. Frank (The Wash-
                                  ington School of Psychiatry):
                                  Some problems of research in
                                  group psychotherapy with
                                  neurotics


Sunday,  September 5   Morning    David Rapaport (Austen-
                                  Riggs Foundation):  The basic
                                  conceptual structure of
                                  psychoanalysis

                       Afternoon  Tamara Dembo (New School
                                  for Social Research):
                                  Social-emotional relation-
                                  ships between injured and
                                  non-injured people


Monday,  September 6   Morning    Fritz Heider (University of
                                  Kansas):  Problems of inter-
                                  personal relationships

                       Afternoon  Alex Bavelas (Massachusetts
                                  Institute of Technology):
                                  Some mathematical properties
                                  of psychological space



No formal program is planned for the evenings.  It has been
suggested that Saturday evening be reserved for five or ten
minute reports of research in progress by members of the group
who are not on the program.
```

Participants in the meeting who have not been previously introduced in this volume are Alex Bavelas (Ph.D., Massachusetts Institute of Technology, 1948), Fritz Heider (Ph.D., Graz, 1920), and David Rapaport (Ph.D., Royal Hungarian Petrus Pazmany, 1938).

Archives of the History of American Psychology, Donald K. Adams Papers.

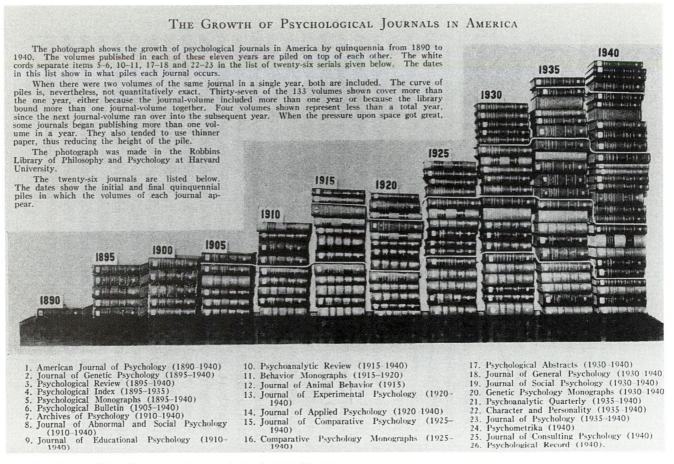

THE GROWTH OF PSYCHOLOGICAL JOURNALS IN AMERICA

The photograph shows the growth of psychological journals in America by quinquennia from 1890 to 1940. The volumes published in each of these eleven years are piled on top of each other. The white cords separate items 5–6, 10–11, 17–18 and 22–23 in the list of twenty-six serials given below. The dates in this list show in what piles each journal occurs.

When there were two volumes of the same journal in a single year, both are included. The curve of piles is, nevertheless, not quantitatively exact. Thirty-seven of the 133 volumes shown cover more than the one year, either because the journal-volume included more than one year or because the library bound more than one journal-volume together. Four volumes shown represent less than a total year, since the next journal-volume ran over into the subsequent year. When the pressure upon space got great, some journals began publishing more than one volume in a year. They also tended to use thinner paper, thus reducing the height of the pile.

The photograph was made in the Robbins Library of Philosophy and Psychology at Harvard University.

The twenty-six journals are listed below. The dates show the initial and final quinquennial piles in which the volumes of each journal appear.

1. American Journal of Psychology (1890–1940)
2. Journal of Genetic Psychology (1895–1940)
3. Psychological Review (1895–1940)
4. Psychological Index (1895–1935)
5. Psychological Monographs (1895–1940)
6. Psychological Bulletin (1905–1940)
7. Archives of Psychology (1910–1940)
8. Journal of Abnormal and Social Psychology (1910–1940)
9. Journal of Educational Psychology (1910–1940)
10. Psychoanalytic Review (1915–1940)
11. Behavior Monographs (1915–1920)
12. Journal of Animal Behavior (1915)
13. Journal of Experimental Psychology (1920–1940)
14. Journal of Applied Psychology (1920–1940)
15. Journal of Comparative Psychology (1925–1940)
16. Comparative Psychology Monographs (1925–1940)
17. Psychological Abstracts (1930–1940)
18. Journal of General Psychology (1930–1940)
19. Journal of Social Psychology (1930–1940)
20. Genetic Psychology Monographs (1930–1940)
21. Psychoanalytic Quarterly (1935–1940)
22. Character and Personality (1935–1940)
23. Journal of Psychology (1935–1940)
24. Psychometrika (1940)
25. Journal of Consulting Psychology (1940)
26. Psychological Record (1940).

Psychological Review, 1943, p. 80. Anonymous, Permission American Psychological Association.

registers of the content and location of the literature on all aspects of psychology. Both of these sources are vital for the flourishing of a science. Serials supplement books in a variety of ways, and, since they consist of independently written reports, they can be published in a much shorter time than is required for the writing, editing, and producing of a bound volume. The literature logs allow a professional to learn about the existence and whereabouts of latest developments in the field. Although these information grids extend over essentially the entire span covered in this volume we have not dealt with them previously for two reasons: first, much of the expansion in this growth was delayed until the Era of Maturity and, second, postponing the accounts of these two aids to scholarship allows this discussion to conclude with victories.

This sketch begins with the founding in 1887 of *The American Journal of Psychology* by G. Stanley Hall.★ He was then at the Johns Hopkins University at a time when fellow faculty members were unusually interested in scholarly journals. From 1878 through 1887 they established serials devoted to archeology, chemistry,

mathematics, modern languages, and philosophy. Hall's *Journal* was well received, but when some differences about editorial practices developed, James Mark Baldwin★ and James McKeen Cattell★ created the Psychological Review Company. In 1894, they started two periodicals: *The Psychological Review* and *The Psychological Index*. They would later add to this list, and other psychologists would initiate several additional periodicals.

The most elaborate journal program came to be sponsored by the American Psychological Association, but this institutional support was delayed until 1925 when Howard C. Warren★ (Ph.D., Johns Hopkins, 1917), then owner of the Psychological Review Company, wanted to establish journals as "organs of American psychology rather than an individual enterprise," and he offered to sell those he owned to the American Psychological Association (Warren, 1930, p. 461). The organization had to raise money to meet the price, and, in 1929, when it had repaid approximately two-thirds of the debt, Warren generously cancelled the remainder. In 1925, the

At the time Howard C. Warren gave the Psychological Review Company to the APA, the PRC owned and published The Psychological Review, The Psychological Index, Psychological Monographs, Psychological Bulletin, *and* The Journal of Experimental Psychology *(Fernberger, 1934).*

Archives of the History of American Psychology, University of Iowa Libraries Record.

Association also received *The Journal of Abnormal and Social Psychology* from the man who founded it in 1906 and edited it until 1929, Morton Prince (M.D., Harvard, 1879), one of the trailblazers in the study of psychopathology in the United States. These acquisitions did not block publications by individuals and other groups (p. 165), but they started the American Psychological Association on a course in which it became the pacesetter.

The diligence of informing members about available literature began shortly after the first journal was founded, most of this information has been conveyed in two serial publications. The first of these, *The Psychological Index,* issued from 1894 to 1930, contains lists of the titles of articles and books. This was supplemented in 1927 by *The Psychological Abstracts,* a register of noncritical summaries of material published in both books and periodicals and in several languages. This is still being published, but the sheer mass of the writing has required reductions in the scope of the *Abstracts,* and coverage was reduced to only *serial literature in English.* But even within this limitation, the amount that is surveyed is vast. By 1990, the contents of over 1,400 journals in the behavioral and social sciences were being abstracted, approximately 3,000 entries in each of 12 issues printed during a single year. The American Psychological Association tries to make this aggregate manageable by publishing supplements that segregate the articles into different areas (American Psychological Association, 1990). The abundance of this literature confirms a constructive, pluralistic psychology—both scientific and applied—vigorous at more than 100 years of age.

Wilhelm Wundt centennial. The 22nd World Congress of Psychology was held at what was then called Karl-Marx University, formerly and presently the University of Leipzig, the institution at which Wilhelm Wundt★ established the pioneer experimental psychology laboratory. Wundt, of course, was the honored figure in

the centennial year of 1979–1980. The medal pictured here (obverse and reverse views), was struck by the government of (East) Germany and is made of brown porcelaneous ceramic clay of the sort used at the nearby Meissen factories in the early eighteenth century.

Archives of the History of American Psychology Photographic File, Courtesy Elizabeth Scarborough.

Wilhelm Wundt centennial. This medal (obverse and reverse views) was struck by the American Psychological Association in 1979 to honor Wilhelm Wundt for his role, in 1879, in establishing psychology as a modern laboratory discipline. The medal was issued in different metals: 1 in gold, 200 in fine silver, and more than

1,000 in bronze or pewter. Sales were good. The silver medal was moving slowly, however, until attempts to corner the silver market resulted in a cost less than the value of the silver incorporated into it, producing such a rush of orders that the entire issue was sold.

Private Collection. Identification with the help of Ludy T. Benjamin, Jr.

References

A

Adorno, T. W. (1968). Scientific experiences of a European scholar in America (D. Fleming, Trans.). In D. Fleming & B. Bailyn (Eds.), *The intellectual migration: Europe and America, 1930–1960* (pp. 338–370). Cambridge, MA: Harvard University Press.

Allport, F. H. (1924). *Social psychology*. Boston, MA: Houghton Mifflin.

Allport, F. H. (1925). *A systematic questionnaire for the study of personality*. Chicago, IL: Stoelting.

Allport, F. H., & Allport, G. W. (1921). Personality traits: Their classification and measurement. *Journal of Abnormal and Social Psychology, 16*, 1–40.

Allport, F. H., Walker, L., & Lathers, E. (1934). Written composition and characteristics of personality. *Archives of Psychology* (No. 173).

Allport, G. W. (1937). *Personality: A psychological interpretation*. New York: Holt.

Allport, G. W. (1938). William Stern: 1871–1938. *American Journal of Psychology, 51*, 770–773.

Allport, G. W. (1968). The personalistic psychology of William Stern. In B. B. Wolman (Ed.), *Historical roots of contemporary psychology* (pp. 321–337). New York: Harper & Row.

Allport, G. W., & Allport, F. H. (1928). *The A-S reaction study: A scale for measuring ascendance-submission in personality*. Boston: Houghton Mifflin.

Allport, G. W., & Odbert, H. S. (1936). Trait-names: A psycho-lexical study. *Psychological Monographs, 47*(Whole No. 211).

American Council on Education (1956). *Conclusions and recommendations on a study of the general educational development testing program*. Washington, DC: Author.

American Psychological Association (1990). *Journals in psychology: A resource listing for authors*. Washington, DC: Author.

Ames, L. B. (1989). *Arnold Gesell—themes of his work*. New York: Human Sciences Press.

Andrews, T. G. (Ed.). (1948). *Methods of psychology*. New York: Wiley.

Angell, J. R. (1903). The relations of structural and functional psychology to philosophy. *Philosophical Review, 12*, 243–271.

Angell, J. R. (1907). The province of functional psychology. *Psychological Review, 14*, 61–91.

Anonymous (1943). The growth of psychological journals in America. *Psychological Review, 50*, 80.

Arnheim, R. (1966). *Toward a psychology of art: Collected essays*. Berkeley, CA: University of California Press.

Arnheim, R. (1974). "Gestalt" misapplied. *Contemporary Psychology, 19*, 570.

Asch, S. E. (1952). *Social Psychology*. New York: Prentice Hall.

Ash, P., & Kroeker, L. P. (1975). Personnel selection, classification, and placement. In M. R. Rosenzweig & L. W. Porter (Eds.), *Annual Review of Psychology, 26*, 481–507. Palo Alto, CA: Annual Reviews.

Atkinson, R. C. (1968). Computerized instruction and the learning process. *American Psychologist, 23*, 225–239.

Avery, D. D., & Cross, H. A., Jr. (1978). *Experimental methodology in psychology*. Monterey, CA: Brooks/Cole.

B

Bahrick, H. P. (1983). The cognitive map of a city: Fifty years of learning and memory. In G. H. Bower (Ed.), *The psychology of learning and motivation, 17*, 125–163. New York: Academic Press.

Bahrick, H. P. (1984). Semantic memory content in permastore: Fifty years of memory for Spanish learned in school. *Journal of Experimental Psychology: General, 113*, 1–29.

Bahrick, H. P., Bahrick, P. O., & Wittlinger, R. P. (1975). Fifty years of memory for names and faces: A cross-sectional approach. *Journal of Experimental Psychology: General, 104*, 54–75.

Bakan, D. (1954). A reconsideration of the problem of introspection. *Psychological Bulletin, 51*, 105–118.

Bakan, D. (1966). The influence of phrenology on American psychology. *Journal of the History of the Behavioral Sciences, 2*, 200–220.

Baldwin, J. M. (1894). Psychology past and present. *Psychological Review, 1*, 363–391.

Bales, J. (1987, December). Senate bill contains exemptions: House bill outlaws worker polygraphs. *APA Monitor*, p. 17.

Beck, S. J. (1930a). Personality diagnosis by means of the Rorschach Test. *American Journal of Orthopsychiatry, 1*, 81–88.

Beck, S. J. (1930b). The Rorschach Test and personality diagnosis. I. The feeble-minded. *American Journal of Psychiatry, 10*, 20–52.

Beck, S. J. (1932). The Rorschach Test as applied to a feeble-minded group. *Archives of Psychology* (No. 136).

Beck, S. J. (1969). *Oral history*. Samuel Beek Papers, Box OH1, Archives of the History of American Psychology, University of Akron.

Benjamin, L. T., Jr. (1979). David Boder's psychological museum and the exposition of 1938. *The Psychological Record, 29*, 559–565.

Benjamin, L. T., Jr. (1988). A history of teaching machines. *American Psychologist, 43*, 703–712.

Bergmann, G. (1956). The contribution of John B. Watson. *Psychological Review, 63*, 265–276.

Berliner, A. (1959). Notes for a lecture on reminiscences of Wundt and Leipzig. *Anna Berliner Memoirs*. Box M50, Archives of the History of American Psychology, University of Akron.

Bertenthal, B. I., Proffitt, D. R., Kramer, S. J., & Spetner, N. B. (1987). Infants' encoding of kinetic displays varying in relative coherence. *Developmental Psychology, 23,* 171–178.

Bettelheim, B. (1943). Individual and mass behavior in extreme situations. *Journal of Abnormal and Social Psychology, 38,* 417–452.

Betts, G. L. (Ed.). (1946). *Minnesota Rate of Manipulation Test: Examiner's manual.* Minneapolis, MN: Educational Test Bureau.

Binet, A., & Simon, T. (1916). *The development of intelligence in children* (E. S. Kite, Trans.). Baltimore: Williams & Wilkins. (Original work published 1905–1911)

Bingham, W. V. (1919a). Army personnel work, with some implications for education and industry. *Journal of Applied Psychology, 3,* 1–10.

Bingham, W. V. (1919b). Development and standardization of the Army Trade Tests. *Industrial Education Circular* (No. 4), 11–16. Washington, DC: Department of the Interior, Bureau of Education.

Bingham, W. V. (1923). Psychology applied. *Scientific Monthly, 16* (No.2), 141–159.

Bingham, W. V. (1941). Psychological services in the United States Army. *Journal of Consulting Psychology, 5,* 221–224.

Bingham, W. V. (1952). Walter Van Dyke Bingham. In E. G. Boring, H. S. Langfeld, H. Werner, & R. M. Yerkes (Eds.), *A history of psychology in autobiography* (Vol. IV, pp. 1–26). Worcester, MA: Clark University Press.

Blumenthal, A. L. (1991). The intrepid Joseph Jastrow. In G. A. Kimble, M. Wertheimer, and C. White (Eds.), *Portraits of pioneers in psychology* (pp.75–87). Hillsdale, NJ: Lawrence Erlbaum.

Boder, David P. (1949). *I did not interview the dead.* Urbana, IL: University of Illinois Press.

Bonser, F. G. (1910). The reasoning ability of children of the fourth, fifth, and sixth school grades. *Contributions to Education* (No. 37). New York: Teachers College, Columbia University.

Boring, E. G. (1938). The Society of Experimental Psychologists: 1904–1938. *American Journal of Psychology, 51,* 410–421.

Boring, E. G. (1942). *Sensation and perception in the history of experimental psychology.* New York: Appleton Century.

Boring, E. G. (1950). *A history of experimental psychology* (2nd ed.). New York: Appleton-Century-Crofts. (Original work published 1929)

Boring, E. G. (1953). A history of introspection. *Psychological Bulletin, 50,* 169–189.

Bowers, R. L., & Richards, R. W. (1990). Dual-elements in pigeons' matching-to-sample with temporal and visual stimuli. *The Psychological Record, 40,* 259–271.

Bradford, L. P. (1974). *National Training Laboratories: Its history 1947–1970.* Bethel, ME: Author.

Bray, C. W. (1948). *Psychology and military proficiency: A history of the applied psychology panel of the National Defense Research Committee.* Princeton, NJ: Princeton University Press.

Bregman, E. O. (1922). Studies in industrial psychology. *Archives of Psychology* (No. 59). New York: Columbia University.

Bregman, E. O. (1925). *Revision of Army Alpha Examination for General Intelligence, Form A.* New York: Psychological Corporation.

Bregman, E. O. (1935). *Revision of Army Alpha Examination for General Intelligence, Form B.* New York: Psychological Corporation.

Bringmann, W. G., Ungerer, G. A., & Ganzer, H. (1980). Illustrations from the life and work of Wilhelm Wundt. In W. G. Bringmann & R. D. Tweney, (Eds.), *Wundt studies: A centennial collection* (pp. 329–359). Toronto: C. J. Hogrefe.

Brown v. Board of Education of Topeka, 347 U.S. 483 (1954).

Brown, C. R. (1967). *University of Michigan–Carl R. Brown Collection.* Box M51, Archives of the History of American Psychology, University of Akron.

Brown, C. W. (1958). George Malcolm Stratton, social psychologist. *Science, 127* (3311), 1432–1433.

Burks, B. (1940). Report of the Committee on Displaced Foreign Psychologists. *Psychological Bulletin, 37,* 715–718.

Burnham, J. C. (1978). The influence of psychoanalysis on American culture. In J. M. Quen & E. T. Carlson (Eds.), *American psychoanalysis: Origins and development* (pp. 52–72). New York: Brenner/Mazel.

Burtt, H. E. (1940). George Frederick Arps: 1874–1939. *American Journal of Psychology, 53,* 141–142.

Butcher, J. N., Dahlstrom, W. G., Graham, J. R., Tellegen, A., & Kaemmer, B. (1989). *Manual for the restandardized Minnesota Multiphasic Personality Inventory: MMPI-2. An administrative and interpretive guide.* Minneapolis, MN: University of Minnesota Press.

C

Cady, V. M. (1923). The estimation of juvenile incorrigibility. *Journal of Delinquency Monograph* (No. 2). Whittier, CA: California Bureau of Juvenile Research.

Calkins, M. W. (1911). *A first book in psychology* (2nd rev. ed.). New York: Macmillan.

Campbell, D. T. (1969). Reforms as experiments. *American Psychologist, 24,* 409–429.

Cannon, W. B. (1936). Ivan Petrovitch Pavlov. *Research Bulletin on the Soviet Union, 1,* 5–8.

Carpignano, J. (1987). Problems in the practice of responsible school psychology. *The School Psychologist, 41* (No. 4), 1–4.

Carr, H., & Watson, J. B. (1908). Orientation in the white rat. *Journal of Comparative Neurology and Psychology, 18,* 27–44.

Cattell, J. M. (1890). Mental tests and measurements. *Mind, 15,* 373–381.

"Christian H. Stoelting." (1943). *American Journal of Psychology, 56,* 450.

Cogan L. C., Conklin, A. M., & Hollingworth, H. L. (1915). An experimental study of self-analysis, estimates of associates, and the results of tests. *School and Society, 2,* 171–179.

Contemporary authors (1st rev.) (1979). s. v. "Starch, Daniel." Detroit, MI: Gale Research Company.

Crissey, M. S. (1979). *Ghosts of the Jersey pines: The Kallikaks rise up to haunt.* Invited address at the Annual Convention of the American Psychological Association, New York, NY.

Cronbach, L. (1975). Five decades of public controversy over mental testing. *American Psychologist, 30,* 1–14.

D

Dahlstrom, W. G., Welsh, G. S., & Dahlstrom, L. E. (1972). *An MMPI handbook, vol. I: Clinical interpretation* (rev. ed.). Minneapolis, MN: University of Minnesota Press.

Dahlstrom, W. G., Welsh, G. S., Dahlstrom, L. E. (1975). *An MMPI handbook, vol. II: Research applications* (rev. ed.). Minneapolis, MN: University of Minnesota Press.

Dallenbach, K. M. (1928). Bibliography of the writings of Edward Bradford Titchener. *American Journal of Psychology, 40,* 121–125.

Dallenbach, K. M. (1946). The Emergency Committee in Psychology, National Research Council. *American Journal of Psychology, 59,* 496–582.

Dallenbach, K. M. (1955). Phrenology versus psychoanalysis. *American Journal of Psychology, 68,* 511–525.

Davis v. County School Board of Prince Edward County, Virginia. Transcript of Record, 191 (1952).

Davis, A., & Eells, K. (1953). *Davis-Eells Test of General Intelligence or Problem-Solving Ability: Manual.* Yonkers-on-Hudson, NY: World Book.

Delabarre, E. B. (1898). A method of recording eye-movements. *American Journal of Psychology, 9,* 572–574.

Delabarre, E. B., & Popplestone, J. A. (1974). A cross cultural contribution to the *cannabis* experience. *The Psychological Record, 24,* 67–73.

Denning, P. J. (1986). The science of computing: Will machines ever think? *American Scientist, 74* (No. 4), 344–346.

Dewey, J. (1896). The reflex arc concept in psychology. *Psychological Review, 3,* 357–370.

Dewsbury, D. A. (1991). Obituary for James McConnell (1925–1990). *Animal Behavior Society Newsletter, 36* (No.1), p. 6.

Dewsbury, D. A. (1993). On publishing controversy: Norman R. F. Maier and the genesis of seizures. *American Psychologist, 48,* 869–877.

Diamond, S. (Ed.). (1974). *The roots of psychology: A source book in the history of ideas.* New York: Basic Books.

Dictionary of Scientific Biography. (1972). s. v. "Gall, Franz Joseph." Charles Scribner's Sons.

Dollard, J., & Miller, N. E. (1950). *Personality and psychotherapy: An analysis in terms of learning, thinking, and culture.* New York: McGraw-Hill.

Downey, J. E. (1923). *The will-temperament and its testing.* Yonkers-on-Hudson, NY: World Book.

Downey, M. T. (1965). *Ben D. Wood: Educational Reformer.* Princeton, NJ: Educational Testing Service.

DuBois, P. H. (1970). *A history of psychological testing.* Boston: Allyn and Bacon.

Duncan, J. (1980). The locus of interference in the perception of simultaneous stimuli. *Psychological Review, 87,* 272–300.

Dunlap, K. (1919). Psychological research in aviation. *Science,* (n. s. *49*), 94–97.

Dunlap, K. (1932). Knight Dunlap. In C. Murchison (Ed.), *A history of psychology in autobiography* (Vol. II, pp. 35–61). Worcester, MA: Clark University Press.

E

Edgell, B., & Symes, W. L. (1906). The Wheatstone-Hipp chronoscope. Its adjustments, accuracy, and control. *British Journal of Psychology, 2,* 58–88.

The effects of segregation and the consequences of desegregation: A social science statement. (1952). New York: Supreme Printing Co.

Ellenberger, H. (1954). The life and work of Hermann Rorschach (1884–1922). *Bulletin of the Menninger Clinic, 18,* 173–219.

Encyclopaedia Britannica, (14th ed.). s. v. "Experimental Psychology."

Estes, W. K. (1980). Is human memory obsolete? *American Scientist, 68,* 62–69.

Estes, W. K. (1981). The bible is out [Review of experimental psychology]. *Contemporary Psychology, 26,* 327–330.

Exner, J. E., Jr. (1989). The Society for Personality Assessment: A history. In A. M. O'Roark & J. E. Exner, Jr. (Eds.), *History and directory: Society for Personality Assessment: Fiftieth anniversary* (pp. 3–54). Hillsdale, NJ: Lawrence Erlbaum.

Eysenck, H. J., & Kamin, L. (1981). *Intelligence: The battle for the mind.* London: Macmillan.

F

Fernald, D. (1984). *The Hans legacy: A story of Science.* Hillsdale, NJ: Lawrence Erlbaum.

Fernberger, S. (1934). Howard Crosby Warren 1867–1934. *Psychological Bulletin, 31,* 1–4.

Festinger, L. (1957). *A theory of cognitive dissonance.* Evanston, IL: Row, Peterson.

Festinger, L., Riecken, H. W., & Schachter, S. (1956). *When prophecy fails.* Minneapolis, MN: University of Minnesota Press.

Flanagan, J. C. (Ed.). (1948). The aviation psychology program in the Army Air Forces. *Army Air Forces Aviation Psychology Program Report No. 1.* Washington, DC: U. S. Government Printing Office.

Fleck, G. (Ed.). (1973). *A computer perspective.* Cambridge, MA: Harvard University Press.

Fowler, R. D., & Butcher, J. N. (1986). Critique of Matarazzo's views on computerized testing: All sigma and no meaning. *American Psychologist, 41,* 94–96.

Frank, L. K. (1939). Projective methods for the study of personality. *Journal of Psychology, 8,* 389–413.

Franz, S. I. (1900). On the methods of estimating the force of voluntary muscular contractions and on fatigue. *American Journal of Physiology, 4,* 348–372.

Freeman, F. S. (1950). *Theory and practice of psychological testing.* New York: Henry Holt.

Freeman, F. S. (1955). *Theory and practice of Psychological Testing* (rev. ed.). New York: Henry Holt.

Freud, A. (1937). *The ego and mechanisms of defense.* New York: International Universities Press.

Friedline, C. (1962). Lecture on the history of psychology. *Cora Friedline Memoirs.* Box OH1, Archives of the History of American Psychology, University of Akron.

G

Galton, F. (1909). *Memoirs of my life.* New York: E. P. Dutton.

Garfield, S. L. (1981). Psychotherapy: A 40-year appraisal. *American Psychologist, 36,* 174–183.

Garrett, H. E. (ca. 1967). *Children: Black & white.* Kilmarnock, VA: Patrick Henry Press.

Garvey, C. R. (1929). List of American psychology laboratories. *Psychological Bulletin, 26,* 652–660.

Gibson, E. J., & Walk, R. D. (1960). The "visual cliff." *American Scientist, 202* (No. 4), 64–71.

Goddard, H. H. (1908a). The Binet and Simon tests of intellectual capacity. *The Training School, 5,* 3–9.

Goddard, H. H. (1908b). The grading of backward children. *The Training School, 5,* 12–14.

Goddard, H. H. (1910a). Four hundred feeble-minded children classified by the Binet method. *Journal of Psycho-Asthenics, 15,* 17–30. (Also in *Pedagogical Seminary,* 1910, *17,* 387–397)

Goddard, H. H. (1910b). A measuring scale of intelligence. *The Training School, 6,* 146–155.

Goddard, H. H. (1911). Heredity of feeble-mindedness. *Annual Report of the American Breeders Association, 6,* 103–116.

Goddard, H. H. (1952). Letter to "Dear Friends," 6 March. In *Goddard Papers,* Box M35 2, Archives of the History of American Psychology, University of Akron.

Goldfried, M. R., & Kent, R. N. (1972). Traditional versus behavioral personality assessment: A comparison of methodological and theoretical assumptions. *Psychological Bulletin, 77,* 409–420.

Goodenough, F. L. (1926). *Measurement of intelligence by drawings.* Yonkers-on-Hudson, NY: World Book.

Goodenough, F. L. (1949). *Mental testing: Its history, principles, and applications.* New York: Rinehart.

Gottlieb, G. (1972). Zing-Yang Kuo: Radical scientific philosopher and innovative experimentalist (1898–1970). *Journal of Comparative and Physiological Psychology, 80,* 1–10.

Gottschaldt, K. (1938). Gestalt factors and repetition. In W. D. Ellis (Ed. & Trans.), *A source book of Gestalt psychology* (pp. 109–135). London: Kegan Paul, Trench, Trubner. (Original work published 1926)

Graham, C. H. (1958). Walter Samuel Hunter, 1889–1954. *Biographical Memoirs, 31,* 127–155.

Griffin, D. R., & Hock, R. J. (1948). Experiments on bird navigation, *Science, 107* (No. 2779), 347–349.

Guilford, J. P. (1948). Some lessons from aviation psychology. *American Psychologist, 3,* 3–11.

H

Hall, G. S. (1912). *Founders of modern psychology.* New York: Appleton.

Hall, G. S. (1920). Preface to American edition. In S. Freud, *A general introduction to psychoanalysis* (deluxe ed., J. Riviere, Trans.). New York: Garden City Publishing.

Hall, G. S. (1923). *Life and confessions of a psychologist.* New York: Appleton.

Hall, G. S., & Wallin, J. E. W. (1902). How children and youth think and feel about clouds. *Pedagogical Seminary, 9,* 460–506.

Harlow, H. F., Harlow, M. K., & Suomi, S. J. (1971). From thought to therapy: Lessons from a primate laboratory. *American Scientist, 59* (No. 5), 538–549.

Harper, R. S. (1950). The first psychological laboratory. *Isis, 41,* 158–161.

Harrison, R. (1963). Functionalism and its historical significance. *Genetic Psychology Monographs, 68,* 387–423.

Harrower, M. (1983). *Kurt Koffka: An unwitting self-portrait.* Gainesville, FL: University Presses of Florida.

Harrower, M. R., & Steiner, M. E., (1945). *Manual for psychodiagnostic inkblots.* Authors.

Hathaway, S. R. (1947). A coding system for MMPI profile classification. *Journal of Consulting Psychology, 11,* 334–337.

Hathaway, S. R. (1958). A study of human behavior: The clinical psychologist. *American Psychologist, 13,* 257–265.

Hathaway, S. R. (1978). Through psychology my way. In T. S. Krawiec (Ed.), *The psychologists: Autobiographies of distinguished living psychologists, 3,* 105–123. Brandon, VT: Clinical Psychology Publishing.

Healy, W. (1914). A pictorial completion test. *Psychological Review, 21,* 189–203.

Healy, W., & Fernald, G. M. (1911). Tests for practical mental classification. *Psychological Monographs, 13*(2, Whole No. 54).

Hebb, D. O. (1949). *The organization of behavior: A neuropsychological theory.* New York: Wiley.

Heidbreder, E. (1933). *Seven psychologies.* New York: Appleton-Century.

Heidbreder, E. (1940). Freud and psychology. *Psychological Review, 47,* 185–195.

Heider, F. (1944). Social perception and phenomenal causality. *Psychological Review, 51,* 358–374.

Henle, M. (1962). On the relation between logic and thinking. *Psychological Review, 69,* 366–378.

Henle, M. (Ed.). (1971). *The selected papers of Wolfgang Köhler.* New York: Liveright.

Henle M. (1978). Gestalt psychology and Gestalt therapy. *Journal of the History of the Behavioral Sciences, 14,* 23–32.

Henle, M. (1986). *1879 and all that: Essays in the theory and history of psychology.* New York: Columbia University Press.

Henle, M. (1987). Koffka's *Principles* after fifty years. *Journal of the History of the Behavioral Sciences, 23,* 14–21.

Henle, M. (1989). Some new Gestalt psychologies. *Psychological Research, 51,* 81–85.

Henmon, V. A. C. (1919). Air service tests of aptitude for flying. *Journal of Applied Psychology, 3,* 103–109.

Herma, H., Kris, E., & Shor, J. (1943). Freud's theory of the dream in American textbooks. *Journal of Abnormal and Social Psychology, 38,* 319–334.

Herring, J. P. (1922). *Herring Revision of the Binet-Simon Tests: Examination manual, Form A.* Yonkers-on-Hudson, New York: World Book.

Hertz, M. R. (1932). *Concerning the reliability and the validity of the Rorschach Ink-Blot Test.* Unpublished doctoral dissertation, Western Reserve University, Cleveland, Ohio.

Hertz, M. R. (1985). *Oral History.* Oral History Project, Board of Professional Affairs, American Psychological Association.

Hilgard, E. R. (1949). Human motives and the concept of the self. *American Psychologist, 4,* 374–382.

Hilgard, E. R. (1951). Methods and procedures in the study of learning. In S. S. Stevens (Ed.), *Handbook of Experimental Psychology* (pp. 517–567). New York: Wiley.

Hilgard, E. R. (1957). Freud and experimental psychology. *Behavioral Science, 2,* 74–79.

Hilgard, E. R. (1974). Ernest Ropiequet Hilgard. In G. Lindzey (Ed.), *A history of psychology in autobiography* (Vol. VI, pp. 129–160). Englewood Cliffs, NJ: Prentice-Hall.

Hilgard, E. R. (1978). *American psychology in historical perspective: Addresses of the presidents of the American Psychological Association, 1892–1977.* Washington, DC: American Psychological Association.

Hilgard, E. R. (1987). *Psychology in America: A Historical Survey.* San Diego, CA: Harcourt Brace Jovanovich.

Hilgard, E. R., & Marquis, D. G. (1940). *Conditioning and learning.* New York: Appleton-Century.

Hollingworth, H. L. (1915). Specialized vocational tests and methods. *School and Society, 1,* 918–922.

Hollingworth, H. L. (1926). *The psychology of thought: Approached through studies of sleeping and dreaming.* New York: Appleton.

Hollingworth, H. L. (1943). *Leta Stetter Hollingworth: A biography.* Lincoln, NE: University of Nebraska Press.

Holmes, O. W. (1861). Sun-painting and sun-sculpture; With a stereoscopic trip across the Atlantic. *Atlantic Monthly, 8,* 13–29.

Hoover, T. O., & McPherson, M. W. (1972). A few paradoxes in the history of inkblots. *Proceedings of the 80th annual convention of the American Psychological Association, 7,* 779–780.

Hornaday, W. T. (1883). Mental capacity of the elephant. *Popular Science Monthly, 23,* 497–509.

Horowitz, E. L. (1936). The development of attitude toward the Negro. *Archives of Psychology* (No. 194).

House, S. D. (1927). A mental hygiene inventory: A contribution to dynamic psychology. *Archives of Psychology* (No. 88).

Hovland, C. I. (1938). Experimental studies in rote-learning theory: I. Reminiscence following learning by massed and by distributed practice. *Journal of Experimental Psychology, 22,* 201–224.

Hunt, J. McV. (1961). *Intelligence and experience.* New York: Ronald Press.

Hunter, W. S. (1928). The behavior of raccoons in a double alternation temporal maze. *Journal of Genetic Psychology, 35,* 374–388.

Hunter, W. S. (1946). Psychology in the war. *American Psychologist, 1,* 479–492.

Ittelson, W. H. (1952). *The Ames demonstrations in perception.* Princeton, NJ: Princeton University Press.

J

Jahoda, M. (1963). Some notes on the influence of psycho-analytic ideas on American psychology. *Human Relations, 16,* 111–129.

James, W. (1890). *Principles of psychology (Vols. 1–2).* New York: Holt.

James, W. (1892). *Psychology, briefer course.* New York: Holt.

Janney, J. E. (1941). Fad and fashion leadership among undergraduate women. *Journal of Abnormal and Social Psychology, 36,* 275–278.

Jastrow, J. (1892). Some anthropometric and psychologic tests on college students–a preliminary survey. *American Journal of Psychology, 4,* 420–427.

Jastrow, J. (1893). Section of psychology. In F. W. Putnam (Ed.), *World's Columbian Exposition Official Catalogue, Department M* (pp. 50–60). Chicago: W. B. Conkey.

Jastrow, J., Baldwin, J. M., & Cattell, J. M. (1898). Physical and mental tests. *Psychological Review, 5,* 172–179.

Johnson, B. (1920). Emotional instability in children. *Ungraded, 4,* 73–79. (From *Journal of Delinquency, 5,* Abstract p. 137)

Johnson, D. M. (1945). The "phantom anesthetist" of Mattoon: A field study of mass hysteria. *Journal of Abnormal and Social Psychology, 40,* 175–186.

Jonçich, G. (1968). *The sane positivist: A biography of Edward L. Thorndike.* Middletown, CT: Wesleyan University Press.

Jones, E. (1953–1957). *The life and work of Sigmund Freud* (Vols. 1–3). New York: Basic Books.

Jones, M. C. (1924a). The elimination of children's fears. *Journal of Experimental Psychology, 7,* 382–390.

Jones, M. C. (1924b). A laboratory study of fear: The case of Peter. *Pedagogical Seminary, 31,* 308–315.

Jones, M. C. (1975). A 1924 pioneer looks at behavior therapy. *Journal of Behavior Therapy and Experimental Psychiatry, 6,* 181–187.

K

Kantor, J. R. (1925). The significance of the *Gestalt* conception in psychology. *Journal of Philosophy, 22,* 234–241.

Kantor, J. R. (1971). *The aim and progress of psychology and other sciences: A selection of papers.* Chicago: Principia Press.

Kantor, J. R., & Smith, N. W. (1975). *The science of psychology: An interbehavioral survey.* Chicago: Principia Press.

Karslake, J. S. (1940). The Purdue Eye-Camera: A practical apparatus for studying the attention value of advertisements. *Journal of Applied Psychology, 24,* 417–440.

Kellman, P. J., & Spelke, E. S. (1983). Perception of partly occluded objects in infancy. *Cognitive Psychology, 15,* 483–524.

Kellogg, W. N., & Kellogg, L. A. (1967). *The ape and the child: A study of environmental influence upon early behavior*. New York: Hafner. (Original work published 1933)

Kent, G. H. (1946). *Series of Emergency Scales (Manual)*. New York: Psychological Corporation.

Kent, G. H., & Rosanoff, A. J. (1910). A study of association in insanity. *American Journal of Insanity, 67*, 37–96, 317–390.

Kinkade, R. G. (Ed.). (1974). *Thesaurus of psychological index terms*. Washington, DC: American Psychological Association.

Kling, J. W., & Riggs, L. A. (Eds.). (1971). *Woodworth and Schlosberg's Experimental Psychology* (3rd ed.). New York: Holt, Rinehart & Winston.

Knox, H. A. (1914). A scale, based on the work at Ellis Island, for estimating mental defect. *Journal of the American Medical Association, 62*, 741–747.

Koffka, K. (1935). *Principles of Gestalt psycholgy*. New York: Harcourt, Brace.

Köhler, W. (1927). *The mentality of apes* (2nd rev. ed.). (E. Winter, Trans.). New York: Harcourt, Brace. (Original work published 1917, first published in English 1925)

Köhler, W. (1929). *Gestalt psychology*. New York: Liveright.

Köhler, W. (1938). Simple structural functions in the chimpanzee and in the chicken. In W. D. Ellis (Ed.), *A source book of Gestalt psychology*. London: Kegan Paul, Trench, Trubner. (Original work published 1918)

Krohn, W. O. (1893). An experimental study of simultaneous stimulations of the sense of touch. *Journal of Nervous and Mental Diseases, 18*, 169–184.

Kuhlmann, F. (1922). *A handbook of mental tests: A further revision and extension of the Binet-Simon scale*. Baltimore, MD: Warwick & York.

Kuo, Z. Y. (1931). The genesis of the cat's responses to the rat. *Journal of Comparative Psychology, 11*, 1–35.

Kurtz, R. M. (1969). A conceptual investigation of Witkin's notion of perceptual style. *Mind, 78*, 522–533.

L

Lafleur, L. J. (1942). Anti-social behavior among ants. *Journal of Comparative Psychology, 33*, 33–39.

Lafleur, L. J. (1943). A reply. *Journal of Comparative Psychology, 35*, 97–99.

Laird, D. A. (1925). Detecting abnormal behavior. *Journal of Abnormal and Social Psychology, 20*, 128–141.

LaPiere, R. T., & Farnsworth, P. R. (1942). *Social psychology*. New York: McGraw-Hill.

Lashley, K. S. (1929). *Brain mechanisms and intelligence: A quantitative study of injuries to the brain*. Chicago: University of Chicago Press.

Lashley, K. S. (1930). Basic neural mechanisms in behavior. *Psychological Review, 37*, 1–34.

Lashley, K. S. (1938). The mechanism of vision: XV. Preliminary studies of the rat's capacity for detail vision. *Journal of General Psychology, 18*, 123–193.

Lewin, K. (1936). Some social-psychological differences between the United States and Germany. *Character and Personality, 4*, 265–293.

Licklider, J. C. R., & Miller, G. A. (1951). The perception of speech. In S. S. Stevens (Ed.), *Handbook of Experimental Psychology* (pp. 1040–1074). New York: Wiley.

Link, H. C. (1919). *Employment psychology: The application of scientific methods to the selection, training and rating of employees*. New York: Macmillan.

Little, J. K. (1934). Results of use of machines for testing and for drill, upon learning in educational psychology. *Journal of Experimental Education, 3*, 45–49.

Lundin, R. W. (1967). *An objective psychology of music* (2nd ed.). New York: Ronald Press.

M

MacKinnon D. W. (1977). From selecting spies to selecting managers—the OSS assessment program. In J. L. Moses & W. C. Byham (Eds.), *Applying the assessment center method* (pp. 13–30). New York: Pergamon Press.

MacLeod, R. B. (1947). The phenomenological approach to social psychology. *Psychological Review, 54*, 193–210.

Maier, N. R. F. (1949). *Frustration: The study of behavior without a goal*. New York: McGraw-Hill.

Maller, J. B. (1944). Personality tests. In J. McV. Hunt (Ed.), *Personality and the behavior disorders* (pp. 170–213). New York: Ronald Press.

Mandler, J. M. (1990). A new perspective on cognitive development in infancy. *American Scientist, 78*, 236–243.

Mandler, J. M., & Mandler, G. (1968). The diaspora of experimental psychology: The Gestaltists and others. In D. Fleming & B. Bailyn (Eds.), *The intellectual migration: Europe and America, 1930–1960* (pp. 371–419). Cambridge, MA: Harvard University Press.

Marrow, A. J. (1969). *The practical theorist: The life and work of Kurt Lewin*. New York: Basic Books.

Martin, L. J. (1906). The electrical supply in the new psychological laboratory at the Leland Stanford, Jr., University. *American Journal of Psychology, 17*, 274–279.

Marx, M. H., & Cronan-Hillix, W. A. (1987). *Systems and theories in psychology* (4th ed.). New York: McGraw-Hill.

Maslow, A. H. (1967). Self-actualization and beyond. In J. F. T. Bugenthal (Ed.), *Challenges of humanistic psychology* (pp. 279–286). New York: McGraw-Hill.

Maslow, A. H. (1970). *Motivation and personality* (2nd ed.). New York: Harper & Row. (Original work published 1954)

Matarazzo, J. D. (1972). *Wechsler's measurement and appraisal of adult intelligence* (5th ed.). Baltimore: Williams & Wilkins.

Matarazzo, J. D. (1981). David Wechsler (1896–1981). *American Psychologist, 36*, 1542–1543.

Matarazzo, J. D. (1986). Computerized clinical psychological test interpretations: Unvalidated plus all mean and no sigma. *American Psychologist, 41*, 14–24.

McCaffrey, K. R. (1965). Founders of the Training School at Vineland, New Jersey: S. Olin Garrison, Alexander Johnson, Edward H. Johnstone. (Doctoral Dissertation, Teachers College, Columbia University, 1965). *Dissertation Abstracts, 65–14*, 974.

McClelland, D. C. (1973). Testing for competence rather than for "intelligence." *American Psychologist, 28*, 1–14.

McGraw, M. B. (1935). *Growth: A study of Johnny and Jimmy*. New York: Appleton-Century.

McPherson, M. W., & Popplestone, J. A. (1981). *Binet's influence on the sampling of intelligent behavior*. Paper presented at the meeting of the American Psychological Association, Los Angeles, CA.

Meehl, P. E. (1956). Wanted—a good cookbook. *American Psychologist, 11*, 263–272.

Melton, A. W. (Ed.). (1947). Apparatus tests. *Army Air Forces Aviation Psychology Program Report* (No. 4). Washington, DC: Government Printing Office.

Meltzoff, A. N., & Borton, R. W. (1979). Intermodal matching by human neonates. *Nature, 282*, 403–404.

Merrill, M. (1943). Lillien Jane Martin: 1851–1943. *American Journal of Psychology, 56*, 453–454.

Messer, S. B., & Winokur, M. (1980). Some limits to the integration of psychoanalytic and behavior therapy. *American Psychologist, 35*, 818–827.

Meyer, M. F. (1935). Roads, reefs and refuges of an academic runagate. *Meyer Memoirs*. Box M1621, Archives of the History of American Psychology, University of Akron.

Miles, C. C., & Miles, W. R. (1932). The correlation of intelligence scores and chronological age from early to late maturity. *American Journal of Psychology, 44*, 44–78.

Miles, W. R. (1943). Red goggles for producing dark adaptation. *Proceedings of the Federation of American Societies for Experimental Biology, 2*, 109–115.

Miles, W. R. (1956). Raymond Dodge 1871–1942. *Biographical Memoirs, 29,* 65–122.

Milgram, S. (1974). *Obedience to authority: An experimental view.* New York: Harper & Row.

Miller, N. E. (1979). Walter R. Miles (1885–1978). *Year Book of the American Philosophical Society,* 89–94.

Miller, N. E. (1983). Behavioral medicine: Symbiosis between laboratory and clinic. In M. R. Rosenzweig & L. W. Porter (Eds.), *Annual Review of Psychology, 34,* 1–31.

Moore, B. V., Lapp, C. J., & Griffin, C. H. (1943). *Enginneering and physical science aptitude test.* New York: Psychological Corporation.

Morgan, C. D., & Murray, H. A. (1935). A method for investigating fantasies. *Archives of Neurology and Psychiatry, 34,* 289–306.

Morris, F. O. (1873?). *Anecdotes in natural history.* New York: Routledge and London: S. W. Partridge.

Mowrer, O. H. (1959). A cognitive theory of dynamics [Review of *Dynamics of Behavior*]. *Contemporary Psychology, 4,* 129–133.

Mullan, E. H. (1917). Mental examination of immigrants: Administration and line inspection at Ellis Island. *Public Health Reports, 32*(Part 1), 733–746. United States Public Health Service. Washington, DC: U. S. Government Printing Office.

Munroe, R. L. (1955). *Schools of psychoanalytic thought: An exposition, critique, and attempt at integration.* New York: Dryden Press.

Münsterberg, H. (1893). *Psychological Laboratory at Harvard University.* Cambridge, MA.

Münsterberg, H. (1896?) *Pseudoptics.* Springfield, MA: Milton Bradley Co.

Murphy, G., & Murphy, L. B. (1931). *Experimental social psychology.* New York: Harper.

Murphy, L. B. (1941). Experiments in free play. In E. Lerner & L. B. Murphy (Eds.), Methods for the study of personality in young children. *Monographs of the Society for Research in Child Development, 6,* 1–98 (Serial No. 30).

Murphy, L. B. (1960). Coping devices and defense mechanisms in relation to autonomous ego functions. *Bulletin of the Menninger Clinic, 24,* 144–153.

Murphy, L. B., & Moriarty, A. E. (1976). *Vulnerability, coping, and growth.* New Haven, CT: Yale University Press.

Murray, H. A. (1938). *Explorations in personality: A clinical and experimental study of fifty men of college age.* New York: Oxford University Press.

N

Napoli, D. S. (1981). *Architects of adjustment: The history of the psychological profession in the United States.* Port Washington, NY: Kennikat Press.

Neisser, U. (1984). Interpreting Harry Bahrick's discovery: What confers immunity against forgetting? *Journal of Experimental Psychology: General, 113,* 32–35.

Newman, E. B. (1966). Minutes of the annual meeting of the Council of Representatives. *American Psychologist, 21,* 1127–1147.

Nichols, H. (1893, October). The psychological laboratory at Harvard. *McClure's Magazine,* 399–409.

Nisbett, R. E., & Wilson, T. D. (1977). Telling more than we can know: Verbal reports on mental processes. *Psychological Review, 84,* 231–259.

Notable American women 1607–1950: A biographical dictionary. s. v. "Calkins, Mary Whiton."

Notable American women 1607–1950: A biographical dictionary. s. v. "Ladd-Franklin, Christine."

O

O'Dell, J. W. (1972). P. T. Barnum explores the computer. *Journal of Consulting and Clinical Psychology, 38,* 270–273.

Office of Strategic Services (OSS) Assessment Staff. (1948). *Assessment of men: Selection of personnel for the Office of Strategic Services.* New York: Rinehart.

P

Pate, J. L., & Newsom, M. W. (1983). Imagery effects with mixed and unmixed lists. *The Psychological Record, 33,* 379–389.

Pearson, K. (1924). *The life, letters and labours of Francis Galton: Vol. 2. Researches of middle life.* Cambridge, England: The University Press.

Pfungst, O. (1965). *Clever Hans (the horse of Mr. Von Osten)* R. Rosenthal (Ed.), New York: Holt, Rinehart and Winston. (Original work published 1911)

Pillsbury, W. B. (1928). The psychology of Edward Bradford Titchener. *Philosophical Review, 37,* 95–108.

Popplestone, J. A. (1985). The legacy of memory in apparatus and methodology. In W. Traxel (Ed.), *Ebbinghaus-Studien 2* (pp. 203–215). Germany: Passau Universitätsverlag.

Popplestone, J. A., & McPherson, M. W., (1974). An historical note on *cannabis. Catalog of Selected Documents in Psychology, 4,* 68. (Ms. No. 660)

Popplestone, J. A., & McPherson, M. W. (1983). Pioneer psychology laboratories in clinical settings. In J. Brozek (Ed.), *Explorations in the history of psychology in the United States* (pp. 196–272). Lewisburg, PA: Bucknell University Press.

Popplestone, J. A., & McPherson, M. W. (1988). *Dictionary of concepts in general psychology.* New York: Greenwood Press.

Porter, R. B., & Harsh, C. M. (1947). Achievement examinations for elementary enlisted schools. In D. B. Stuit (Ed.),

Personnel research and test development in the Bureau of Naval Personnel (pp. 295–314). Princeton, NJ: Princeton University Press.

Posner, M. I., & Mitchell, R. F. (1967). Chronometric analysis of classification. *Psychological Review, 74,* 392–409.

Pratt, C. C. (1969). Wolfgang Köhler 1887–1967. In W. Köhler, *The task of Gestalt psychology* (pp. 3–29). Princeton, NJ: Princeton University Press.

Pressey, S. L. (1921). A group scale for investigating the emotions. *Journal of Abnormal and Social Psychology, 16,* 55–64.

Pressey, S. L. (1926). A simple apparatus which gives tests and scores—and teaches. *School and Society, 23,* 373–376.

Pressey, S. L. (1932). A third and fourth contribution toward the coming "industrial revolution" in education. *School and Society, 36,* 668–672.

Pressey, S. L. (1967). Sidney Leavitt Pressey. In E. G. Boring & G. Lindzey (Eds.), *A history of psychology in autobiography* (Vol. V, pp. 311–339). New York: Appleton-Century-Crofts.

Pressey, S. L., & Pressey, L. W. (1919). "Cross-out" tests with suggestions as to a group scale of the emotions. *Journal of Applied Psychology, 3,* 138–150.

Pumpian-Mindlin, E. (Ed.). (1952). *Psychoanalysis as science: The Hixon lectures on the scientific status of psychoanalysis.* Stanford, CA: Stanford University Press.

R

Radford, J. (1974). Reflections on introspection. *American Psychologist, 29,* 245–250.

Raphelson, A. C. (1980). Psychology at Michigan: The Pillsbury years (1897–1947). *Journal of the History of the Behavioral Sciences, 16,* 301–312.

Rogers, C. R. (1967). Carl R. Rogers. In E. G. Boring & G. Lindzey (Eds.), *A history of psychology in autobiography* (Vol. V, pp. 343–384). New York: Appleton-Century-Crofts.

Rorschach, H. (1942). *Psychodiagnostics: A diagnostic test based on perception* (3rd ed. rev.). (P. Lemkau & B. Kronenberg, Trans., W. Morgenthaler, Ed.). Birmingham, AL: Classics of Psychiatry and Behavioral Sciences Library. (Original work published 1921)

Rorschach, H., & Oberholzer, E. (1924). The application of the interpretation of form to psychoanalysis. *Journal of Nervous and Mental Diseases, 60,* 225–248, 359–379.

Rosenzweig, M. R., Bennett, E. L., & Diamond, M. C. (1972). Brain changes in response to experience. *Scientific American, 226,* 22–30.

Ross, D. (1972). *G. Stanley Hall: The psychologist as prophet.* Chicago: University of Chicago Press.

Rubin, E. (1921). *Visuell wahrgenommene Figuren* (German trans. of *Synsoplevede Figurer*). Copenhagen: Gyldendalske. (Original work published 1915)

Ruckmick, C. A. (1926). Development of laboratory equipment in psychology in the United States. *American Journal of Psychology, 37,* 582–592.

Ryans, D. G. (1947). Services provided to navy training through achievement examinations. In D. B. Stuit (Ed.), *Personnel research and test development in the Bureau of Naval Personnel* (pp. 287–294). Princeton, NJ: Princeton University Press.

S

Sanford, E. C. (1893). Some practical suggestions on the equipment of a psychological laboratory. *American Journal of Psychology, 5,* 429–438.

Schachter, S. (1959). *The psychology of affiliation: Experimental studies of the sources of gregariousness.* Stanford, CA: Stanford University Press.

Schneirla, T. C. (1940). Further studies on the army-ant behavior pattern. *Journal of Comparative Psychology, 29,* 401–460.

Schneirla, T. C. (1942). "Cruel" ants—and Occam's razor. *Journal of Comparative Psychology, 34,* 79–83.

Schneirla, T. C. (1943). Postscript to "cruel ants." *Journal of Comparative Psychology, 35,* 233–235.

Schulze, R. (1912). *Experimental psychology and pedagogy: For teachers, normal colleges, and universities* (R. Pintner, Trans.). London: George Allen. (Original work published 1909)

Seagoe, M. V. (1975). *Terman and the gifted.* Los Altos, CA: William Kaufmann.

Sears, R. R. (1936). Experimental studies of projection: 1. Attribution of traits. *Journal of Social Psychology, 7,* 151–163.

Sears, R. R. (1943). Survey of objective studies of psychoanalytic concepts: A report prepared for the Committee on Social Adjustment. *Social Science Research Council Bulletin* (No. 51). New York: Social Science Research Council.

Seashore, C. E. (1919). *Manual of instructions and interpretations for measures of musical talent.* New York: Columbia Gramophone Company.

Sebeok, T. A., & Rosenthal, R. (Eds.). (1981). The Clever Hans Phenomenon: Communication with horses, whales, apes, and people. *Annals of the New York Academy of Sciences, 364.*

Shakow, D. (1949). The evaluation of the procedure. In A. F. Bronner (Chair), The objective evaluation of psychotherapy; round table, 1948. *American Journal of Orthopsychiatry, 19* (No.3), 471–479.

Shakow, D. (1969). *Clinical psychology as science and profession: A forty-year odyssey.* Chicago: Aldine Publishing.

Shakow, D., & Rapaport, D. (1964). The influence of Freud on American psychology. *Psychological Issues, 4,* Monograph 13.

Sidis, B. (1903). *The psychology of suggestion: A research into the subconscious nature of man and society.* New York: Appleton.

Skinner, B. F. (1932). Drive and reflex strength: II. *Journal of General Psychology, 6,* 38–47.

Skinner, B. F. (1979, March). My experience with the baby-tender. *Psychology Today,* 29–40.

Skinner, B. F. (1983). *A matter of consequences: Part three of an autobiography.* New York: Knopf.

Skinner, B. F. (1984). The shame of American education. *American Psychologist, 39,* 947–954.

Skodak, M., & Skeels, H. M. (1949). A final follow-up study of one hundred adopted children. *Journal of Genetic Psychology, 75,* 85–125.

Small, W. S. (1899a). An experimental study of the mental processes of the rat. *American Journal of Psychology, 11,* 133–165.

Small, W. S. (1899b). Notes on the psychic development of the young white rat. *American Journal of Psychology, 11,* 80–100.

Small, W. S. (1900). Experimental study of the mental processes of the rat: II, *American Journal of Psychology, 12,* 206–239.

Snow, R. E. (1982). The training of intellectual aptitude. In D. K. Detterman & R. J. Sternberg (Eds.), *How and how much can intelligence be increased* (pp. 1–37). Norwood, NJ: Ablex Publishing.

Sokal, M. (1982). James McKeen Cattell and the failure of anthropometric mental testing, 1890–1901. In W. R. Woodword & M. G. Ash (Eds.), *The problematic science: Psychology in nineteenth-century thought* (pp. 322–345). New York: Praeger.

Sontag, L. W., Baker, C. T., & Nelson, V. L. (1958). Mental growth and personality development: A longitudinal study. *Monographs of the Society for Research in Child Development, 23,* (Serial No. 68).

Spearman, C. (1930). C. Spearman. In C. Murchison (Ed.), *A history of psychology in autobiography,* (Vol. I, pp. 299–333). Worcester, MA: Clark University Press.

Sprung, L., & Sprung, H. (1981). Wilhelm Maximilian Wundt—ancestor or model? *Zeitschrift für Psychologie, 189,* 237–242.

Staff, Personnel Research Section, Adjutant General's Office (1947). The Army General Classification Test, with special reference to the construction and standardization of forms 1a and 1b. *Journal of Educational Psychology, 38,* 385–420.

Stagner, R. (1940). The cross-out technique as a method of public opinion analysis. *Journal of Social Psychology, 11,* 79–90.

Starch, D. (1916). *Educational measurements.* New York: Macmillan.

Stern, W. (1914). *The psychological methods of testing intelligence* (G. M. Whipple, Trans.). Baltimore: Warwick & York. (Original work published 1912)

Stern, W. (1930). William Stern (S. Langer, Trans., R. Schmidt, Ed.). In C. Murchison (Ed.), *A history of psychology in autobiography* (Vol. I, pp. 335–388). Worcester, MA: Clark University Press.

Stern, W. (1937). Cloud pictures: A new method for testing imagination. *Character and Personality, 6,* 132–146.

Sternberg, R. J., Ketron, J. L., & Powell, J. S. (1982). Componential approaches to the training of intelligent performance. In D. K. Detterman & R. J. Sternberg (Eds.), *How and how much can intelligence be increased* (pp. 155–172). Norwood, NJ: Ablex Publishing.

Stolz, S. B., Wienckowski, L. A., & Brown, B. S. (1975). Behavior modification: A perspective on critical issues. *American Psychologist, 30,* 1027–1048.

Stratton, G. M. (1896). The new psychological laboratory at Leipzig. *Science* (n.s. 4), 867–868.

Strong, E. K., Jr. (1919). The task of the Army Personnel Organization. *Industrial Education Circular* (No. 4), 2–10. Department of the Interior, Bureau of Education, Washington, DC.

Strong, E. K., Jr. (1943) *Vocational interests of men and women.* Stanford, CA: Stanford University Press.

Strong, E. K., Jr. (1958). Satisfactions and interests. *American Psychologist, 13,* 449–456.

Stuart, R. M., & Paine, A. B. (1896). *Gobolinks or shadow-pictures for young and old.* New York: Century.

Supa, M., Cotzin, M., & Dallenbach, K. M. (1944). "Facial vision": The perception of obstacles by the blind. *American Journal of Psychology, 57,* 133–183.

Sylvester, R. M. (1913). The form board test. *Psychological Monographs, 15* (4, Whole No. 65).

T

Taine, H. (1877). The acquisition of language by children. *Mind, 2,* 252–259. (Original work published 1876)

Terman, L. M. (1916). *The measurement of intelligence.* Boston: Houghton Mifflin.

Terman, L. M., & Merrill, M. A. (1937). *Measuring intelligence.* Boston: Houghton Mifflin.

Terman, L. M., & Merrill, M. A. (1960). *Stanford-Binet Intelligence Scale: Manual for the third revision, form L-M.* Boston: Houghton Mifflin.

Terman, L. M., & Merrill, M. A. (1972). *Stanford-Binet Intelligence scale: Manual for the third revision* (1972 Norms ed.). Boston: Houghton Mifflin.

Thompson, R. F., Lindsley, D. B., & Eason, R. G. (1966). Physiological psychology. In J. B. Sidowski (Ed.), *Experimental methods and instrumentation in psychology* (pp. 117–182). New York: McGraw Hill.

Thorndike, E. L. (1910). Handwriting. *Teachers College Record, 11,* 1–18.

Thorndike, E. L. (1919). Scientific personnel work in the army. *Science (n. s. 49),* 53–61.

Thorndike, R. L., Hagen, E. P., & Sattler, J. M. (1986). *The Stanford-Binet Intelligence Scale* (4th ed.); *Guide for administering and scoring.* Chicago: Riverside Publishing.

Thornton, C. L. (1970). *Tolman's chemistry-in method only?* Paper presented at the meeting of the Cheiron Society.

Titchener, E. B. (1900). *The psychological laboratory of Cornell University.* Worcester, MA: Oliver B. Wood.

Titchener, E. B. (1901a). *Experimental psychology: Vol. I. Qualitative experiments: Part I. Student's manual.* London: Macmillan.

Titchener, E. B. (1901b). *Experimental psychology: Vol. I. Qualitative experiments: Part II. Instructor's manual.* London: Macmillan.

Titchener, E. B. (1905a). *Experimental psychology: Vol. II. Quantitative experiments: Part I. Student's manual.* London: Macmillan.

Titchener, E. B. (1905b). *Experimental psychology: Vol. II. Quantitative experiments: Part II. Instructor's manual.* London: Macmillan.

Tolman, E. C. (1932). *Purposive behavior in animals and men.* New York: Century.

Topoff, H. R. (1971). Forward. In T. C. Schneirla, *Army ants: A study in social organization* (pp. xiii–xviii). H. R. Topoff (Ed.). San Francisco, CA: W. H. Freeman.

Tsai, L. S. (1951). Cooperation for survival. (From *Bulletin of the National Society for Medical Research, 6,* No. 2, Abstract, pp. 1–3).

Tulving, E., & Thomson, D. M. (1973). Encoding specificity and retrieval processes in episodic memory. *Psychological Review, 80,* 352–373.

Tzeng, O. J., and Wang, W. S. Y. (1983). The first two R's. *American Scientist, 71,* 238–243.

U

Uhrbrock, R. S. (1928). An analysis of the Downey will-temperament tests. *Teachers College Contributions to Education* (No. 296).

V

Varon, E. J. (1935). The development of Alfred Binet's psychology. *Psychological Monographs, 46* (3, Whole No. 207).

W

Wachtel, P. L. (1972). Field dependence and psychological differentiation: Reexamination. *Perceptual and Motor Skills, 35,* 179–189.

Wade, T. C., & Baker, T. B. (1977). Opinions and use of psychological tests: A survey of clinical psychologists. *American Psychologist, 32,* 874–882.

Wallin, J. E. W. (1905). *Optical illusions of reversible perspective: A volume of historical and experimental researches.* Princeton, NJ: Author.

Wallin, J. E. W. (1927). *Clinical and abnormal psychology: A textbook for educators, psychologists and mental hygiene workers.* Boston: Houghton Mifflin.

Walsh, A. A. (1972). The American tour of Dr. Spurzheim. *Journal of the History of Medicine and Allied Sciences, 27,* 187–205.

Warden, C. J., & Baar, J. (1929). The Müller-Lyer Illusion in the Ring Dove, Turtur Risorius. *Journal of Comparative Psychology, 9,* 275–292.

Warden, C. J., Jenkins, T. N., & Warner, L. H. (1935). *Comparative psychology: A comprehensive treatise: Volume I. Principles and methods.* New York: Ronald Press.

Warren, H. C. (1930). Howard C. Warren. In C. Murchison (Ed.), *A history of psychology in autobiography* (Vol. I, pp. 443–469). Worcester, MA: Clark University Press.

Watson, J. B. (1907). Kinaesthetic and organic sensations: Their role in the reactions of the white rat to the maze. *Psychological Review Monograph Supplements, 8* (No. 33).

Watson, J. B. (1913). Psychology as the behaviorist views it. *Psychological Review, 20,* 158–177.

Watson, J. B. (1916). The place of the conditioned-reflex in psychology. *Psychological Review, 23,* 89–116.

Watson, J. B. (1926). What the nursery has to say about instincts. In C. Murchison (Ed.), *Psychologies of 1925,* (pp. 1–35). Worcester, MA: Clark University Press.

Watson, J. B. (1936). John Broadus Watson. In C. Murchison (Ed.), *A history of psychology in autobiography* (Vol. III, pp. 271–281). Worcester, MA: Clark University Press.

Watson, J. B., & Rayner, R. (1920). Conditioned emotional reactions. *Journal of Experimental Psychology, 3,* 1–14.

Wechsler, D. (1935). *The range of human capacities.* Baltimore, MD: Williams & Wilkens.

Wechsler, D. (1939). *The measurement of adult intelligence.* Baltimore, MD. Williams & Wilkens.

Wechsler, D. (1944). *The measurement of adult intelligence* (3rd ed.). Baltimore: Williams & Wilkins.

Wechsler, D. (1946). *The Wechsler-Bellevue Intelligence Scale: Form II. Manual for administering and scoring the test.* New York: Psychological Corporation.

Wechsler, D. (1949). *Wechsler Intelligence Scale for Children.* New York: Psychological Corporation.

Wechsler, D. (1955). *Manual for the Wechsler Adult Intelligence Scale.* New York: Psychological Corporation.

Wechsler, D. (1963). *Manual for the Wechsler Preschool and Primary Scale of Intelligence.* New York: Psychological Corporation.

Wechsler, D. (1970). *Correspondence File,* Archives of the History of American Psychology, University of Akron.

Wechsler, D. (1974). *Manual for the Wechsler Intelligence Scale for Children—Revised.* New York: Psychological Corporation.

Wechsler, D. (1981). *Wechsler Adult Intelligence Scale—Revised.* New York: Psychological Corporation.

Wechsler, D. (1989). *Wechsler Preschool and Primary Scale of Intelligence—Revised.* New York: Psychological Corporation.

Weiss, A. P. (1917). Relation between structural and behavior psychology. *Psychological Review, 24,* 301–317.

Wells, F. L. (1908). Technical aspects of experimental psychopathology. *American Journal of Insanity, 64,* 477–512.

Wells, F. L. (1951). *Modified Alpha Examination, Manual of Directions* (rev.). New York: Psychological Corporation.

Wertheimer, Max (1959). Productive thinking. In M(ichael) Wertheimer (Ed.), *Productive thinking* (enlarged ed.). New York: Harper & Brothers. (Original work published 1945)

Wertheimer, Michael (1987). *A brief history of psychology* (3rd ed.). New York: CBS College Publishing.

Whipple, G. M. (1910). *Manual of mental and physical tests.* Baltimore, MD: Warwick & York.

Whipple, G. M. (1914). *Manual of mental and physical tests: Part I. Simpler processes.* Baltimore, MD: Warwick & York.

Whipple, G. M. (1915). *Manual of mental and physical tests: Part II. Complex processes.* Baltimore, MD: Warwick & York.

Whipple, G. M. (1921). The National Intelligence Tests. *Journal of Educational Research, 4,* 16–31.

Who's who in American education (11th ed.). s.v. "Williamson, Edmund G." Nashville, TN: Author.

Wissler, C. (1901). The correlation of mental and physical tests. *Psychological Review Monograph Supplements, 3* (6, Whole No. 16).

Witkin, H. A., Lewis, H. B., Hertzman, M., Machover, K., Meissner, P. B., & Wapner, S. (1972). *Personality through perception: An experimental and clinical study.* Westport, CT: Greenwood Press.

Witmer, L. (1896). Practical work in psychology. *Pediatrics, 2,* 462–471.

Wolf, T. H. (1973). *Alfred Binet.* Chicago: University of Chicago Press.

Wolpe, J., & Lang, P. J. (1964). A fear survey schedule for use in behaviour therapy. *Behaviour Research and Therapy, 2,* 27–30.

Wood, B. D. (1923). *Measurement in higher education.* Yonkers-on-Hudson, NY: World Book.

Woodworth, R. S. (1910). Racial differences in mental traits. *Science* (n.s. *31,* No. 788), 171–186.

Woodworth, R. S. (1919). Examination of emotional fitness for warfare. *Psychological Bulletin, 16,* 59–60.

Woodworth, R. S. (1929). *Psychology* (rev. ed.). New York: Holt.

Woodworth, R. S. (1932). Robert S. Woodworth. In C. Murchison (Ed.), *A history of psychology in autobiography* (Vol. II, pp. 359–380). Worcester, MA: Clark University Press.

Woodworth, R. S. (1938). *Experimental psychology.* New York: Holt.

Woodworth, R. S. (1942). *The Columbia University psychological laboratory: A fifty-year retrospect.* New York.

Woodworth, R. S. (1948). *Contemporary schools of psychology* (rev. ed.). New York: Ronald Press.

Woodworth, R. S. (1958). *Dynamics of behavior.* New York: Holt, Rinehart, & Winston.

Woodworth, R. S., & Mathews, E. (1924). *Personal Data Sheet.* Chicago, IL: Stoelting.

Woodworth, R. S., & Schlosberg, H. (1954). *Experimental psychology* (rev. ed.). New York: Holt.

Y

Yerkes, R. M. (1918). Psychology in relation to the war. *Psychological Review, 25,* 85–115.

Yerkes, R. M. (1919). Report of the Psychology Committee of the National Research Council. *Psychological Review, 26,* 83–149.

Yerkes, R. M. (Ed.). (1921). Psychological examining in the United States army. *Memoirs of the National Academy of Sciences, 15,* Washington: Government Printing Office.

Yerkes, R. M., & Bridges, J. W. (1914). The point scale: A new method for measuring mental capacity. *Boston Medical and Surgical Journal, 171,* 857–866.

Yerkes, R. M., Bridges, J. W., & Hardwick, R. S. (1915). *A point scale for measuring mental ability.* Baltimore, MD: Warwick & York.

Yerkes, R. M., & Watson, J. B. (1911). Methods of studying vision in animals. *Behavior Monographs, 1* (No. 2).

Young, P. T. (1928). Auditory localization with acoustical transposition of the ears. *Journal of Experimental Psychology, 11,* 399–429.

Young, P. T. (1936). *Motivation of behavior: The fundamental determinants of human and animal activity.* New York: Wiley.

Young, P. T. (1961). *Motivation and emotion: A survey of the determinants of human and animal activity.* New York: Wiley.

Young-Bruehl, E. (1988). *Anna Freud: A biography.* New York: Summit Books.

Z

Zeigarnik, B. (1967). On finished and unfinished tasks. In W. D. Ellis (Ed. & Trans.), *A source book of Gestalt psychology* (pp. 300–314). London: Routledge & Kegan. (Original work published 1927)

Zilboorg, G. (1941). *A history of medical psychology.* New York: Norton.

Index